VOLUME EDITORS

SCOTT F. PARKER has contributed chapters to *Ultimate Lost and Philosophy, Football and Philosophy, Alice in Wonderland and Philosophy, Golf and Philosophy,* and *iPod and Philosophy.* He is a regular contributor to *Rain Taxi Review of Books.* His writing has also appeared in *Philosophy Now, Sport Literate, Fiction Writers Review, Epiphany, The Ink-Filled Page,* and *Oregon Humanities.*

MICHAEL W. AUSTIN is an Associate Professor of Philosophy at Eastern Kentucky University, where he works primarily in ethics. He has published *Conceptions of Parenthood: Ethics and the Family* (2007), *Running and Philosophy: A Marathon for the Mind* (Wiley-Blackwell, 2007), and *Football and Philosophy: Going Deep* (2008).

SERIES EDITOR

FRITZ ALLHOFF is an Assistant Professor in the Philosophy Department at Western Michigan University, as well as a Senior Research Fellow at the Australian National University's Centre for Applied Philosophy and Public Ethics. In addition to editing the *Philosophy for Everyone* series, Allhoff is the volume editor or co-editor for several titles, including *Wine & Philosophy* (Wiley-Blackwell, 2007), *Whiskey & Philosophy* (with Marcus P. Adams, Wiley, 2009), and *Food & Philosophy* (with Dave Monroe, Wiley-Blackwell, 2007). His academic research interests engage various facets of applied ethics, ethical theory, and the history and philosophy of science.

PHILOSOPHY FOR EVERYONE

Series editor: Fritz Allhoff

Not so much a subject matter, philosophy is a way of thinking. Thinking not just about the Big Questions, but about little ones too. This series invites everyone to ponder things they care about, big or small, significant, serious… or just curious.

Edited by Scott F. Parker and Michael W. Austin

COFFEE
PHILOSOPHY FOR EVERYONE
Grounds for Debate

WILEY-BLACKWELL

A John Wiley & Sons, Ltd., Publication

This edition first published 2011
©2011 John Wiley & Sons Ltd

Wiley-Blackwell is an imprint of John Wiley & Sons, formed by the merger of Wiley's global Scientific, Technical and Medical business with Blackwell Publishing.

Registered Office
John Wiley & Sons Ltd, The Atrium, Southern Gate, Chichester, West Sussex, PO19 8SQ, United Kingdom

Editorial Offices
350 Main Street, Malden, MA 02148-5020, USA
9600 Garsington Road, Oxford, OX4 2DQ, UK
The Atrium, Southern Gate, Chichester, West Sussex, PO19 8SQ, UK

For details of our global editorial offices, for customer services, and for information about how to apply for permission to reuse the copyright material in this book please see our website at www.wiley.com/wiley-blackwell.

The right of Scott F. Parker and Michael W. Austin to be identified as the editors of the editorial material in this work has been asserted in accordance with the UK Copyright, Designs and Patents Act 1988.

Library of Congress Cataloging-in-Publication Data

Coffee – Philosophy for Everyone: grounds for debate / edited by Scott F. Parker and Michael W. Austin.
    p.   cm. – (Philosophy for everyone)
  Includes bibliographical references.
  ISBN 978-1-4443-3712-9 (pbk.: alk. paper)   1. Coffee—Philosophy.   I. Parker, Scott F. II. Austin, Michael W.
  TX415.C64 2011
  641.3'373—dc22
                                             2010034203

A catalogue record for this book is available from the British Library.
This book is published in the following electronic formats: ePDF 9781444393361; Wiley Online Library 9781444393385; ePub 9781444393378

Set in 10/12.5pt Plantin by SPi Publisher Services, Pondicherry, India
Printed in Malaysia by Ho Printing (M) Sdn Bhd

01   2011

For Dad, thanks for the Saturday morning walks to Broadway Coffee Merchant when I was a kid, and for Sophie's World *when I was a teenager.*
Scott

For Dan, a true friend.
Mike

"You know what I'm going to do?" she says to me at long last. Without waiting for a reply, she says, "I'm going to make myself a cup of coffee, then go sit out on the back porch and spend the rest of the night thinking of new ways to ask, and answer, 'What is the meaning of life?'"

Christopher Phillips, *Socrates Cafe* (New York: W. W. Norton, 2001)

No one can understand the truth until he drinks of coffee's frothy goodness.

Sheik Abd-al-Kadir

CONTENTS

FOREWORD

Pythagoras of Samos never had a latte; Socrates never sipped a macchiato; and Aristotle thought great thoughts, but never quaffed a red eye. Anne Conway may have been familiar with coffee, but was probably not an imbiber, because during her lifetime coffee was still relegated to the English apothecary as an exotic headache remedy. From this we understand that the philosopher Novartis's idea for Excedrin was not without precedent.

Philosophy predates coffee by more than a millennium, yet it is coffee, perhaps more than any other substance, that has been identified with Western philosophic thought since its introduction to Europe through Venice in the seventeenth century.

It is believed that ancient Mediterranean lands did not know of coffee, yet a thousand years ago, the extraordinary Persian intellect, physician, and scientist Abu Ali al-Hussain Ibn Abdallah Ibn Sina, born in 980 BCE near Bukhara (modern-day Uzbekistan) and known in the West as just Ibn Sina – or in the name's Latinized form, Avicenna – wrote about coffee and its marvelous qualities.

The Age of Enlightenment was brightened by the presence of coffee, and French philosopher Denis Diderot included images of coffee mills in the *Encyclopédie* project, an effort to put on paper all the knowledge known to that generation, in Europe. It also included articles by famous living men, including exotic American personages Benjamin Franklin and Thomas Jefferson. The result, *L'Encyclopédie, ou Dictionnaire Raisonné des Sciences, des Arts et des Métiers*, published in Paris between 1762 and 1777, was an intellectual triumph of the age. While Diderot was editing,

Voltaire was sipping coffee. It is said that the French philosopher, who frequented Le Procope, the famed Paris coffeehouse, now restaurant, consumed fifty cups per day. Hegel also had a fondness for drinking coffee, but then so did millions of other folks during the eighteenth century.

In 1832, adjutant general of the US Army Roger Jones issued General Order 100a in an effort to curb alcohol abuse in the ranks. The whiskey ration was eliminated, replaced by coffee and tea, except in special circumstances. An Act of Congress in 1862 discontinued the special circumstances, and coffee was triumphant. Tens of thousands of Union soldiers were introduced to the coffee habit during subsequent military service during the Civil War, and the wars that have followed.

It was during the Civil War that political philosopher Abraham Lincoln was said to remark to a waiter in the President's House, "If this is coffee, please bring me some tea; but if this is tea, please bring me some coffee." The most prominent American philosopher of the period was poet Walt Whitman, for whom I know no coffee reference; however, there is a Starbucks at the Walt Whitman Mall, in Huntington Station, New York. You can go there, buy a *Tall*, that is the twelve-ounce size you get if you order a "small" at Starbucks, even though there is a size called a *Short* that is eight ounces and is not listed on the chain's menu boards (but the why of that is a philosophical question for another day). You can sip your coffee and just imagine what the gentle man who wrote *Leaves of Grass* would think about the eighty-eight retailer spaces that have his verses etched into the fascia stucco of their exteriors, and the five thousand paved parking spaces all named in his honor.

In the United States the period following the Civil War was one of enlightenment in Northern cities, and social philosophers such as Jane Adams of Chicago's Hull House opened coffeehouses so poor working-class people could avoid taverns, and buy food without the temptation of alcohol.

The triumph of the second industrial revolution enabled coffee, reduced to nominal cost by mass production, to become a universal drink that crossed lines of class and station throughout much of the world, fueling nineteenth-century philosopher caffeinatics including Goethe and Rousseau.

Coffee makes people think. We can only guess at the philosophical discussions, debates, disputes, and dialogues that have taken place over coffee in its history. Coffee has historically been a beverage that sparks the exercise of intellectual energy, often of the more radical variety, resulting in verbosity, and on occasion leading to heresy and sedition. It has been the source of fulmination by potentates and kings from Constantinople to London who in turn closed, opened, closed again, and finally gave up the vain effort to suffocate free thought, by stifling the use of "the beverage that gives you time to think."

Karl Marx was buzzed on his favorite blend when he attacked the idea of private property and supported free trade because he believed it would break down nation-states. He was possibly cheered on by anarchist Emma Goldman, but in the twentieth century writer Ayn Rand pulled him down, possibly while brewing and serving coffee and miniature Danish pastries to Frank O'Connor and their guests. Ms. Rand made much of cigarettes, but I don't remember a particularly philosophical coffee reference in her writing. The polemicist, intellectual incendiary, and coffee drinker Noam Chomsky has done in Ms. Rand's ideas, in his turn. Professor Emeritus Chomsky has some interesting ideas on the economy of coffee, expressed in *Propaganda and the Public Mind*, that could be easily used as fire-starter the next time coffee folks sit down to have a thoughtful discussion touching on the ideas of free trade, fair trade, and direct trade.

Bob Dylan was a leader in the philosophy of social and political awakening that was the hallmark of his poetic folk lyrics of the 1960s, but "One More Cup of Coffee," a track from his 1976 album *Desire*, is a painful song of unrequited love and abandonment mulled over one last cup o' joe.

The poet philosopher of rock 'n' roll, Paul Simon, wrote of despair and alienation felt by many of his generation, "And we sit and drink our coffee / Couched in our indifference / Like shells upon the shore / You can hear the ocean roar / In the dangling conversation / And the superficial sighs / The borders of our lives."

Creative thinking and coffee appear to be mutually dependent as the philosopher poet seeks out coffee for its stimulation, comfort, and metaphoric effect, and the farmer, roaster, barista, and even the potter require the thinker to find their own *raison d'être*.

Levi R. Bryant, professor of philosophy at Collin County Community College, McKinney, Texas, recently posted on his Larval Subjects blog, "It seems that for some reason or other I am always waxing on about my blue coffee mugs. In part, I suppose, this is because my coffee mug is always nearby, within reach of my hand when I am sitting at my computer and readily available for my gaze to alight upon. In part, this is because coffee mugs are familiar furniture of the world and are therefore ideally suited as an example. Finally, and I find this to be odd, this is because my blue coffee mugs fill me with a deep sense of warmth and comfort."

Coffee and philosophy, partners since the beverage's beginnings, are destined to remain linked until the world runs out of java. Chicago's Café Descartes, named for the French philosopher, heralds the motto, "I drink, therefore I am." If it fits your personal philosophy you can order it on a coffee mug from zazzle.com.

DONALD SCHOENHOLT

SCOTT F. PARKER AND MICHAEL W. AUSTIN

EDITORS' INTRODUCTION

Pour yourself a hot steaming cup of joe, 'cause we're gonna talk about the amber liquid of life ... the common man's gold, and like gold it brings to every person the feeling of luxury and nobility. Thank you, Juan Valdez.

Bob Dylan, *Theme Time Radio Hour,*
"Coffee," introduction

Coffee is not for everyone, but it sure comes close. In the United States of America, more than half of the population over the age of eighteen consumes coffee on a daily basis. In fact, the average American consumption of coffee per person is three and a half cups per day. The United States is also the leading importer of coffee in the world, bringing in twice as much of the bean as the second-place country, Germany. Of course, coffee consumption is not just an American phenomenon. Worldwide, over 500 *billion* cups of coffee are served each year. Each year Brazil turns out one third of the coffee produced in the world, which is three times as much as the next largest producer of coffee, Vietnam.[1] Since it was first discovered in its native Ethiopia over one thousand years ago, coffee has spread the globe. It's grown in the tropical regions of Africa, Latin America, and Asia; and it's drunk there and most everywhere else. Caffeine is the world's most commonly used drug, and the majority of it is taken in the form of coffee. Coffee consumption is clearly a widespread phenomenon.

Perhaps surprisingly, so is philosophy. At its best, philosophy provides us with a way to uncover important truths about the world and how to live. And while you may not do it consciously, everyone practices philosophy, in some sense of the term. Why? The reason is that we have beliefs about the nature of reality, what sorts of things we can know, and how best to live. Sometimes we're aware of these beliefs, and sometimes we're not. But hopefully we have reasons that we take to support these beliefs. These kinds of issues, and many others, fall under the domain of philosophy, which literally means "love of wisdom." So, the question is not whether you or we are philosophers, but rather, whether or not we're *good* philosophers. That's where this book comes into the picture. Reading it will provide you with new ways to think philosophically about coffee and the rest of your life. And along the way, you'll also learn some new things about coffee and how to more fully enjoy it.

It's only natural that there be a book devoted to coffee and philosophy, as they are strongly linked in cultural imagination as well as in practice. So strongly linked, in fact, that in modern times they seem almost inseparable. The appropriate analogy is that coffee and philosophy go together like foreplay and sex. You can have one without the other, but the latter is better with the former, and the former often leads to the latter. Coffee is conducive to slow drinking, which leads to slowing down generally and the opportunity for conversation, reading, and thinking. And philosophy benefits from coffee, which sharpens attention and can heighten creativity. There's an old joke that a philosopher is a machine that turns coffee into theories. In the legend of coffee's discovery in Ethiopia, the goat herder and poet Kaldi saw his goats dancing on their hind legs after chewing the leaves and berries of a coffee tree. When Kaldi chewed on the trees and berries himself, "poetry and song spilled out of him. He felt that he would never be tired or grouchy again."[2]

But if the sex analogy seems overly excited it's not just because of the caffeine coursing through our blood and permeating the blood-brain barrier – philosophy is as active a mental stimulant as exists. The concerns of philosophy demand our attention every bit as much as does sex. What's the nature of reality? Is there a God? How should I behave? What matters? Jean-Paul Sartre once said, "Everything has

SCOTT F. PARKER AND MICHAEL W. AUSTIN

been figured out, except how to live." Philosophy is the big questions and it can't be oversold.

We mention Sartre because he might be the first person to come to mind when you think of coffee and philosophy. The iconic photographs of Sartre in Paris's Café de Flore with the porcelain cup in front of him are some of the most indelible images of what a philosopher looks like. For Sartre, philosophy is inseparable from café culture. And maybe café culture is inseparable from philosophy, too? Consider this existentialist joke. Sartre was sitting in a café when a waitress approached him: "Can I get you something to drink, Monsieur Sartre?" Sartre replied, "Yes, I'd like a cup of coffee with sugar but no cream." Nodding agreement, the waitress walked off to fill the order and Sartre returned to working. A few minutes later, however, the waitress returned and said, "I'm sorry, Monsieur Sartre, we are all out of cream – how about with no milk?"

Another Frenchman, less well known for his connection to coffee, but with a more impressive coffee resume, Voltaire drank up to sixty cups of coffee a day (although, unlike Sartre, he didn't complement his caffeine with large doses of alcohol, nicotine, amphetamines, and barbiturates). But this kind of relationship hasn't always been the case. Plenty of philosophers have made do without. The ancients, of course, had no knowledge of coffee. More recently, philosophy's two greatest walkers, Immanuel Kant and Friedrich Nietzsche, were also its two greatest coffee abstainers. Somehow, they were still able to write prolifically for many years. What makes Sartre and Voltaire, and Kant and Nietzsche, unusual is their extremity. Most any other philosopher from the past few hundred years has drunk a more moderate amount of coffee. In the United States and Europe (from where our philosophical tradition mostly emerges) coffee and cafés are cultural institutions. Coffee is part of popular culture (songs by Frank Sinatra and Sam Lightnin' Hopkins, commercials featuring Johnny Cash and Jerry Seinfeld; when Bob Dylan started his *Theme Time Radio Hour* show on satellite radio, "coffee" was the theme of his fifth episode); it's a crucial part of many people's daily routines (morning coffee, coffee break, etc.); cafés are semi-public spaces where some people like to spend their free time and some people seem to spend their entire waking lives.[3]

So coffee's a big part of culture and it's compatible with, even conducive to, philosophy. What does philosophy have to say about coffee? Quite a bit, actually. Some of the big questions we face as coffee consumers are explicitly moral questions. How important is it that we buy coffee that's fair trade or direct trade? Shade-grown? Organic? Also, with "coffee" now comprising $130-per-pound Hacienda La Esmeralda Special, a cup of joe that's been sitting out all day at the gas station, the ever-mockable half-caf, three-pump, extra-foam, skinny whatever, and myriad other varieties, there are important aesthetic questions to ask. Can one coffee really be *better* than another? If so, what makes it better? Is anyone really tasting notes of lemongrass? But coffee isn't drunk exclusively for aesthetic reasons. And neither is it drunk for entirely utilitarian reasons. Yes, people drink it to stay awake, but there's more to coffee drinking than that. There's a large, diverse, energetic culture surrounding it. So when we talk about coffee, we're talking about everything that goes along with it, too: its associations with conversation and friendship, art and reading, politics and revolution – all of these are of philosophical interest. And then, in addition to using philosophy to think about coffee, philosophy can use coffee to think about the larger world, asking metaphysical questions about what coffee can tell us about God, ourselves, and reality. These four areas of philosophy – metaphysics, culture, aesthetics, ethics – are the categories we've grouped the book's chapters in. Most of the contributors are philosophers, but there are also chapters written by coffee experts, journalists, and historians, though each chapter is connected to some of the big or small questions philosophers ask.

But just what are these areas of philosophy? These days, people often associate metaphysics with the section of the bookstore containing volumes on the healing power of crystals, but philosophers understand metaphysics in a very different way. When a philosopher does metaphysics, she is seeking to understand the nature of reality. In order to understand this, consider the sorts of questions asked which philosophers consider *metaphysical* questions: Is there a God? Is the color red identical to a particular wavelength of light? Is there such a thing as the self? If so, what is it like? Do we have freedom of the will? Is coffee merely black puddle water, or is it in fact a panacea?

Okay, that last question might not seem to fit, but for anyone with a love of coffee, it is an important metaphysical question with very practical implications. And it is a question explored in the first unit, "The First Cup: Coffee and Metaphysics," in the chapter by Mark Pendergrast, author of *Uncommon Grounds: The History of Coffee and How It Transformed our World*. Pendergrast takes the reader on a wide-ranging tour of the debates about the place of coffee in human life. In the chapter by Michael W. Austin, "The Necessary Ground of Being," some of the recent debates about the metaphysical foundations of ethics are explored, ideally with a cup of your favorite beverage close at hand. Kristopher G. Phillips writes about what it's like to be a coffee drinker, and gives us very practical advice on how to more deeply appreciate the substance and nuances of coffee. Steven Geisz shares several insights grounded in Indian philosophical thought as he discusses life, suffering, death, reincarnation, the human self, and that all-important morning cup of coffee. Finally, in her chapter, "The Existential Ground of Community: Coffee and Otherness," Jill Hernandez writes about the connections between existentialism, coffee, and the elusive good of community that so many of us long for and sometimes seek to acquire at our favorite coffeehouse, ending on a hopeful note.

In the spirit of lively debate, some of the chapters in the second unit, "The Grounds for Debate: Coffee Culture," argue against each other, offering different readings of the virtues and vices of coffee culture. Scott F. Parker reflects on the role coffeehouses can play in making philosophy more accessible to the average person and argues that being philosophically engaged with the world is a responsibility of being human (no surprise one of the book's editors would say something like this). Asaf Bar-Tura argues that laptops and other technologies have turned coffeehouses into places people go to isolate themselves instead of to participate in community, and then gives models of how coffeehouses can once again be locales for social change. In "Café Noir: Anxiety, Existence, and the Coffeehouse," Brook J. Sadler finds in coffee the perfect drink for our anxious, isolated postmodern condition. The culture sections ends with Bassam Romaya taking up the question of why coffee – more than tea, beer, cola, or some other beverage – is the drink most compatible with philosophy.

The third unit, "The Wonderful Aroma of Bean: Coffee Aesthetics," investigates coffee in terms of aesthetics, or the branch of philosophy that is interested in beauty and taste. In "Three Cups: The Anatomy of a Wasted Afternoon," Will Buckingham spends an afternoon in a café and demonstrates what it can be like to *do* philosophy. He combines everyday observations and an openness to letting his mind wander with a reading of Emmanuel Levinas to form his own philosophical reflections on the values of coffee, cafés, and idleness. Moving from the level of the café to the level of the coffee itself, coffee expert Kenneth Davids examines three coffees of various qualities and by way of asking "Is Starbucks Really Better than Red Brand X?" offers a set of standards for how to judge and enjoy coffee. Next, in "The Flavor of Choice: Neoliberalism and the Espresso Aesthetic," Andrew Wear traces the aesthetic of espresso from its origins in the Italian *caffè* to its redefinition as a mass-market beverage, and considers how that aesthetic has been impacted for the sake of profit.

Aesthetics and ethics in coffee end up being pretty closely tied. Good coffee beans, for example, tend to come from coffee farmers who are paid well for their work. John Hartmann and Scott F. Parker focus their attention on this relationship in two chapters that serve as a transition to the final unit on ethics. Hartmann, in his chapter "Starbucks and the Third Wave," examines third wave coffee in the context of Starbucks' immense influence on how we drink coffee and what we expect from a coffee company in the way of social responsibility. Parker takes up similar ground from a different angle in an interview with Stumptown Coffee's Matt Lounsbury.

The move into ethics is completed in our final unit, "To Roast or Not to Roast: The Ethics of Coffee." Ethics is concerned with our moral obligations, the moral virtues, and what it takes to be truly fulfilled as a human being. Gina Bramucci and Shannon Mulholland draw from first-hand experience visiting African coffee farms to compare fair trade coffee with the increasingly common direct trade model. Kenneth W. Kirkwood takes up the caffeine in coffee and analyzes its use as a performance-enhancing drug. In the penultimate chapter, Stephanie Aleman provides several ways to think about the question "Is coffee green?" And finally, in "Coffee and the Good Life: The Bean and the Golden Mean," Lori Keleher uses Aristotle's *Nicomachean Ethics* to help locate coffee's place in the good life – an appropriate place, we think, to end.

While this book celebrates coffee, it's important to acknowledge that there is no shortage of opposition to it. Coffee has been banned by religions, it's been called "the drink of the Devil"; it has been accused of both stirring the passions and stymieing them; it's been thought to stunt growth, cause cancer, weaken bones. And let's not forget that caffeine is a poison certain tropical plants have evolved to protect themselves against predators.

We note these concerns about coffee, but we do not share them. And we assume you don't either. So, please, pour yourself a cup of coffee at home, or order a cappuccino at your neighborhood café. These essays are best enjoyed as they were written – with coffee in hand. Finally, it is our hope that reading this book will whet your appetite for coffee, philosophy, and coffee and philosophy.

NOTES

1 http://www.pbs.org/frontlineworld/stories/guatemala.mexico/facts.html.
2 Mark Pendergrast, *Uncommon Grounds: The History of Coffee and How It Transformed our World* (New York: Basic Books, 1999), pp. 4–5.
3 See, for example, the web series *Coffee Bean Guys*, http://www.youtube.com/watch?v=UCNuc5bXi_s and the afterword to this book.

PART I

THE FIRST CUP: COFFEE AND METAPHYSICS

CHAPTER 1

COFFEE

Black Puddle Water or Panacea?

Throughout coffee's history, critics have accused the drink of causing horrendous health problems, while those who love the brew have espoused its almost miraculous curative powers. This extreme devotion and condemnation continues today.

Coffee grows wild on the mountainsides of Ethiopia. It is likely that the seeds of *bunn*, as coffee was called there, were at first ground and mixed with animal fat for a quick-energy snack, while the leaves were brewed to make a weakly caffeinated brew. Tribesmen made wine out of the fermented pulp as well as a sweet beverage called *kisher* out of the lightly roasted husks of the coffee cherry. At some point during the fifteenth century, someone roasted the beans, ground them, and made an infusion. Coffee as we know it finally came into being.

At first, coffee was apparently used primarily by Sufi monks in Ethiopia and across the Red Sea in Yemen, where coffee trees were cultivated by the fifteenth century. The drink helped them stay awake for midnight prayers, and it added zest to the whirling dance of the mystic dervishes. The drink became a kind of communion wine for the Islamic Sufis, for whom alcoholic beverages were forbidden. In Yemen, the monks sometimes recited the traditional *ratib*, the repetition 116 times of the phrase "*Ya Qawi*" ("O possessor of all strength"), while sharing ritual cups of coffee. The reference was to Allah, but coffee itself was also seen as possessing much strength. The word "coffee" probably derives not from *Qawi* but from *qahwa*, the Arab word for wine, since coffee similarly seemed to possess some kind of stimulating drug.

The Sufis carried coffee beans throughout the Arab world, including Mecca. The beverage quickly spread beyond the monasteries and into secular use. Thus, while coffee was at first considered a medicine or religious aid, it soon enough became an everyday habit. Wealthy people had a coffee room in their homes, reserved only for ceremonial imbibing. For those who did not have such private largesse, coffeehouses, known as *kaveh kanes*, sprang up. By the end of the fifteenth century, Muslim pilgrims had introduced coffee throughout the Islamic world in Persia, Egypt, Turkey, and North Africa, making it a lucrative trade item.

As the drink gained in popularity throughout the sixteenth century, it also gained its reputation as a troublemaking social brew. Various rulers decided that people were having too much fun in the coffeehouses. "The patrons of the coffeehouse indulged in a variety of improper pastimes," Ralph Hattox notes in his history of the Arab coffeehouses, "ranging from gambling to involvement in irregular and criminally unorthodox sexual situations."[1]

When Khair-Beg, the young governor of Mecca, discovered that satirical verses about him were emanating from the coffeehouses, he determined that coffee, like wine, must be outlawed by the Qur'an, and he induced his religious, legal, and medical advisors to agree. Thus, in 1511 the coffeehouses of Mecca were forcibly closed.

The ban lasted only until the Cairo sultan, a habitual coffee drinker, heard about it and reversed the edict. Other Arab rulers and religious leaders, however, also denounced coffee during the course of the 1500s and into the next century. The Grand Vizier Kuprili of Constantinople, fearing sedition during a war, closed the city's coffeehouses in 1633. Anyone caught drinking coffee was soundly cudgeled. Offenders found imbibing a second time were sewn into leather bags and thrown into the Bosphorus. Even so, many continued to drink coffee in secret, and eventually the ban was withdrawn.

Why did coffee drinking persist in the face of persecution in these early Arab societies? The addictive nature of caffeine provides one answer, of course; yet there is more to it. Coffee provided an intellectual stimulant, a pleasant way to feel increased energy without any apparent ill effects.

Coffeehouses allowed people to get together for conversation, entertainment, and business, inspiring agreements, poetry, and irreverence in equal measure. So important did the brew become in Turkey that a lack of sufficient coffee provided grounds for a woman to seek a divorce. "O Coffee!" wrote an Arab poet in 1511 (the same year the drink was banned briefly in Mecca), "Thou dost dispel all care, thou are the object of desire to the scholar. This is the beverage of the friends of God."[2] Even though Mohammed (ca. 570–632) never drank coffee, a myth arose that the Prophet had proclaimed that under the invigorating influence of coffee he could "unhorse forty men and possess forty women."[3]

Europeans Discover Coffee

At first Europeans didn't quite know what to make of the strange new brew. German physician Leonhard Rauwolf published *Travels in the Orient* in 1582, describing "a very good drink, by them called *Chaube* that is almost as black as ink, and very good in illness, chiefly that of the stomach; of this they drink in the morning early ... as hot as they can; they put it often to their lips but drink but little at a time, and let it go round as they sit."[4]

The Venetian Gianfrancesco Morosini wrote disapprovingly in 1585 about the "time sunk in idleness" in drinking coffee in Constantinople. "They continually sit about, and for entertainment they are in the habit of drinking in public in shops and in the streets, a black liquid, boiling [as hot] as they can stand it, which is extracted from a seed they call Caveé ... [that] is said to have the property of keeping a man awake."[5]

In 1610 British poet Sir George Sandys noted that the Turks sat "chatting most of the day" over their coffee, which he described as "blacke as soote, and tasting not much unlike it." He added, however, that it "helpeth, as they say, digestion, and procureth alacrity."[6]

In a book published in Germany in 1656, Adam Olearius, an astronomer and surveyor who had traveled to Persia, wrote about coffee, warning that "if you partake to excess of such kahave water, it completely extinguishes all pleasures of the flesh."[7] He claimed that coffee had rendered a Sultan Mahmed Kasnin impotent. His book, translated and published in France in 1666, helped fuel anti-coffee sentiment there.

By the time Olearius's book was published, Europeans were already discovering coffee. Pope Clement VIII, who died in 1605, supposedly tasted the Moslem drink at the behest of his priests, who wanted him to ban it. "Why, this Satan's drink is so delicious," he reputedly exclaimed, "that it would be a pity to let the infidels have exclusive use of it. We shall fool Satan by baptizing it and making it a truly Christian beverage."[8]

In the first half of the seventeenth century, coffee was still an exotic beverage, and like other such rare substances as sugar, cocoa, and tea, initially was used primarily as an expensive medicine by the upper classes. Over the next fifty years, however, Europeans were to discover the social as well as medicinal benefits of the Arabian drink.

Surprisingly, given their subsequent enthusiasm for coffee, the French lagged behind the Italians and British in adopting the coffeehouse. In 1669 a new Turkish ambassador, Soliman Aga, introduced coffee at his sumptuous Parisian parties, inspiring a craze for all things Turkish. Male guests, given voluminous dressing gowns, learned to loll comfortably without chairs in the luxurious surroundings, and to drink the exotic new beverage. Still, it appeared to be only a novelty.

French doctors, threatened by the medicinal claims made for coffee, went on the counterattack in Marseilles in 1679, no doubt encouraged by French winemakers: "We note with horror that this beverage ... has tended almost completely to disaccustom people from the enjoyment of wine."[9] Then, in a fine burst of pseudoscience, a young medical student named Colomb blasted coffee, asserting that it "dries up the cerebrospinal fluid and the convolutions ... the upshot being general exhaustion, paralysis, and impotence."[10]

Six years later, however, Sylvestre Dufour, another French physician, wrote a book strongly defending coffee, claiming that it relieved kidney stones, gout, and scurvy, while it also helped mitigate migraine headaches. "Coffee banishes languor and anxiety, gives to those who drink it, a pleasing sensation of their own well-being and diffuses through their whole frame, a vivifying and delightful warmth."[11] By 1696 one Paris doctor was prescribing coffee enemas to "sweeten" the lower bowel and freshen the complexion.

The French historian Michelet described the advent of coffee as "the auspicious revolution of the times, the great event which created new customs, and even modified human temperament."[12] Certainly coffee lessened the intake of alcohol while the cafés provided a wonderful intellectual stew that ultimately spawned the French Revolution. The coffeehouses of continental Europe were egalitarian meeting places where, as

MARK PENDERGRAST

the food writer Margaret Visser notes, "men and women could, without impropriety, consort as they had never done before. They could meet in public places and talk."[13]

Coffee and coffeehouses reached Germany in the 1670s. By 1721 there were coffeehouses in most major German cities. For quite a while the coffee habit remained the province of the upper classes. Many physicians warned that it caused sterility or stillbirths. In 1732 the drink had become controversial (and popular) enough to inspire Johann Sebastian Bach to write his humorous *Coffee Cantata*, in which a daughter begs her stern father to allow her this favorite vice: "Dear father, do not be so strict! If I can't have my little demitasse of coffee three times a day, I'm just like a dried-up piece of roast goat! Ah! How sweet coffee tastes! Lovelier than a thousand kisses, sweeter far than muscatel wine! I must have my coffee."[14] Later in the century, coffee-obsessed Ludwig van Beethoven ground precisely sixty beans to brew a cup.

By 1777 the hot beverage had become entirely too popular for Frederick the Great, who issued a manifesto in favor of Germany's more traditional drink: "It is disgusting to notice the increase in the quantity of coffee used by my subjects, and the like amount of money that goes out of the country in consequence. My people must drink beer. His Majesty was brought up on beer, and so were his ancestors." Four years later the king forbade the roasting of coffee except in official government establishments, forcing the poor to resort to coffee substitutes. They also managed to get hold of real coffee beans and roast them clandestinely, but government spies, pejoratively named *coffee smellers* by the populace, put them out of business. Eventually coffee outlived all the efforts to stifle it in Germany. *Frauen* particularly loved their *Kaffeeklatches*, gossipy social interludes that gave the brew a more feminine image.

Every other European country also discovered coffee during the same period. Nowhere did coffee have such a dynamic and immediate impact, however, as in England.

The British Invasion

Like a liquid black torrent the coffee rage drenched England, beginning at Oxford University in 1650, where Jacobs, a Lebanese Jew, opened the first coffeehouse for "some who delighted in noveltie."[15] Two years later in London, Pasqua Rosée, a Greek, opened a coffeehouse and printed the first coffee advertisement, a broadside touting "The Vertue of the *COFFEE* Drink," described as "a simple innocent thing, composed into a Drink, by being dryed in an Oven, and ground to Powder, and boiled up with Spring water."[16] Rosée's ad asserted that coffee would aid digestion, cure headaches, coughs, consumption, dropsy, gout, and scurvy, and prevent miscarriages. More practically, he wrote: "It will prevent Drowsiness, and make one fit for business, if one have occasion to *Watch*; and therefore you are not to Drink of it *after Supper*, unless you intend to be *watchful*, for it will hinder sleep for 3 or 4 hours."[17]

By 1700 there were, according to some estimates, two thousand London coffeehouses, occupying more premises and paying more rent than any other trade. They came to be known as *penny universities*, because for that price one could purchase a cup of coffee and sit for hours listening to extraordinary conversations. Each coffeehouse specialized in a different type of clientele. In one, physicians could be consulted. Others served Protestants, Puritans, Catholics, Jews, literati, merchants, traders, fops, Whigs, Tories, army officers, actors, lawyers, clergy, or wits. The coffeehouses provided England's first egalitarian meeting place, where a man was expected to chat with his tablemates whether he knew them or not.

Before the advent of coffee the British imbibed alcohol, often in Falstaffian proportions. In 1774 one observer noted that "coffee-drinking hath caused a greater sobriety among the nations; for whereas formerly Apprentices and Clerks with others, used to take their mornings' draught in Ale, Beer or Wine, which by the dizziness they cause in the Brain, make many unfit for business, they use now to play the Good-fellows in this wakefull and civill drink."[18]

Not that most coffeehouses were universally uplifting places; rather, they were chaotic, smelly, wildly energetic, and capitalistic. "There was a rabble going hither and thither, reminding me of a swarm of rats in a ruinous cheese-store,"[19] one contemporary noted. "Some came, others went; some were scribbling, others were talking; some were drinking, some smoking, and some arguing; the whole place stank of tobacco like the cabin of a barge."[20]

The strongest blast against the London coffeehouses came from women, who unlike their Continental counterparts were excluded from this all-male society (unless they were the proprietors). In 1674 *The Women's Petition Against Coffee* asked, "[Why do our men] trifle away their time, scald their Chops, and spend their Money, all for a little base, black, thick, nasty bitter stinking, nauseous Puddle water?"[21] The women were

  MARK PENDERGRAST

convinced that the drink was emasculating their mates. "We find of late a very sensible *Decay* of that true *Old English Vigour*.... Never did Men wear *greater Breeches*, or carry *less* in them of any *Mettle* whatsoever."[22] This condition was all due to "the Excessive use of that Newfangled, Abominable, Heathenish Liquor called *Coffee*, which ... has so *Eunucht* our Husbands, and *Crippled* our more kind *gallants*.... They come from it with nothing *moist* but their snotty Noses, nothing *stiffe* but their Joints, nor *standing* but their Ears."[23]

The *Women's Petition* revealed that a typical male day involved spending the morning in a tavern "till every one of them is as Drunk as a Drum, and then back again to the Coffee-house to drink themselves sober." Then they were off to the tavern again, only to "stagger back to *Soberize* themselves with Coffee."[24] In response, the men defended their beverage in their own broadside publication. Far from rendering them impotent, "[coffee] makes the erection more Vigorous, the Ejaculation more full, adds a spiritualescency to the Sperme."[25]

On December 29, 1675, King Charles II issued "A Proclamation for the Suppression of Coffee-Houses." In it he banned coffeehouses as of January 10, 1676, since they had become "the great resort of Idle and disaffected persons" where tradesmen neglected their affairs. The worst offense, however, was that in such houses "divers false malitious and scandalous reports are devised and spread abroad to the Defamation of his Majestie's Government, and to the Disturbance of the Peace and Quiet of the Realm."[26]

An immediate howl went up from every part of London. Within a week, it appeared that the monarchy might once again be overthrown – and all over coffee. On January 8, two days before the proclamation was due to take effect, the king backed down.

Ironically, however, over the course of the eighteenth century the British began to drink tea instead of coffee for various reasons. While the black brew never disappeared entirely, its use in England diminished steadily until recent years have seen a coffee renaissance.

Postum and Coffee Neuralgia

The arguments over coffee and its effects on the human body continued unabated throughout the eighteenth and nineteenth centuries. In the late eighteenth century, King Gustav III of Sweden conducted an experiment to show that coffee was a poison, forcing a convicted murderer to drink it every day, while another prisoner drank tea. Both prisoners outlived the king and their observing doctors.

The isolation of caffeine in 1819 did not substantially alter the tenor of the debate, although with the decline of the theory of the "four humours," experts stopped talking about whether coffee was too dry, wet, hot, or cold in nature.

After the Boston Tea Party of 1773, coffee surpassed tea in the colonies and the young United States to become the patriotic beverage of choice. Of course, the pragmatic North Americans also appreciated the fact that coffee was cultivated much nearer to them than tea and was consequently cheaper.

In late nineteenth-century America, coffee was challenged by new health concerns. In 1890 Charles W. Post, an energetic entrepreneur, suffered a nervous breakdown and joined other sufferers in Battle Creek, Michigan, at the famed Sanitarium, or "San," of Dr. John Harvey Kellogg.

Kellogg had made himself the impresario of health faddism, and one of his particular dislikes was coffee. "The tea and coffee habit is a grave menace to the health of the American people," he intoned, adding that the drinks caused arteriosclerosis, Bright's disease, heart failure, apoplexy, and premature old age. "*Tea and coffee are baneful drugs* and their sale and use *ought to be prohibited by law*," wrote Kellogg. He even alleged that "insanity has been traced to the coffee habit."[27]

Post's nine months at the San failed to cure his indigestion or nervous disorder, so he left. By 1892 Post had recovered sufficiently to open his own Battle Creek alternative to Kellogg's Sanitarium, which he christened La Vita Inn. In 1895 Post first manufactured Postum, a grain-based coffee substitute that bore a suspicious resemblance to Kellogg's Caramel Coffee (served at the San).

By May 1897 sales were booming, largely due to scare ads that depicted harried, desperate, and dissipated people hooked on caffeine. They warned of the hazards of "coffee heart," "coffee neuralgia," and "brain fag." Abstaining from coffee and drinking Postum would effect the promised cure. "Lost Eyesight through Coffee Drinking,"[28] one headline blared. "It is safe to say that one person in every three among coffee users has some incipient or advanced form of disease."[29] Coffee was a "drug drink" that contained "a poisonous drug – caffeine, which belongs in the same class of alkaloids with cocaine, morphine, nicotine, and strychnine."[30] One ad featured coffee spilling slowly from a cup, accompanied by an alarming text: "Constant dripping wears away the stone. Perhaps a hole has been started in you.... Try leaving off coffee for ten days and use Postum Food Coffee."

When he wasn't frightening his readers Post buttered them up, appealing to their egos. He addressed an ad to "highly organized people,"[31] telling them that they could perform much better on Postum than on nerve-wracking coffee. Post also addressed the modern man, asserting that Postum was "The Scientific Way To Repair Brains and Rebuild Waste Tissues."[32] Coffee was not a food but a powerful drug. "Sooner or later the steady drugging will tear down the strong man or woman, and the stomach, bowels, heart, kidneys, nerves, brain, or some other organ connected with the nervous system, will be attacked."[33]

Post was not alone in damning coffee. Most doctors of the era warned against the beverage's habitual use. In 1906 a London doctor – perhaps more loyal to tea – stated, "Coffee drunkards, as I may call them, are greatly increasing in number." He added that the coffee habit produced "palpitations of the heart, an irregular pulse, nervousness, indigestion and insomnia."[34]

Even American physicians such as George Niles had harsh words for the drink so beloved by his countrymen. True, he thought that "strong coffee, either alone or with a little lemon juice, is often useful in overcoming a malarial chill or a paroxysm of asthma."[35] But he went on to warn that "it is easy to form a coffee habit, which, yielded to, may lead into muscular tremors, palpitation, a feeling of praecordial oppression, tinnitus aurium, hyperesthesia, muscular lassitude, vertigo, heartburn, vague symptoms of indigestion, constipation and pronounced insomnia."[36] On the whole, coffee came in for an inordinate amount of criticism in the first two decades of the twentieth century.

The beleaguered coffee industry responded with anecdotal stories to illustrate the drink's beneficial effects on longevity. For instance, Mrs. Christine Hedin of Ironwood, Michigan, celebrated her hundredth birthday by "drinking coffee all day long,"[37] as was her normal habit (from four to ten cups daily). A centenarian Frenchman was told that coffee, which he drank to excess, was a poison. "If it is poison," he said, "I am a fine example of the fact that it is a very slow poison."[38]

In 1911 Harry and Leta Hollingworth conducted groundbreaking double-blind experiments on caffeine's effects on humans, the first really scientific effort to look at the issue. The experiments indicated that caffeine, in moderate amounts, improved motor skills while leaving sleep patterns relatively unaffected.

Birth Defects and Pancreatic Cancer

Health concerns about the effects of coffee and caffeine continued to simmer, however, and in the 1960s they began to receive support through a series of epidemiological studies. "A new problem for the coffee industry is rearing its ugly head," wrote Samuel Lee, the technical editor of the *Tea & Coffee Trade Journal* in 1966. "Serious scientific workers are trying to demonstrate that prolonged, continued or excessive consumption of beverage coffee may be deleterious, or even a serious health hazard."[39]

In November 1979 Michael Jacobson of the Center for Science in the Public Interest (CSPI) filed a petition with the Food and Drug Administration (FDA) asking for warning labels on coffee and tea packages reading: "Caffeine May Cause Birth Defects." At a press conference, he presented a woman who claimed that her heavy coffee consumption offered the only "reasonable explanation" for her child's deformities.

In response, the National Coffee Association (NCA) pointed out that experimental rats were being forced to ingest the equivalent of thirty-five cups of coffee all at once. The International Life Sciences Institute (ILSI), founded in 1978 with soft-drink money, joined the NCA to conduct epidemiological studies on caffeine. Coca-Cola was particularly concerned about saving caffeine's reputation, since it sold both coffee and Coke. Caught in the political riptide, the FDA waffled. "We're not saying caffeine is unsafe," Sanford Miller of the FDA said. "We're just not saying it's safe."[40] The agency issued a warning against caffeine consumption by pregnant women, but it did not demand a warning label.

The next year, an epidemiological study appeared to link coffee to pancreatic cancer, triggering widespread media attention and sick jokes about coffee being "good till the last drop dead." Then a new study purported to link caffeine with the formation of benign breast lumps. Yet another claimed that coffee produced heart arrhythmia, while a Norwegian survey found higher cholesterol levels in heavy coffee drinkers.

The 1980 edition of the *Diagnostic and Statistical Manual of Mental Disorders*, bible of the American Psychiatric Association, included "caffeinism" as a diagnosis, making the consumption of too much coffee a bona fide psychiatric disorder. In 1981 Charles Wetherall published *Kicking the Coffee Habit*, calling coffee "Public Health Enemy Number One," which was waging "a pathological war on this country."[41]

The NCA moved vigorously to counter the calumnies against its drink, funding more studies and assembling a file of thousands of articles from the medical and scientific literature. Many other independent scientists and doctors also pointed out flaws in the anti-coffee findings, and a 1982 study of twelve thousand pregnant women revealed no detectable ill effects from coffee consumption. Nonetheless, the damage was done. During the 1980s, coffee was associated with over one hundred diseases and disorders and, though subsequent studies threw every negative finding into question, the implanted fears led more consumers to decaffeinated alternatives or away from coffee completely.

The Pendulum Swings Back to Pro-Coffee

Today the debate over coffee and caffeine rages on, though for the moment the pendulum has swung to the positive side. Caffeine is the most widely taken psychoactive drug on earth, and coffee is its foremost delivery system. "Today, most of the world's population ... consumes caffeine daily," wrote Jack James, author of two books and many articles on caffeine.[42] He estimates that global consumption is the approximate equivalent of one caffeine-containing beverage per day for every person in the world. In the United States, around 90 percent of the population habitually takes caffeine in one form or another.

Humans clearly crave stimulating concoctions, drinking, chewing, or smoking some form of drug in virtually every culture in the form of alcohol, coca leaves, kava, marijuana, poppies, mushrooms, qat, betel nuts, tobacco, coffee, kola nuts, yoco bark, guayusa leaves, yaupon leaves (cassina), maté, guaraná nuts, cacao (chocolate), or tea. Of those in the list above, caffeine is certainly the most ubiquitous, appearing in the last nine items.

Caffeine is one of the alkaloids: organic (carbon-containing) compounds built around rings of nitrogen atoms. Alkaloids are the pharmacologically active chemicals produced by many tropical plants. Because they have no winter to provide relief from predators, tropical plants have evolved sophisticated methods to protect themselves. In other words, caffeine is a natural pesticide. It is quite likely that plants contain caffeine because it affects the nervous system of most would-be consumers, discouraging them from eating the plants. Of course, that is precisely the attraction for the human animal.

Caffeine, $C_8H_{10}N_4O_2$, readily passes through biological membranes such as the gastrointestinal tract. The human liver treats caffeine as a poison and attempts to dismantle it, stripping off methyl groups. It can't cope with all of them, so quite a few whole caffeine molecules make it past the liver and eventually find a docking place in the brain.

The caffeine molecule mimics the neurotransmitter adenosine, which decreases electrical activity in the brain and inhibits the release of other neurotransmitters. In other words, adenosine slows things down. It lets us rest and probably helps put us to sleep once a day. When caffeine gets to the receptors first, however, it doesn't let adenosine do its job. Caffeine doesn't actively keep us awake – it just blocks the natural mental brake.

The brain isn't the only place caffeine affects. There are receptors throughout the body, where adenosine performs varied functions. Thus, caffeine constricts some blood vessels. In low doses, it appears to slow the heartbeat, while larger amounts cause the heart to beat more rapidly. Caffeine causes certain muscles to contract more easily. At the same time, however, it can relax the airways of the lungs and *open* other types of blood vessels. Caffeine is a diuretic, and small amounts of calcium float away in the urine, leading to concern over possible bone loss. The latest research indicates that this is a potential concern only for elderly women with low calcium intake.

As Stephen Braun concluded in his book *Buzz*: "The effects of caffeine on such things as breast cancer, bone loss, pancreatic cancer, colon cancer, heart disease, liver disease, kidney disease, and mental dysfunction have been examined in ... detail and, to date, *no* clear evidence has been found linking moderate consumption of caffeine ... with these or any other health disorder."[43]

Most authorities recommend "moderate consumption." There are many anecdotal and clinical reports that drinking too much caffeine can cause problems. The lethal dose for humans is about ten grams, though it would be virtually impossible to consume that much quickly by drinking coffee, requiring more than one hundred cups. Initial signs of toxicity include vomiting, abdominal cramps, and a racing heartbeat. The fourth edition of the *Diagnostic and Statistical Manual of Mental Disorders* (DSM-IV) includes *caffeine intoxication* as a bona fide ailment.

Yet moderate caffeine intake has benefits. As Harry Hollingworth found in his 1911 double-blind studies, caffeine can minimally improve motor skills and reaction time while leaving sleep patterns relatively unaffected. Coffee boosts athletic performance (perhaps through stimulation of more adrenaline) to the point that the International Olympic

Committee used to call caffeine a "doping agent." Caffeine can help those who suffer from asthma and is given to infants suffering from neonatal apnea (cessation of spontaneous breathing). Some adults with allergies find that caffeine allays symptoms. It can mitigate the pain of migraine headaches (though withdrawal from caffeine *causes* other headaches). For those who need a diuretic or laxative, coffee provides relief. Some studies even commend the drink's use as an antidepressant to prevent suicide.

Caffeine has been shown to increase sperm motility, so it may prove useful in artificial insemination programs (though others fear it may harm the sperm while speeding it on its way). There doesn't seem to be any truth to the centuries-old calumny that coffee causes impotence, however. Combined with analgesics such as aspirin, caffeine appears to help alleviate pain. While coffee often is accused of providing no nutrition, it provides traces of potassium, magnesium, and manganese. Like red wine, it is an important source of antioxidants.

Caffeine has a paradoxical effect on hyperactive children with attention-deficit disorder: Coffee seems to calm them down. Coffee consumption can apparently help prevent Parkinson's, Alzheimer's, liver cancer, colon cancer, type 2 diabetes, and gallstones.

I am somewhat skeptical about these findings. All too often, we hear that what caused cancer ten years ago is now supposed to cure it, or vice versa. Yet many of the recent coffee studies are epidemiologically sound, following huge numbers of people for many years and carefully weeding out possible confounding factors. For example, a 2006 study on liver disease, published in the *Archives of Internal Medicine*, tracked 125,580 people. It suggested that for each cup of coffee they drank per day, participants were 22 percent less likely to develop alcoholic cirrhosis. A study in the *Journal of the American Medical Association* the previous year followed 193,473 participants. It found not only that coffee protected against type 2 diabetes, but also that the more cups you drank, the less risk there was of diabetes.

Surprisingly, there is little evidence that caffeine harms children. Like adults, however, children are subject to withdrawal symptoms – from soft drink deprivation more frequently than from coffee. Many doctors have expressed concern about pregnant and nursing women who drink coffee. Caffeine readily passes through the placental barrier to the fetus, and it turns breast milk into a kind of natural latte. Because premature infants lack the liver enzymes to break down caffeine, it stays in their systems much longer. By the time they are six months old, most children eliminate caffeine at the same rate as adults, with a blood-stream half-life of around five hours.

Research has failed to prove that caffeine harms the fetus or breastfed infant, but some studies appear to implicate caffeine in lower birth-weights. Jack James has urged pregnant women to abstain completely from drinking caffeine beverages. On the other hand, the NCA (which certainly has a vested interest in the matter) has asserted that "most physicians and researchers today agree that it's perfectly safe for pregnant women to consume caffeine." For those who choose to "err on the side of caution," the NCA recommended one or two cups daily.

Some people can drink dozens of cups of coffee a day without bouncing off the walls because they have developed a caffeine tolerance. If they quit cold turkey, however, they can suffer exquisite withdrawal symptoms, which include headaches, drowsiness, fatigue, decreased performance, and, for extreme cases, nausea and vomiting. The symptoms can last up to a week. As addictions go, it is a relatively harmless one.

And that brings us around to the question with which we began this historical review of pro and con health claims for coffee. Why has this particular beverage always inspired such fervent advocates and detractors? I can only hazard an educated hypothesis, but my earlier analogy with communion wine seems reasonable to me. We have all heard the truism, "You are what you eat," but even more so, "You are what you drink." We are, after all, composed primarily of water, and psychologically we appear to identify more deeply with our beverages than anything else we consume.

Among such drinks, the drug-laced beverages seem to have the most powerful impact, not only on our bodies, but also on our psyches. Of all animals, humans appear to have an inherent thirst for mood-altering liquids. Jonathan Swift believed that "coffee makes us severe, and grave, and philosophical," although it seems to make many people excited and light-hearted. At any rate, we often like to share coffee communally, to laugh over it, to do business, to tell stories, to philosophize, and perhaps to plan a revolution or two.

And because we are understandably concerned with anything upon which we are dependent, we tend to demonize or glorify such beverages. Thus, while I may not have any provable answers to my question of why coffee has always caused such conflicting opinions, I suspect that the arguments over the "black, thick, nasty bitter stinking, nauseous Puddle water," that "beverage of the friends of God," will continue into the indefinite future.

NOTES

1 Ralph S. Hattox, *Coffee and Coffeehouses: The Origins of a Social Beverage in the Medieval Near East* (Seattle: University of Washington Press, 1986), p. 6.

2 Mark Pendergrast, *Uncommon Grounds: The History of Coffee and How It Transformed our World* (New York: Basic Books, 1999), p. xv.

3 Ibid., p. 6.

4 Bennett Alan Weinberg and Bonnie K. Bealer, *The World of Caffeine: The Science and Culture of the World's Most Popular Drug* (London and New York: Routledge, 2001), p. 99.

5 Ibid., p. 19.

6 Pendergrast, *Uncommon Grounds*, p. 8.

7 Weinberg and Bealer, *World of Caffeine*, p. 85.

8 Pendergrast, *Uncommon Grounds*, p. 8.

9 Ibid., pp. 8–9.

10 Ibid., p. 9.

11 Weinberg and Bealer, *World of Caffeine*, p. 105.

12 Ibid., p. 9.

13 Margaret Visser, *Much Depends on Dinner: The Extraordinary History and Mythology, Allure and Obsessions, Perils and Taboos of an Ordinary Meal* (New York: Grove Press, 1999), p. 207.

14 Pendergrast, *Uncommon Grounds*, p. 11.

15 Ibid., p. 12.

16 Ibid.

17 Ibid.

18 Ibid., p. 13.

19 Ibid.

20 Ibid.

21 Ibid., p. xv.

22 Ibid., p. 13.

23 Ibid.

24 Ibid., p 14.

25 Ibid.

26 Ibid.

27 Ibid., p. 97.

28 Ibid., p. 99.

29 Ibid.

30 Ibid.

31 Ibid., p. 100.

32 Ibid.

33 Ibid.

34 Ibid., p. 103.

35 Ibid.

36 Ibid.
37 Ibid., p. 105.
38 Ibid.
39 Ibid., p. 301.
40 Ibid., p. 340.
41 Ibid.; Charles F. Wetherall, *Kicking the Coffee Habit* (Wetherall Pub. Co., 1981), pp. 20–21.
42 Pendergrast, *Uncommon Grounds*, p. 411; Jack E. James, *Understanding Caffeine: A Behavioral Analysis* (Thousand Oaks, CA: Sage, 1997), pp. 1–14.
43 Pendergrast, *Uncommon Grounds*, pp. 412–413; Stephen Braun, *Buzz: The Science and Lore of Alcohol and Caffeine* (Oxford: Oxford University Press, 1996), pp. 107–195.

CHAPTER 2

THE NECESSARY GROUND OF BEING

"Please, don't even talk to me until I've had my coffee."

As I write this, there is a commercial airing on television in which a guy apparently cannot interact with other people in anything resembling a pleasant fashion until he has had his morning cup of coffee. The above words are the first words out of his mouth when his roommate greets him in the morning. Not only is he rude to his roommate, he's also rude to a friend on the street (and his dog), a woman he sits next to on the bus, and the restaurant employee who is asking him if he would like some premium roast coffee. After his coffee, he greets strangers on the street, complements their clothes, and remarks on the beauty of the weather. While the character in this commercial is very annoying, many coffee drinkers can identify with a fundamental truth that the commercial is trying to express: Some of us need coffee. In some sense of the term, coffee is *necessary* for us as a way to get the ball rolling and begin the day. In short, we need the bean.

There is a very different sort of conversation about necessity that fails to appear in thirty-second TV spots. This conversation is a philosophical

Coffee – Philosophy for Everyone: Grounds for Debate, First Edition. Edited by Scott F. Parker and Michael W. Austin, series editor Fritz Allhoff.

one, and includes a claim about something that many people believe to be necessary for the moral aspects of human life: God. God is necessary, the argument goes, because without God there is nothing to ground ethics. In this chapter, I will consider some of the philosophical debates surrounding that aspect of reality which many think depends on God for its existence – moral reality. In short, the idea is that if there are objective ethical truths, then we need God to explain their existence.

Or at least that's what some philosophers would have us believe. Others, however, disagree. So pour yourself a cup of your favorite coffee and join a conversation that has been going on for millennia – in schools of philosophy, monasteries, colleges and universities, and coffeehouses – about whether or not we need a Being to ground ethics.

Necessity, Contingency, and My Very First Cup of Coffee

I still remember it, though rather vaguely. I was pretty young, around ten years of age, and on a canoe trip with my parents and younger brother. We'd stopped to have lunch on the riverbank when Dad offered me a taste of coffee from his gunmetal gray steel thermos. This wasn't the fancy stainless steel kind of container with aerodynamic lines that you can buy at your local Starbucks or independent coffeehouse and take to the office. This was the kind of thermos that guys who *work* for a living use while they build skyscrapers or bridges. Anyway, I took a sip, and was instantly revolted by the taste of the strange concoction I'd just ingested. Why would anyone drink something that tasted like a mixture of water and dirt with a bit of milk to take the edge off? Moreover, how could anyone find drinking this stuff enjoyable? I'm sure in my young mind I thought some nice cherry Kool-Aid would be just fine, thank you. It tastes better, and makes your tongue red, which is very cool when you're ten.

Fast-forward ten years or so to my undergraduate days at Kansas State University. I had procrastinated writing a philosophy paper until the night before it was due (hopefully none of my current students are reading this!). My roommate Jason worked at a local coffee shop, so we had some good coffee in the apartment. The thought of a bunch of caffeinated soda wasn't appealing, so I tried some of his coffee. Unsurprisingly, it did the job and kept me awake enough to finish my paper at around three in the morning. Surprisingly, I actually liked it. The experience was nothing like

MICHAEL W. AUSTIN

the unpleasant one I'd had as a child on the riverbank. From the time of that almost all-nighter to the present, I've been a coffee drinker.

Things could have turned out differently, however. I might not have become a coffee drinker that night. So the fact that I'm now someone who drinks and enjoys coffee on a daily basis is a particular kind of fact, a particular kind of truth. It's what philosophers call a *contingent truth*. A contingent truth is one that is true but could have been false. It could have been the case that instead of trying my roommate's coffee, I opted for a different caffeinated drink or popped a caffeine pill or two. If I'd opted for one of these rather than his coffee, I would not now be a coffee drinker, or at least I wouldn't have become one when I did. As you might guess, there are a lot of contingent truths. For example, it is a contingent truth that the Royals won the World Series in 1985, that Barack Obama became the forty-fourth president of the United States in January 2009, that the high temperature in Boulder, Colorado, today was 57 degrees, and that Starbucks has enjoyed such immense success over the past two decades. The Royals could have lost the World Series, Obama could have lost the election or decided to run in 2012 rather than 2008, the high in Boulder could have been 47, and Starbucks could have been bought out by another corporation and subsequently failed. None of these things did happen, but they could have happened. And this is what distinguishes contingent truths from another kind of truth.

This other kind of truth is what philosophers call *necessary truth*. Necessary truths, unlike contingent truths, are those truths which cannot be false. Some examples of necessary truths are:

- $2 + 2 = 4$.
- If A is larger than B, and B is larger than C, then A is larger than C.
- Nothing can be red all over and green all over at the same time.
- If everyone at Starbucks is drinking espresso, and Shane is at Starbucks, then Shane is drinking espresso.

Some philosophers think that there are also *necessary ethical* truths, somehow grounded in the basic nature of reality. Possible examples of such truths include:

- Genocide is immoral.
- We should strive for a just world.
- Torturing infants for fun is wrong.
- Compassion is a virtue.

As you know, and as some of the contributors to this book point out, there are important ethical issues connected to the production and consumption of coffee. For example, if it is true that we should strive for a just world, this would entail that coffee growers, harvesters, and roasters should be given a fair price for the product and the labor required to bring that beloved cup of coffee to our kitchen table every morning (and every afternoon, and every night, for some of us). The existence of necessary ethical truths is not only relevant to the production of coffee, or to the production of other goods and services. Such truths are also relevant to one of life's big questions, one that continues to draw the attention of philosophers the world over: Is there a God?

Do We Need God to Justify Fair Trade – and the Rest of Ethics?

In one sense, the answer is clearly no. Plenty of people, religious and non-religious alike, believe that we have a moral obligation to treat others fairly and justly, and that within the coffee trade this entails engaging in fair trade practices. And many of them can give reasonable arguments for this belief. But there is another sense in which the answer to this question is more controversial. Some philosophers believe that if there are necessary ethical truths, then the best explanation of this is that there is a God. That is, they think that the existence of such truths fits better within a theistic framework than within a naturalistic framework. Others don't believe that God exists, but maintain belief in the existence of necessary ethical truths. They argue that in a world without God, economic exploitation via unfair trade practices would still be wrong, just as it would be wrong in a world in which God exists.

I think that all rational people of good will should agree that unfair trade is wrong, regardless of their religious beliefs. In fact, I think that all rational people of good will believe that we should be moral, and live good, decent lives, whether or not there is a God. The deeper philosophical question, however, is how to account for these facts, if they are indeed facts. In what follows I'll discuss how theists and atheists account for these two facts: (1) that there are necessary moral truths; and (2) that we should be moral.

Contemporary philosopher Erik Wielenberg argues that we should be moral and that there are some necessary ethical truths, even if there is no God. One such necessary ethical truth is the claim that suffering is

MICHAEL W. AUSTIN

intrinsically evil. The fact that 2 + 2 = 4 is also a necessary truth, though it is not an ethical truth. In every possible universe, it is impossible that 2 + 2 = 5. And in every possible universe, it is impossible that suffering be anything other than an intrinsic evil.[1] How does Wielenberg account for these facts, given that he is a naturalist (someone who believes that there is no God or any other supernatural component of reality)? The answer is fairly straightforward. Wielenberg states that these "necessary ethical truths … are part of the furniture of the universe."[2] They are just there, they are truths that cannot be false, and that's all there is to say about it.

Let's now turn to the second claim I mentioned above, that we should be moral. Wielenberg considers several possible answers to the question, "Why be moral?" Someone might seek to live a moral life to receive eternal reward or avoid eternal punishment; they might seek to live such a life because they think that the moral life is the truly happy life; or that by being moral one has the best chance to achieve wealth, power, and pleasure. Wielenberg follows Enlightenment philosopher Immanuel Kant in stating that the reason to be moral is simply this: We ought to be moral. To see how this works, consider the following internal dialogue you may have had about the coffee you consume: *Why should I buy fair trade coffee? Well, it is morally just that the farmers and others who are involved in the growth, harvest, production, and roasting of the coffee I drink each day should be able to sustain a decent livelihood. To buy coffee for which the farmers, for example, are not receiving a living wage is unjust. Since I want to be a good, morally decent person, I will not contribute to systemic economic injustice, even if I have to pay a bit more per pound for my favorite coffee. It seems that I am obligated to buy fair trade coffee, and so I should act accordingly.*

Morally mature people realize that the fact that some action is our moral duty is a sufficient reason for doing that action. While some might debate whether or not we actually have a duty to buy fair trade coffee, the point is that if such a duty exists, then that's all we need to know in order to do the right thing. No further reason is needed. And for things that we clearly have a duty to do, according to commonsense morality – such as being compassionate to those in need, caring for our children, and seeking to be a person of integrity – there is no further reason needed apart from the fact that we are morally obligated to do such things.

Some philosophers who believe that God exists argue that the existence of necessary ethical truths and the fact that we should be moral are best explained by the existence of a necessary ethical being, or God. The idea is not that one must believe in God in order to live a morally decent or good life. Neither is the idea to question whether or not there are necessary ethical truths, nor to doubt whether the fact that something is my moral duty is sufficient for doing that action. Instead, the issue is *how to account for these facts* given the worldview one holds. So while Wielenberg takes these as brute given facts for which no further explanation is needed, others think that this is problematic and offer a different account.

For example, contemporary philosopher J. P. Moreland argues that the existence of necessary ethical truths and objective moral value, as well as the normative force of moral obligation, are pieces of evidence that favor theism over atheism because they fit more naturally within a theistic worldview compared to a worldview without God.[3] It's important to keep in mind that these criticisms do not apply to the naturalist who thinks that all ethical values are relative or subjective, but rather only to those who think that naturalism is true *and* that there are some necessary ethical truths which we ought to follow in our daily lives.

First, Moreland asks the reader to consider how to account for the existence of objective moral value. If the universe began with the Big Bang, and then over the course of time the physical components of the universe begin to combine into increasingly complex physical compounds, how does value arise? Necessary ethical truths such as "Suffering is intrinsically bad" and "Courage is necessarily a virtue" are non-natural, non-physical aspects of reality. How can a naturalist embrace the existence of such things, given her view of the purely natural origins of the universe? Moreover, the moral order presents itself as something which commands obedience. According to Moreland, the sense of guilt one feels for falling short of the moral order is best explained by the existence of a good and personal God who is the ultimate ground of its existence. People don't feel a sense of guilt toward abstract moral principles but toward personal beings.

Before we move to the issue of why we should be moral, consider how it is that we human beings are able to do what objective morality requires. What is the chance that there are eternally unchanging ethical truths which we can also act upon? Additionally, it is remarkable that these truths also contribute to human flourishing. For Moreland, theism has an obvious answer to how these things are the case, but it is unclear and far from obvious how naturalism would account for these facts. Related to this, how is it that human beings can acquire knowledge of intrinsic value and moral reality? These values are not empirically detectable. That is, we don't come to know them via sight, sound, taste, smell, or touch. And they cannot stand in physical causal relations with one's brain. So how is it the case, if naturalism is true, that we can know such things?

MICHAEL W. AUSTIN

Finally, pour yourself a second cup and consider a question that has been asked by philosophers and human beings generally for millennia: *Why should I be moral?* As I pointed out above, some philosophers respond that the reason we should be moral is just that it is the moral thing to do. Anyone who needs a further reason does not realize that moral reasons are sufficient for action. Even if doing the right thing doesn't get us an eternal reward, or the present rewards of fame, wealth, or pleasure, we should still do the right thing because it is the right thing. So both naturalists and theists can respond to the question "Why should I be moral?" with the response "Because it is the moral thing to do." When someone gives such an answer, they are working from within the moral point of view. When someone has adopted the moral point of view, this means that they've embraced the requirements of morality and are seeking to live in a moral manner by subscribing to moral judgments which they take to be binding on all people. And they think that morality should be applied in an impartial way, without prejudice or bias. The point to note here is that when someone says the reason to be moral is that it is the moral thing to do, they are already reasoning from *within* the moral perspective.

But we can also think about the question from *outside* of the moral perspective. When we do so, we are asking the question, "What rational justification can be given for why it is reasonable to adopt the moral point of view rather than some other perspective?" Why should we think that being moral is part of a rational life plan? Why not instead adopt a self-centered, egoistic perspective? According to Moreland, this is a problem for the naturalist. He claims that naturalism cannot give a satisfactory answer to the question, and that an egoistic approach to life is most consistent with the metaphysical tenets of naturalism.

In contrast to this, the theist can offer a variety of reasons to adopt the moral point of view. Moreland states that

> theistic responses incorporate reference to the existence of God. For example, one ought to be moral because the moral law is true and is constituted by the non-arbitrary commands of a good, just, wise, loving God, or because the moral law is grounded in the way we were designed by such a God to function properly. For the Christian, we should be moral for the same reason that a car should be driven on the road and not on the bottom of the ocean: that is the proper, true, flourishing way we were made to function and by so functioning we get in touch with reality and bring honour to our wonderful Creator.[4]

If Moreland is right, then perhaps we need God to ground the existence of moral values more generally and to explain how it is that we both know these values and function best when we live according to them. In this sense, God is a necessary being.

There is much more to be said on both sides of the above controversial issues. Philosophers continue to discuss and debate these questions, and my purpose in this chapter is not to try to settle these disputes. I leave it to the reader to work through these things for yourself if you are so inclined.[5] Be warned, however, that doing so requires a decent amount of reading and some good, hard, critical thinking. But on the flip side, it will be worth it. Our convictions can change or deepen when we consider life's big questions in a systematic and thoughtful manner. In the end, this can result in a better life. And it also requires – for me and probably you also – some good, strong, flavorful coffee to provide fuel for thought. Or at least it provides an excuse to have another cup, if you're looking for one.

Coffee, God, and the Good Life

For me at least, coffee is not necessary for happiness or a good life, but it's pretty close. My day goes better when I start it with a couple healthy cups of Sumatra or some other dark-roasted and bold bean or blend. I also occasionally enjoy an espresso or some other Starbucks concoction in the afternoon when I'm trying to write, read, and (especially) grade papers. And it has to be real coffee, not decaf. A few weeks ago I had a horrible headache, which developed and got stronger as the day went on. Ibuprofen didn't help. I felt like death. It wasn't until later in the day that I wondered and then had confirmed the fact that my morning coffee had been *decaffeinated*. This was not good. You and I need the bean, and I at least need it in its pure, unadulterated, non-Swiss Water Process decaffeinated form.

If you're reading this book, you probably don't need any convincing about the goodness of a quality cup of coffee, though issues about God, moral goodness, and the ultimate aspects of reality may not be so clear. It is here that philosophy can help, not because there is agreement among philosophers about these issues, but because philosophy can help us ask and seek to answer in a reasonable manner questions related to the possible existence of the Necessary Ground of Being.

MICHAEL W. AUSTIN

NOTES

1   Erik J. Wielenberg, *Value and Virtue in a Godless Universe* (New York: Cambridge University Press, 2005), ch. 2.
2   Ibid., p. 52.
3   J. P. Moreland, *The Recalcitrant Imago Dei: Human Persons and the Failure of Naturalism* (London: SCM Press, 2009), ch. 6.
4   Ibid., p. 156.
5   One good place to start is a book that includes both atheistic and theistic philosophers, edited by Nathan King and Robert Garcia, *Is Goodness Without God Good Enough: A Debate on Faith, Secularism, and Ethics* (Lanham, MD: Rowman and Littlefield, 2009).

CHAPTER 3

THE UNEXAMINED CUP IS NOT WORTH DRINKING

The unexamined life is not worth living.

Socrates, *Apology*

Coffee is not a matter of life or death, it's much more important than that.

Unknown

So there you are, at a specialty coffeehouse, standing at the counter listening to the other guests chat up the baristas about the new blend they have. They're throwing around ridiculous lingo like, "The acidity is so bright, but it still has a nice body and a long finish." All you want is a cup of coffee. No frills, no crazy nonsense. Just straight up, black coffee (or maybe you want a little cream – that's cool too). But you don't have the slightest idea what's going on, and perhaps you suspect that the kids behind the bar don't either. Can coffee really be worth all this? I mean, two bucks for coffee?! Am I really getting all that stuff they're talking about? you might be thinking to yourself. Or maybe you're sitting at home, drinking your Folgers/Maxwell House, doubting that there really is that much of a difference (I'm going to argue that there is, dear reader, just you wait), or maybe you don't

Coffee – Philosophy for Everyone: Grounds for Debate, First Edition. Edited by Scott F. Parker and Michael W. Austin, series editor Fritz Allhoff.
© 2011 John Wiley & Sons, Ltd except for editorial material and organization © 2011 Scott F. Parker and Michael W. Austin. Published 2011 by John Wiley & Sons, Ltd.

think that it's worth the risk of being judged by some tattooed twenty-something with chunky black glasses. Maybe none of these descriptions fits you; maybe you know exactly what you like (be it Central/South American or African beans, or a particular blend).

Whoever you are, whatever you drink, there is something that it is like to be you. And, I would argue, there is something that it is like to understand all the supposedly ridiculous lingo baristas and coffee enthusiasts throw around. I intend to show that there is an experiential world of difference between those in the know and those not. There might even be a moral dimension to knowing what you're drinking. To paraphrase Socrates: The unexamined cup is not worth drinking.

What Is It Like to Be a Philosopher of Coffee?

Now I am not going to tell you anything about what it is like to be me, or for that matter, what it is like to be any other philosopher of coffee. What I want to do instead is tell you a bit about what I mean when I say it's like *something* to be a coffee drinker. The philosopher Thomas Nagel famously argued that consciousness is, by its very nature, experiential; that there really is something that it's like to be conscious or, as he argued, to be a bat.[1] His paper was intended to argue that the what-it's-like-ness of an organism (the qualitative subjective experience, sometimes called qualia,[2] that belongs to an organism), be it human or otherwise, is not something science can help us understand. By its very nature, what-it's-like-ness is a mysterious kind of thing. We can use Nagel's example to highlight an important point: that there is something that it's like to be a coffee drinker, and that it's not something that is impossible for you to come to know.

The example Nagel uses to drive home the peculiar nature of conscious experience is that of being a bat; but here he's not talking about what it's like for us to be bats – we can imagine that with little difficulty. We'd flap our arms and scream a lot, perhaps. But that's not particularly philosophically interesting – we're just pretending. What Nagel wants to highlight is that there is something peculiar to the bat's experience of being a bat; there is something that it is like to use echo-location as a primary source of sensory experience. You and I don't have access to that kind of sensory experience, and we can't even really imagine what it would be like if we did. Furthermore, Nagel argues, even though we have access to all kinds of physical facts about how echo-location works, we still don't really know what it's like to use it. What does this have to do with coffee? Everything.

There is something-that-it's-like to be a barista or coffee connoisseur, but, unlike being a bat, with the coffee examples this something-that-it's-like does not have to be a "fundamentally alien form of life."[3] You might worry, however, that if Nagel is right – and many philosophers consider that a big if – about science being fundamentally unable to illuminate for us the nature of subjective conscious experience, then how can we figure out what it is like to be a knowledgeable coffee drinker? What can philosophy do to help you realize what it's like to experience, and I mean really experience, coffee? Simply convincing you that there is something that coffee drinkers experience isn't enough. I have to show you that you too can experience it. But how can you learn what these kinds of subjective experiences are, and how will you know when you are having them?

It seems like the best way to learn anything is through experience itself, but you might have to know what to look for, and Frank Jackson's now-famous "Mary" thought experiment[4] has generated all kinds of different approaches to explaining how we can learn about subjective experiences. It is worth noting that Jackson first used this thought experiment to argue for the strong conclusion that qualia are non-physical entities which exist independently of all physical stuff. But we needn't accept Jackson's conclusion to use his illustrative experiment to learn something about experience, or more precisely, about the experience of coffee. First, the experiment.

Imagine that Mary, a woman in her early thirties, is now and always has been locked in a black and white room, has had her body painted black and white, has never had access to anything colored at all. She has been educated through lectures shown on exclusively colorless televisions and books that lacked even the faintest speck of color. Now imagine that this woman is a genius, and has in fact become the world's leading color physicist (simultaneously specializing in human neurophysiology), amassing every bit of book knowledge (sometimes called "propositional knowledge") that can be gained about color, vision, and the interplay among the various biological, chemical, and structural entities involved in human color vision. The upshot is that Mary knows every physical fact there is to know about color. She even correctly identifies the sky as "blue" and a ripe Roma tomato as "red."

But what, Jackson asks, "will happen when Mary is released from her black and white room or is given a color television monitor? Will she learn anything or not? It seems obvious that she will learn something about the world and our visual experience of it."[5] Jackson is not alone in his sentiment that Mary learns something new; most philosophers admit to having this intuition. But physicalists, those philosophers who maintain that everything there is must be physical, have deployed a number of attempts to explain, in purely physical terms, what it is that Mary learns. Remember that it looks like she learns something non-physical, since she already knows all the physical facts about color vision.

One notable suggestion, put forth by philosopher David Lewis,[6] is that what Mary learns is not a new fact, but rather a new ability. Maybe what Mary learns is the ability to discern, identify, recollect, and imagine the way the world is. She is now able to do things that she couldn't do before, and as such, it's not that she's learned that there is a what-it's-like to see color, but rather she's learned how to do some cool new stuff. Specifically, Lewis suggests that what Mary has learned is how to recognize the same visual experience should it come again, and that she became able to gain certain information when presented with other information. For example, say that she has had an experience of a red rose. If, for some reason, she did not know which color rose it was, and she later learns that it was red, then, because of this new information (namely, that that color is what red looks like), she has the ability to learn something about her previous experiences. What she can now do is discern which of her previous experiences were red ones and which ones were not. It is important to note, as Lewis does, that gaining the ability to gain information is not the same thing as actually gaining information. Consider this example: Learning how to use Google to find a website is not the same thing as actually finding a website. Similarly, by appealing to this hypothesis we can gain new information about the coffee experiences that we've already had. Of course, you are in a position that is exactly the opposite of Mary's; you just need the book knowledge in order to use the abilities you already possess!

What Is It Like to Drink Coffee?

Taking a brief break from straightforward philosophizing, let's go through some of the standard terminology that coffee connoisseurs (a.k.a. "geeks") will use to describe the various features of coffees. This section is something of a how-to guide to understanding coffee and coffee jargon.

There is no reason the knowledgeable experience of coffee should be unattainable – unlike a run-in with a bat, a run-in with a coffee drinker need not be "fundamentally alien" in experience.

If you're looking to find out how exactly it is that a cup of coffee can be better than another – in a word, if you're looking to examine your cup of coffee – you might want to know about some of the key aspects that can change the nature of the coffee. While I'm not going to go into great detail about the idiosyncrasies of each variety of bean, I will suggest some paradigms that generally illustrate the characteristics that we'll consider. When examining your cup of coffee for its relative value, you'll want to note the acidity, the body, the finish, and the flavor. Each of these is a technical term and has a particular use in coffee tasting. I'll offer you an intuitive description of each of these and then a quick idea of how to find it in your own experience. This kind of thing may work best if you go with others and compare notes on what you find in the coffees; but a word of warning before you go chat up one another about your findings in a particular kind of coffee: The Specialty Coffee Association of America (SCAA)[7] often holds its "cuppings" (where coffee experts test out crops and roasts of coffee)[8] in silence, because people's senses can be influenced by what others say. We are social creatures, and I take coffee at its best to be a social phenomenon. But as we'll see below, it's sometimes important not to allow social conventions to get in the way of pure aesthetic appreciation. So, sample coffees with your friends, but compare notes only after you have made your own assessment. You may catch something your friend missed, and vice versa.

So what is this acidity? Acidity is the term that coffee experts have introduced that refers to the actual acids in the beans, but don't let this description turn you off to it; for many coffee drinkers, the right level of acidity is actually a coveted quality. Just as acidity is a key aspect to a successful lemonade (after all, lemonade without the citric acid, well, it just wouldn't be lemonade), the right level of acidity can make or break a cup of coffee. I say "right" level because, just like your lemonade, too much of it can result in a sour cup, and that's not good for anybody. So, in a sense, the acidity of a coffee is the "sharp" or "bright" tartness of the coffee, and is frequently found in coffees hailing from Central America and eastern Africa. (Kenyan coffees are a great example of coffees with a nice acidity.)

To find the acidity, it is often best to do a side-by-side comparison between two different coffees: a dark roast blended coffee (a mix of beans from different-origin countries) and a medium to medium-light roasted single-origin African or American coffee. You want your single-origin to be a lighter roast, because the darker the roast, the heavier the body, and that will overpower the acidity (but we'll get to that in a moment). Start with your lighter roast, and take a small sip, but don't swallow it yet, let it rest on your tongue; see if you can spot the "bright" qualia I mentioned above. Now take a sip of water, and do the same with your dark roast. Note that with this dark roast, there is considerably less liveliness to the coffee; it's heavier, it doesn't have the "zip" of your lighter roast. Of course, you can repeat this as many times as you like, but if you notice the differences I have described, then you have now identified differences in acidity.

I just mentioned that the darker the roast of coffee, the less you'll taste the acidity – but there is something characteristic of dark roasts that is itself to be desired: body. This trait is closely tied to another common trait talked about in coffee-geek circles: finish. But first, the body of the coffee. Body is in part determined by the length of the roasting process: The longer the process takes, the more proteins and oils build up on and inside of the bean, and this often results in a "heavier" feeling on the palate. The body of the coffee is the natural weight that the coffee has, and the texture or viscosity one feels when drinking the coffee. Coffees from the South Pacific are paradigmatic examples of those that are known for their body.

Determining the body of the coffee is sometimes difficult for new coffee drinkers, but I think that it's really pretty easy to pick up on if you know what to look for. You can even work with the same coffees you used to find the experience of acidity; you'll need a nice dark roast and something lighter for comparative purposes. This time, start with the darker coffee, take a big sip and again, don't swallow – this time let the coffee surround your tongue and try to note the way it feels. Is it heavy? Does it seem viscous? Try moving your tongue from the back of your mouth to the front. Now cleanse your palate with some water and try the same with your lighter roast; there should be a fairly dramatic difference. The lighter coffee should actually feel lighter in your mouth. You will notice also that if you add cream or milk to your coffee, the body of the darker roast will, so to speak, show through the milk, but will dissolve in the lighter roast, leaving you with a less lingering feel of body.

As I said above, body is very closely tied to finish. This is a term that we coffee nerds stole from wine tasters, and it refers to how long the coffee lasts on your palate after you swallow it. It is usually described as being "long," "short," or "clean," as you might expect. And it should come as no surprise that the darker the roast, the longer the finish. Try to notice that the lighter the roast, the less the body lingers after you swallow the coffee.

When you attend to these qualities, you can find that there really is a whole lot more going on in your overall coffee experience than you might have originally expected, or noticed. Coffee is not just a matter of waking up in the morning, and now you have the tools to notice just what it is about the varieties of coffee you like and what you don't. But it doesn't end here. With the coffee industry becoming such a massive market, the SCAA has developed a way to standardize (at least to some extent) the terminology that picks out the flavor and aroma of the coffee. In fact, it has developed a "coffee taster's flavor wheel,"[9] which provides a hierarchy upon which we can normalize and, in some sense, objectify the language that we use in reporting our subjective or qualitative experiences, or qualia.

Going through the process of finding the qualities and flavor profiles that you enjoy in your coffee can be a really neat experience, and matching up the facts that you now possess with the abilities that Lewis thinks you already possess can lead you to a more enjoyable coffee life. But there is still a serious philosophical question lurking, namely:

Why Is the Unexamined Cup Not Worth Drinking?

You now have at your disposal all the factual knowledge that you'll need to determine just what it is about coffee that you like. I have just given you information so that you can go forth and gain more information. But from all of this, it does not follow that you should go out and spend all of your time seeking out the perfect cup of coffee, carefully discerning just the right balance of acidity and body for you. If you ought to do something, it had better darn well be the case that you are capable of doing it, but just because you can do something, that doesn't mean that you ought to. Well, now that you can go out and examine your cup of coffee, and you can schmooze with the hipsters at the coffeehouse,[10] why should you? The Scottish philosopher David Hume may have something to say about that.

Hume famously argued that morality is not a matter of reason alone; moral truths are not located in the world independent of human minds, but rather are grounded in human sentiment or emotion. That is, Hume

KRISTOPHER G. PHILLIPS

thought that morality is found only in subjective feelings. Despite maintaining that there is no value in the world independent of human minds (that is, morality is not out there in the world to be discovered by reason; rather, morality is just a reflection of how we feel about things), he argues that there is still a standard of morality that will be roughly the same across all humans (since we are all constituted in the same way – we are all human, after all).[11] For example, all humans will feel that it is wrong to, without any reason, boil babies; that is just wrong.

Hume thinks that aesthetic *judgments*, such as "Fresh roasted coffee is better than stale coffee," or "Dark-roasts are better than light-roasts," are based on the same kinds of sentiments, and so in just the same way that we can settle on a standard of morality, we can settle on a principle "of taste [that] be universal, and nearly, if not entirely, the same in all men."[12] If Hume's arguments provide some plausible story of how it is that most, or even all, people really value the same traits when it comes to aesthetic qualities, then it is not a far cry from lending credence to the claim that we should strive to drink exclusively good coffee (since they are based in the same sentiments).

It may not appear immediately obvious that there is a strong connection between morality and, say, art, but there is. In both cases, we are worried about the value that something has; just think about how we describe the music, books, or coffee that we enjoy. More often than not, we describe such things as good (or some relevant parallel thereof). And when we describe people's character and actions, we often employ the same kinds of value terms. After all, how many times have you heard someone say something like "she is a bad person," or "he is a good person, but what he did was a bad thing to do." And what might be common to an extraordinarily offensive piece of music or art and some particularly nasty action on the part of a person? Certainly one similarity is that we find ourselves feeling disapproval. We often speak of moral wrongs as being "offensive," and likewise we call some aesthetic qualities "offensive." I don't mean to suggest that if you drink a sub-par cup of coffee that you've done something morally wrong, but, I suggest, there is a much closer tie between these two areas than you might originally have thought. At the very least, we may find that we have the same kind feelings of approval or disapproval when we think of a particular action as those that we have when we hear some musical piece or taste some coffee.

Hume argues that when it comes to commonsense approaches to aesthetic judgments, there are two equally prevalent views: On the one hand, it seems difficult to say there is any objective sense of taste (it seems odd to suggest that someone is wrong or mistaken to like Twilight), but on the other hand, it seems odd to think that anyone might consider Twilight to be a superior piece of literature to, say, the *Iliad* or the *Odyssey*. To quote Hume once more:

> The same Homer who pleased at Athens and Rome two thousand years ago, is still admired at Paris and at London. All the changes of climate, government, religion, and language, have not been able to obscure his glory. Authority or prejudice may give a temporary vogue to a bad poet or orator; but his reputation will never be durable or general ... [A] real genius, the longer his works endure, and the more wide they are spread, the more sincere is the admiration which he meets with.[13]

Hume thinks that if it seems odd to judge someone's appreciation of aesthetics as wrong, then we have simply made a mistake. One reason he thinks this is that there are works of art, be they literature, sculpture, painting, or culinary art, that simply appear better than all the others, and nearly everyone knows it. The example of Homer's work is particularly telling; Hume points out that despite all of the dramatic cultural changes, despite all of the trends that have come and gone, none of them have come close to changing our feelings about these works.

To account for the differences in taste, Hume appeals to precisely the kind of experiential talk that I discussed in the first section – he suggests that "though some objects, by the structure of the mind, be naturally calculated to give pleasure, it is not to be expected that in every individual the pleasure will be equally felt."[14] In many cases people simply lack the subtlety of experience to know what to look for, and the number of experiences to find those qualities. Hume even draws an analogy to wine tasters (pulling a story from Don Quixote), which is of particular relevance to us. He says that "in point of delicacy, between one person and another, nothing tends further to increase and improve this talent, than practice in a particular art, and frequent survey or contemplation of a particular species of beauty."[15]

And this is exactly what I have been suggesting of coffee. I have offered you some reason to believe that there is something that it is like to be a coffee drinker, and even tried to offer you some information on how to go about finding those traits that evoke in us "sentiments of approbation." It is now up to you to practice, and cultivate the ability you possess to locate the beauty of the perfect cup of coffee. But the question from the outset of this section still looms large: Why should you?

KRISTOPHER G. PHILLIPS

Recall that we said Hume thinks that morality is ultimately a matter of human sentiments; that morality finds its basis in the gut feeling we all possess. He thinks also that those things we value for their aesthetic purposes are based in the same kinds of sentiments. We can refine our abilities and our thinking in such a way that we can determine what is really good, and we can develop an objective standard of taste. In other words, by honing our abilities to discern the subtle effects that food, music, literature, and so on, have on us, we can find those things that are really good. In order to do this, we must not be biased by those social pressures that can confuse or taint our abilities.

Socrates said that the unexamined life is not worth living. What he may have meant was that too often we go through life without thinking about why we value those things that we do; that we uncritically accept what we are told. Socrates' claim is ultimately a moral principle – that the value of life consists in reasoned examination of what we believe and what we value. Hume echoes this sentiment with regard to taste, and the point can be generalized to all acts of valuing:

> It is well known, that, in all questions submitted to the understanding, prejudice is destructive of sound judgment, and perverts all operations of the intellectual faculties: it is no less contrary to good taste; nor has it less influence to corrupt our sentiment of beauty. It belongs to good sense to check its influence in both cases; and in this respect, as well as many others, reason, if not an essential part of taste, is at least requisite to the operation of this latter faculty.[16]

If we construe Hume as echoing Socrates in this passage, then we might think that Hume is giving us reason to really examine why we enjoy the things we do. If you don't examine your cup of coffee in order to find those qualities that evoke genuine sentiments of approbation, you might be failing morally!

But Hume probably won't blame you for not having properly examined your coffee. He is, however, going to offer praise for those who do, "whether any particular person be endowed with good sense and a delicate imagination, free from prejudice, may often be the subject of dispute, and be liable to great discussion and inquiry: but that such a character is valuable and estimable, will be agreed in by all mankind."[17] Even if we have reason to doubt Hume's account of morality, his arguments, in conjunction with our above discussion of qualia, do seem to suggest that there really is something aesthetically and perhaps even morally important about examining your coffee. And if, as Socrates and Hume both thought, there is something intrinsically valuable about the nature of careful reflection on those things that we value, then, as coffee drinkers and philosophers, don't we owe it to ourselves to examine the cup in front of us? Don't we have an obligation to hone our ability to locate and appreciate the good things in life, and to do so free from prejudice?

To paraphrase one of Hume's passages that we noted above, the same coffee that energized Ethiopia centuries ago is still admired the world around. All of the changes of climate, government, religion, and language have been unable to obscure its glory. It belongs to good sense to check your prejudices against that two-dollar cup of coffee, and examine it, for reason is essential to the operations of taste. So go forth and examine your cup, because otherwise, it's not worth drinking.

NOTES

1   Thomas Nagel, "What is it Like to be a Bat?" *The Philosophical Review* 83, no. 4 (October 1974): 435–450.

2   The term qualia carries with it some strange connotations. Many philosophers who disagree with Nagel about science's ability to explain the mind (call them "physicalists") suggest that the term means something non-physical and weird; something that can't really be talked about. It refers to mental properties that are mysterious and offer no explanatory value. But philosophers like Nagel often slip back to meaning nothing other than "subjective experience," and surely even the craziest of philosophers won't deny that we have experiences... For my purposes, I intend to stick with the weaker notion – just subjective experience.

3   Nagel, "Bat."

4   From Frank Jackson, "Epiphenomenal Qualia," *Philosophical Quarterly* 32 (1982): 127–136.

5   Ibid.

6   David Lewis, "What Experience Teaches," from P. Ludlow, Y. Nagasawa, and D. Stoljar (eds.) *There's Something About Mary: Essays on Phenomenal Consciousness and Frank Jackson's Knowledge Argument* (Cambridge, MA: MIT Press, 2004).

7   www.scaa.org.

8   http://coffeegeek.com/guides/beginnercupping/stepbystep offers a nice introduction to cupping techniques.

9   http://www.sweetmarias.com/tastewheel.html offers not only the full flavor/ aroma wheel, but also a taste-wheel that will explain how the flavors arise during the roasting process. It's a great resource.

10 I am well aware that not all, and indeed, not even most people who work at or frequent coffeehouses are hipsters; aren't I allowed a bit of a rhetorical flourish?

11 Hume is well aware that there seems to be radical disagreement in morality, but he has ways of explaining that away. This is not, however, central to the discussion here, so we will bracket that issue.

12 David Hume, "On the Standards of Taste" (1757).

13 Ibid. For the record, I am not meaning to imply any ill-will toward the author of the Twilight series, I only intend to say that the series is not on a par with one of the greatest literary works of all time.

14 Ibid.

15 Ibid.

16 Ibid.

17 Ibid.

CHAPTER 4

SAṂSĀRA IN A COFFEE CUP

Self, Suffering, and the Karma of Waking Up

Indian philosophical and religious traditions tell us we are ensnared in *saṃsāra*, that ongoing cycle of birth, death, and rebirth. There's *saṃsāra* on the grand scale, playing out over lifetime after reincarnated lifetime until an individual manages to get free and realize liberation, *mokṣa*, or nirvana. There is also *saṃsāra* on the micro-scale, playing out over the course of careers, romances, college basketball seasons, meals, and mere moments of experience – cycles of hope and frustration and hope and (of course) frustration yet again.

I want to use the notion of *saṃsāra* to make sense of one of the recurring rhythms of my life: the lethargic struggle, played out each morning, in which I brew and consume unthinkable amounts of deep, bitter, dark, dark coffee. Every day, there are the predictable aches of confronting a new morning in a pre-caffeinated state. There is the lumbering to the coffee maker, the rinsing of the pot, the soft, mantra-like utterances grumbled while dumping (not measuring) fresh grounds into a new filter. There is a practice of something like forbearance while waiting for the first cup to make it to my lips. Then – finally – there is slow rebirth. Something that

Coffee – Philosophy for Everyone: Grounds for Debate, First Edition. Edited by Scott F. Parker and Michael W. Austin, series editor Fritz Allhoff.
© 2011 John Wiley & Sons, Ltd except for editorial material and organization © 2011 Scott F. Parker and Michael W. Austin. Published 2011 by John Wiley & Sons, Ltd.

resembles the daytime *me* that I know and feel complicated ambivalence toward emerges back into the world of deadlines, dirty dishes, daycare drop-offs, and all that. And then, roughly twenty-four hours later, the cycle repeats. There's anxiety, joy, boredom, hope, and everything else, bookended every twenty-four hours by the sacred rituals of caffeinating myself.

Though the various Indian traditions that see the world in terms of *saṃsāra* are diverse, they agree that the cycle of reincarnation is something from which we need to escape. Sure, there's life after the death of this body, and in some sense that might give us comfort, especially if things aren't going well this time around. But, really, these traditions say, the samsaric cycles, on either the big and literal scale or on the small, metaphorical scale, are just a bunch of trouble.

It's not that *saṃsāra* is supposed to be always unpleasant. Indeed, part of what keeps each of us stuck within the birth-and-death cycle – and, indeed, part of what structures and drives the cycle onward – is the seductive nature of much of what occurs in *saṃsāra*. We want stuff. We crave excitement (or security, or love, or …), and if we don't have it right now, we tend to think that it must be just around the karmic corner. If we do have it, then we fear losing it, and thus we struggle and strive to do that one more thing we think we need to do in order to hold on to the excitement (or security or love or …) and nail it down so that once and for all we'll be sure that it won't ever again escape.

It's addictive, this cycle of grasping, and the very things we do to secure for ourselves what we think will make us happy are often *precisely* the things that set in motion karmic chains of consequences that push what we want just a few inches further outward beyond our grasps. This, in turn, frustrates us and tempts us to keep doing whatever we were just doing, but a bit harder. And all that traps us further in pointless *saṃsāra*. It's a rigged game, and the only way not to lose in the end is to find some way to stop playing.

That, in short, is *saṃsāra*.

Buddhist Backgrounds

I now want to focus in on a specifically Buddhist understanding of *saṃsāra*. According to the Buddhists, the samsaric cycle is marked always and everywhere with *suffering* in one form or another. This suffering is called *duḥkha* in Sanskrit (or *dukkha* in the related language of Pali), and it's considered to be one of the so-called "Three Characteristics" that Buddhists think are ubiquitous features of all existence. The other two Characteristics are *impermanence* (*anitya* in Sanskrit, or *anicca* in Pali) and *no-self* (*anātman* in Sanskrit, *anattā* in Pali).[1] More on impermanence and no-self in a minute.

Duḥkha is tricky. The word means *suffering*, but not necessarily the over-the-top, knock-you-upside-the-head-and-ruin-your-day kind of suffering. *Duḥkha* can be, and often is, more subtle. It's an unsatisfactoriness that pervades life. Some things are physically or mentally painful, causing straightforward, undeniable suffering to some degree. Think here of paper-cuts, public humiliation, and real, honest-to-God tragedies, each of which obviously *hurts* in one way or another. Other things, however, don't seem painful on the surface, but nevertheless cause something like pain indirectly, either by not lasting as long as we'd like (think of a picture-perfect afternoon at the park with someone you love) or by not being everything we expected them to be (think of the family vacation marred by long lines, cloudy days, and petty quarrels) or something of the sort. One way or the other, say the Buddhists, *duḥkha* is all over the place.

That everything is marked by *duḥkha* is the first of what Buddhists call "the Four Noble Truths." The second of these Four Noble Truths is this: There is a root cause of *duḥkha*, and that root cause is self-centered *craving* (*tṛṣṇā* in Sanskrit, *taṇhā* in Pali). In short, stuff sucks, but not so much because it sucks in and of itself (whatever that would mean), but rather because we bring ultimately un-meetable expectations and un-fulfillable desires to bear on the world around us. Because of this craving, the world around us is bound (and even bound and determined) to disappoint us. According to Buddhists, though the universe plays its part, in a very real sense, we ourselves cause our own misery.

There are a third and a fourth Noble Truth, of course, but they won't be crucial for what I want to say about my morning coffee addiction in what follows. Still, let's mention them before moving on. The third Noble Truth is that there is a way to make *duḥkha* stop, and the fourth Truth is that the way to make the *duḥkha* stop consists in a so-called "Noble Eightfold Path" that one can follow. This Eightfold Path maps out a way of living well and thereby reducing the self-centered craving that is the root cause of *duḥkha*.

So, *saṃsāra* is the cycle of birth and death, the framework within which we live out our lives, and it, according to Buddhists, is marked by *duḥkha*, which, again, is one of the Three Characteristics of all phenomena in the

STEVEN GEISZ

samsaric world. Let's consider those other two Characteristics before beginning to make our way back to the morning coffee.

Impermanence is a Characteristic of all reality. It's standardly listed as the first of the Three Characteristics, followed by *duḥkha* and then no-self.[2] Nothing lasts forever. In some cases, that's a comforting fact. My morning grogginess, for example, will pass, as will bouts of the common cold, rainy days, boring lectures, and losing basketball seasons. But, in other cases, we *want* things to last forever – or at least for longer than they do – and the impermanence of those things contributes to the thwarting of our cravings. My café Americano, for instance, starts out far too hot to drink, but after a moment it reaches that perfect temperature. If only it would stay at precisely that perfect temperature until I finish it. Indeed, if only this particular coffee drink would last longer than it will, and if only the span of time within which I can lounge at this coffee shop could be stretched out until I am good and satisfied, and if only *all* the things I enjoy could be made to last longer … The fact that all things are transient, when coupled with the craving for things that we like to remain as they are, leads to *duḥkha*, and so these two Characteristics of impermanence and *duḥkha* are connected.

The last of the Three Characteristics is *anātman*, or no-self. According to Buddhists, nothing has a stable self or essence that persists through time. This claim that everything is marked by no-self is understood in different ways by different strands of Buddhism, but they all agree that you and I and all sentient beings that we care about lack a central core self, Self, or soul. Look at yourself (or at your "self") carefully, say the Buddhists, and you will not find anything stable there that deserves to be called "a Self" (with or without the capital "S"). Instead, you will only find processes and momentary phenomena jumbled together in the form of your bodily and mental existences. According to Buddhist traditions, these processes and phenomena do not constitute anything unified enough to be a self, and the mistaken notion that there is a self somewhere in the mix feeds the misguided self-concern that gives rise to the self-centered craving – or, better yet, to the "self"-centered craving – that in turn gives rise to the suffering and unsatisfactoriness that is *duḥkha*.

Moreover, the suffering experienced by the ever-changing, self-less jumbles that we think of as "selves" makes it even easier for the fragmentary processes and phenomena of the various jumbles to give rise to the mistaken thought that there *is* a self in there somewhere. Then, when the idea that there is a self in the mix arises in some jumble, that tends to give rise to the related idea that the self in question needs to be protected from the pain, thereby perpetuating a self-reinforcing (and "self"-reinforcing) cycle of mistaken beliefs and desperate cravings leading to misery. This misery, in turn, leads to more entrenched mistaken beliefs and even more recalcitrant cravings.

Thus, the Three Characteristics of *suffering*, *impermanence*, and *no-self* are intertwined and mutually supporting, and they all relate back to the Four Noble Truths, which say that *there is suffering*, that *self-centered craving is the root cause of suffering*, that *there is a way out of suffering*, and that *the Buddhist's Eightfold Path is that way out*.

Beyond the Three Characteristics and Four Noble Truths, there is what is known as *dependent arising* (*praīttya-samutpāda* in Sanskrit, or *paticca-samuppāda* in Pali). According to the Buddhists, everything that exists does so only as a result of other conditions, and each of those conditions itself exists only as a result of still other conditions, and so on. Everything, that is, arises or originates dependent upon something else.

Described in that way, the claim that everything arises dependently might seem just to be a variation on the claim – familiar from non-Buddhist philosophical systems, the natural sciences, and much contemporary common sense – that every event has a cause. However, the Buddhist notion of dependent arising has a different kind of bite to it. Combined with the no-self claim that says nothing has any stable, independently existing essence, the Buddhist idea that dependent arising is pervasive implies that to understand both the coming-into-being and the current-and-ongoing-existence of any object, process, or phenomenon, we need to see it as being both deeply intertwined with and completely dependent upon a host of other objects, processes, or phenomena, each of which in turn can only properly be understood as intertwined with and dependent upon other objects, processes, or phenomena, and so on.

So, on the one hand, the *non*-Buddhist version of the claim that "everything has a cause" is compatible with a metaphysical vision that sees all the things that make up the universe as being stable entities that exist (or at least could exist) on their own, independent of everything else. On this non-Buddhist version of the "everything-has-a-cause" worldview, the individual things that make up reality are each understandable individually as things with their own essences and independent existences that just so happen to have been caused by other stable entities that exist on their own with their own essences and independent existences.

On the other hand, the Buddhist notion of dependent arising sees all the things that come into being as somehow arising *together* – that is, as forming a large, tangled web of empty nodes that come into being and continue to exist only as a causal result of and only in relation to other things in the web. According to the Buddhist theory of dependent arising, nothing comes into being independently of other things, nothing remains in existence independently of other things, and nothing can even properly be understood or thought of independently of other things.

That's hard to write, hard to read, and hard to think about. How is dependent arising supposed to play out in practice? Consider, as an example, my humble, tangible cup of coffee. According to the Buddhists, it lacks a self or essence: It is marked by *anātman*. Okay, that's fine, and more or less unobjectionable. Indeed, I can't honestly say that I ever thought of any cup of coffee as having something I'd refer to as "a self." But now think of the cup of coffee not just in terms of no-self, but also in terms of dependent arising. The cup of coffee exists here and now, as it does – that is, as a "self-less," steaming mass of liquid coffee in a "self-less" porcelain mug – only because of a host of other conditions, both in the past and at this very instant. There are physical factors such as the physical stuff of which the cup and its contents are made. There are also chemical bonds, air and vapor pressures, and electromagnetic energy, as well as the laws of nature and the physical components of the wider physical environment that keep me sitting here holding on to the handle of the mug without my coffee flying away or freezing solid or boiling off or (heaven forbid) turning into some *über*-hot plasma that would clearly mess up my morning. There are also economic conditions in the past that allowed for the coffee beans to be grown, transported, roasted, ground, and sold to me, that allowed the water to emerge from the tap, that brought the coffee grounds and the water together with the filter in my coffee maker along with the electricity needed to brew this cup. There are also the wider social and psychological histories and pressures that got me into the habit of drinking coffee every morning. And there are lots of other conditions, both now and in the past, that, according to the Buddhist idea of dependent arising, both cause and somehow constitute this humble porcelain mug filled with hot, black coffee that is sitting in front of me now.[3]

In early Buddhist texts, the notion of dependent arising is illustrated by descriptions of chains of phenomena that serve as the conditions for the arising of other phenomena. In a famous passage from the

Saṃyutta Nikāya, ignorance is identified as a condition that gives rise to something that is labeled variously as "mental formulations," "mental dispositions," or "volitional formations." These in turn give rise to other mental phenomena (such as consciousness and feeling) and physical phenomena (such as contact between one's body and the world) that eventually give rise to that self-centered craving that is (according to the second of the Four Noble Truths) the root cause of *duḥkha*. The *duḥkha* is a condition for other things, and the chain ends with the combination of old age and death, so that the Buddhist tradition winds up saying that ignorance is in some sense the cause of all the mental and physical mess that causes suffering and even death. Indeed, it can be taken to be saying that ignorance is a root cause of *saṃsāra* itself.[4]

It is important to note, however, that this chain of conditions giving rise to other conditions does not simply run from ignorance to old age and death. Rather, given the overarching notion of the world we live in as consisting of cycles of *saṃsāra*, the aging and death will themselves serve as causal conditions that set the stage for further rebirth in ignorance, which itself will start the chain again. And the ignorance at the start of the chain is ignorance of many things, but it is especially ignorance of the Four Noble Truths and of the overall Buddhist prescription for getting out of *saṃsāra* and away from suffering and all that bad stuff by eliminating self-focused craving.

Before getting back to the morning coffee, there's a bit more Buddhist background worth considering: the connection between *saṃsāra* and karma. Karma is complicated, but for our purposes here's what's important: *Saṃsāra* is driven onward by karmic consequences, which are causal consequences that will follow at some point down the road from all intentional action that is done in ignorance of the self-less nature of reality.[5] Everything we do intentionally has consequences – good, bad, and neutral. Some of those consequences are predictable and even part of our very intention for doing whatever it is, while some of those consequences are subtler or more distant, perhaps unpredictable, and certainly not part of anything we *intended* to make happen. Nevertheless, those consequences will come, at some point and in some way or other, as the result of the playing out of karmic law. It is this playing out of karmic law that shapes *saṃsāra*, and the self-centered craving that is the root of *duḥkha* is also the root of the intentional actions that create karmic consequences that keep us ensnared in samsaric cycles.

STEVEN GEISZ

We must be careful when describing these karmic cycles. If the no-self idea is correct – if there is really no essential self that continues on through time – then the karmic consequences of my intentional, mis-guidedly self-centered action here and now will not, strictly speaking, be experienced by some real *me* that persists through time until when-ever it is that those karmic consequences come home to roost. Rather, there will be patterns of changing mental and physical phenomena, loosely connected into one or a series of those jumbles I mentioned above, sloppily held together by the presence of the ignorance-fueled, false belief that there *is* some persistent Self at the center of the jumble or series of jumbles that needs to be protected and that *can* be pro-tected by having that Self's desires satisfied. It will be a dynamic jum-ble in the future that dependently arises somehow as a continuation of or causal result of my ignorant, self-centered intentional actions here and now that will reap the karmic punishments and rewards of what "I" do here and now. And, unless that jumble wakes up and somehow "gets it," it, too, will create karma and nudge the samsaric cycle onward, perhaps *ad infinitum*.

But how does all this relate to my addiction to multiple cups of morn-ing coffee?

Certainly there are surface-level resonances between the Buddhist ideas we've just considered and the morning coffee rituals that are famil-iar to so many of us. Coffee consumption is driven onward by a kind of tired suffering in the face of a new day. We crave some way out of the daily morning *duḥkha*, and we hope and expect that one (or maybe even six) cups of coffee will take the edge off. The morning weariness, like everything else, is impermanent. It doesn't last, especially not when it is hammered down by the coffee. However, the relief that the coffee pro-vides is transient, too. And, if we look at things in the right way, we can see dependent arising in the coffee and the cup, and in you and me and all of our patterns of behavior, too. Everything, from the coffee in the cup to the drinker to the wider social and physical environments within which the coffee drinking takes place, can be seen as hanging together in com-plex webs of mutually supporting conditions, such that the coffee ena-bles us (in the full-blown pop-psychology sense of the word *enables*), and we, in a way, enable the coffee, too.

But let's look more closely at two features of my morning coffee addic-tion: the ways in which my functioning self is in some sense created by the coffee, and the karmic consequences of the behaviors that constitute my recurring coffee-drinking rituals.

Brewing Up a Self

Let's think about the self who confronts the morning, and leave aside the Buddhist no-self stuff for a moment. Before I've had my morning coffee, I'm bad at making decisions. My will, insofar as it's there, is not quick on the draw. I don't like to talk much, and, when I do say things, I sure ain't a poet. I don't even *think* very well, pre-coffee. If someone asks me a question, I often forget to answer. My top-of-the-morning motor skills aren't great, either; indeed, I often bump into things on the way to the coffee maker on the counter. I do manage to function in my environment to some extent – the coffee usually gets brewed in my house, and I'm sometimes the one to do it – but I don't function *well*. To top it off, prior to that first cup I'm often unaware of how comparatively poorly I'm doing unless someone else who knows me well points it out to me.

As I gradually caffeinate, I start to think. Then comes workable verbal communication. Gradually, the will begins to stir, and I'm better able to make decisions. I am able to read a story to my toddler son (who – still gloriously free from coffee addiction – wakes up with a thirst for a sippy-cup full of milk and a hunger for fine literature about things like monkeys and lost bunny rabbits). In short, with coffee in my system I begin to approximate what it is that I think of as *me*.

Reflecting on this transition into caffeine-conditioned wakefulness that occurs every morning, it's easy to think of the pre-coffee self as being at best an impoverished version of the post-coffee self, or even as being a rudimentary proto-self that manages (with the help of coffee) to spawn the more wide-awake self that goes about the rest of my day. The more fully functioning, post-coffee me isn't there at the start of the day; he's only on the clock after the coffee kicks in.

How should I think about these facts? Let's consider three hypotheses that differ in terms of how much, if any, of a self is thought of as being there at the break of day.

On one hypothesis, *all* of me is there all along, but, given my coffee karma, much of the self is shut down at the start of the day and certain functions don't "come on line" in the morning until after coffee. According to this hypothesis, the coffee functions primarily to turn on various systems that are there but dormant; it doesn't really create anything.

On a second hypothesis, I am literally not all there prior to the coffee. Instead, a *partial* version of my self confronts the start of the day. Coffee

  STEVEN GEISZ

is added to this partial self, and, somehow, *Voilà!* – a new self emerges. According to this second hypothesis, the fully functioning, post-coffee me is really some sort of half-and-half coffee cyborg, part human and part *Coffea arabica* extract, that is created anew each day by adding coffee to a pre-coffee half-self that makes it through the night.

On a third hypothesis, there is really *no* self – not even a half-formed partial self – there at all at the start of the day. There is just the body, and whatever mentality is present is so rudimentary and fragmented that it does not even deserve to be called a "proto-self." Indeed, on the roughest mornings, this is how it feels. According to this third hypothesis, some-how – as if by the spontaneous generation that people used to think hap-pened with flies and meat – a brand new self is constructed by coffee and the forces of nature each morning by adding coffee to the cognitively empty shell that is my pre-caffeine physical body. The self that is created more or less *ex nihilo* (or, more properly, *ex Coffea*) has a good run of things throughout the day until he is reduced back to nothingness at the end of each day.

These three hypotheses are, perhaps, interesting, but each one pre-sumes that there *is* a self there at the *end* of the morning caffeination process. While they differ in terms of how they conceive of the formation of that self and in terms of what they say about how much (if any) of that self is there at the start of the day, they agree in thinking that some full-blown self somehow comes on line, grows out of a pre-existing proto-self, or gets cobbled together from scratch. In contrast, if we look at my morning coffee transition through the lens of the Buddhist notion of no-self and the associated ideas about dependent origination and the rest, a different possibility emerges: There is nothing there in the morn-ings at all – either pre- or post-coffee – that can properly be thought of as *a self*. There are just various processes, ultimately lacking in any truly stable unity, that give rise to each other with regularity, under the imper-sonal direction of the laws of physical nature and the more metaphysi-cally heavy law of karma.

According to this Buddhist view, the mess of processes available pre-coffee in my case is incapable of operating in various sophisticated sorts of ways. It spills coffee grounds and half-mutters something approximat-ing an expletive, for instance. However, the slightly more organized – or at least slightly more driven – set of processes that is present post-caffeine is more capable of engaging in sophisticated operations in the world. It puts on shoes, drives to campus, and teaches class, for example. The disjointed consciousness and poor decision-making before the coffee, on the one hand, and the more "jointed" consciousness and the somewhat better decision-making after the coffee, on the other hand, are, on this Buddhism-inspired view, not really different in kind, but rather only in degree. In both cases, there's no self. There are just differing intensities of functionality that get filtered through the diaphanous haze of the morning and injected with caffeine.

Just a Cup of Coffee – or a Karma Macchiato?

Every morning, there comes a time when I (at long last!) have a cup of black coffee in my hand. I then lift the mug to my lips and take either a sip or a swig, depending on how desperate I am on that particular occasion, what my mouth's tolerance to heat is like on that day, and how intact my fine-motor coordination is after the night's sleep. Perhaps I don't *choose* to take that sip or swig; maybe it's just a habit, or a mere reflex, and a habit or reflex of the sort that allows us to dispense with any talk of "choosing" on that particular occasion. No matter. Somehow, from within my morning fog, I manage intentionally to start drinking the coffee.

That act has consequences. There are some more or less immediate consequences, such as the near-instantaneous creation of the gustatory, tactile, and olfactory sensations and perceptions of drinking the coffee, the production of memories and random thoughts that go hand in hand with the base-level sensations and perceptions, and the more obviously physico-chemical processes by which the caffeine in the coffee enters into my bloodstream and begins to make me more alert in whatever way it does. I'm not big on tracking those physico-chemical details; it's a reliably repeatable mystery, as far as I'm concerned.

There are longer-term consequences as well, and not all of them are pleasant. Tomorrow morning I will need the coffee again, in part because of my behavior this morning. Indeed, my urge to drink the coffee this morning, and the caffeine withdrawal headache I would experience and the groggy irascibility I would exhibit if I were not to drink it, are arguably karmic consequences of the coffee-drinking behaviors I exhibited yesterday, the day before that, and just about every day before that, stretching back years and years. I am already reaping the karmic consequences of my past coffee-drinking behaviors from earlier in this lifetime, and every morning I add to my karmic coffee load by choosing – or at

STEVEN GEISZ

least intentionally allowing myself – to submit to the patterns of behavior that make up my morning caffeination rituals.

If we include the consequences of my choosing to drink organic versus inorganic coffee, fair trade versus not, high-end versus cheap, drip versus instant, etc., or if we allow ourselves to entertain the possibility of karmic consequences stretching between lifetimes (Was I a barista in a previous life? A coffee picker? Some sort of coffee plant parasite that ruined a particular crop?) or even simply karmic consequences that transfer between different facets of a single life (Am I somehow now compelled daily to drink coffee in part because of that time I lied to my mother about eating that extra Oreo cookie when I was five?), then the sense in which the simple repetitions of my morning coffee behaviors can be seen as enmeshed in myriad cross-cutting karmic relationships and thereby entrapped in samsaric cycles becomes head-spinning. In brewing and then drinking coffee each morning, I act intentionally, but I do so while being driven on by a vast karmic inheritance that would make it at least extremely difficult if not outright impossible for me to do anything else.

By so acting, I foist an additional karmic burden on the "me" who will stand in my kitchen twenty-four hours later doing his best to make his way through a morning.

That's heavy, bitter stuff to think about. I don't know what to make of it all, but I'm sure it calls for another cup.

NOTES

1   There are many introductory texts that map out the notions I am introducing in this section. Two very good academic introductions to these Buddhist ideas are Donald W. Mitchell, *Buddhism: Introducing the Buddhist Experience*, 2nd ed. (New York: Oxford University Press, 2008) and Mark Siderits, *Buddhism and Philosophy: An Introduction* (Indianapolis: Hackett, 2007).
2   See *Aṅguttara Nikāya* III, 134, in Bikkhu Bodhi (trans.), *Numerical Discourses of the Buddha: An Anthology of Sutras from the Aṅguttara Nikāya* (Boston: Wisdom Publications, 1999), p. 7.
3   See Thich Nhat Hanh's discussion of "interbeing" in his *The Heart of Understanding: Commentaries on the Prajñaparamita Heart Sutra* (Berkeley: Parallax Press, 1988), pp. 3–5.
4   In the passage from the *Saṃyutta Nikāya*, the Buddha is recorded as saying the following: "And what, monks, is dependent arising? With ignorance as condition, volitional formations [come to be]; with volitional formations, consciousness; with consciousness ... [insert several other links in the chain here]

... craving; with craving ... [insert a few more links here] ... aging-and-death, sorrow, lamentation, pain, dejection, and despair [i.e., the basic processes that constitute *saṃsāra*] come to be." This passage was taken from the *Saṃyutta Nikāya* 12: 1 II, in Bikkhu Bodhi (trans.), *The Connected Discourses of the Buddha: A Translation of the Saṃyutta Nikāya* (Boston: Wisdom Publications, 2000), p. 355. It is reprinted in Bikkhu Bodhi, *In the Buddha's Words: An Anthology of Discourses from the Pāli Canon* (Boston: Wisdom Publications, 2005), p. 353. I have changed Bikkhu Bodhi's "dependent origination" into "dependent arising." The first bracketed phrase in the *Saṃyutta Nikāya* quotation is in the Bodhi translation itself, whereas the other bracketed phrases are my own.

5   See Bikkhu Bodhi's discussion of karma in Buddhism in *In the Buddha's Words*, pp. 145–146. Bodhi there writes: "The word *kamma* [i.e., the Pali version of the Sanskrit word *karma*] literally means action, but technically it refers to volitional action. As the Buddha says: 'It is volition (*cetanā*) that I call kamma; for having willed (*cetayitvā*), one acts by body speech, and mind'." Donald W. Mitchell translates the word "*cetanā*" with "*will*," and says: "Karma, according to the Buddha, is the result of *willful intention*" (Donald W. Mitchell, *Buddhism, Introducing the Buddhist Experience*, 2nd ed. [New York: Oxford University Press, 2008], p. 42; italics added).

STEVEN GEISZ

CHAPTER 5

THE EXISTENTIAL GROUND OF TRUE COMMUNITY

Coffee and Otherness

The daily café soirées of Jean-Paul Sartre have become a well-known facet of philosophical history. The popularity of Sartre's coffee ritual, however, is inconsistent with Sartre's dark existential philosophy, which claims that we find ourselves to be essentially alone in this world – trapped by the looks that other people give us. It is odd that Sartre, who was at his best when he was sipping coffee and smoking cigarettes in his local café, could become known for a philosophy as depressing as some think existentialism. It leads us to wonder whether an existentialist like Sartre would fit in with the coffee communities that have grown in the United States, or even if existentialism in the twenty-first century can explain why it is that such communities exist and whether they should be fostered.

While I sip my dark roast, in my own brought-from-home Hello Kitty travel mug, listening to grassroots music, and writing this chapter in my local coffeehouse, I am led to think that Sartre missed out on something that other existentialists seemed to at least suspect: Life together can be meaningful in a way that beats life alone. All existentialists believe that having a body – rather than, say, a soul – is the most significant and threatening part of human experience. *Optimistic existentialism* shares this belief, but also suggests that even if it is true that having bodies causes pain and a fear of being alone, we can create meaning for ourselves in communities. We are alone, but we are not alone. We can be saved from isolation, according to the optimistic existentialists (the most noted of whom include Søren Kierkegaard, Gabriel Marcel, Karl Jaspers, and Martin Buber) if we can connect as a community with others who find themselves in the same situation.

The community of others (one perhaps best evidenced in the culture of coffee drinkers) can repair the effects of isolation and dread. Though they use different terms (Kierkegaard's "love," Marcel's "exigent self," Jaspers's "encounter," or Buber's "dialogical principle"), the optimistic existentialists together show that a person has the best chance to triumph over the hopelessness of existence by banding together through shared interests, commitments, and vulnerability with others. If these existentialists are right, then the coffee community – which draws people together, gives identity, and promotes cultural, civic, and environmental awareness – can stand as an example of existential well-being and, if I dare say it, optimism.

A Dark Brew: Traditional Existentialism and Community

Existentialism is often equated in popular culture with the dark writings of Jean-Paul Sartre and Albert Camus. Although existentialism is no longer a philosophical or political movement, most people still think of existentialism as a depressing viewpoint that only predicts meaningless-ness and anguish for people who are smart enough to understand what the existentialists were saying. This caricature is actually well grounded, since many of the important existential thinkers painted an extremely lonely, negative picture of human existence. Sartre, a political and academic icon in World War II France, became famous even outside of academia for arguing – often from his table at the Café de Flore – that "hell is other people," and that existence itself can suffocate people who are trapped by their circumstances or by how other people look at them. Sartre wrote, "I find the profound meaning of my being outside of me, imprisoned in an absence."[1] In a significant way, who a person is depends on how others perceive that person.

JILL HERNANDEZ

Starbucks recently underwent a corporate change that reflects what Sartre meant about individuals. In the fall of 2009, Starbucks decided to use only one roast, Pike Place, for its daily brewed coffee, and to altogether stop brewing a bold roast, except for on-demand single cups. It stopped brewing its mild roasts altogether. The backlash was quite staggering. The perceived commitment Starbucks had toward providing its customers with blends from around the world was replaced with a suspicion that Starbucks might be what other mom-and-pop cafés have always argued it is: a money-hungry company that is wholly interested in the bottom line.[2] The interesting result is that Starbucks recognized the changed perception – so much so that in the spring of 2010, Starbucks ran a "bold coffee passport" promotion that rewarded customers who bought one cup of each of its bold coffees with a free pound of bold roast. And while it has kept the Pike Place roast as its daily brew, the company has reinstated brewing a different bold coffee each day for its customers.

Sartre might say that Starbucks demonstrates what happens to people every single day: Other people trap us, and yet we seemingly cannot have a sense of who we are as people without the perception of other people. But the way others perceive us can actually end up making us lose any true sense of who we are as individuals. Although coffee companies wouldn't survive without adapting to their customers' desires, if a person's sense of self depends on how other people view her, she becomes a type of object to those people. And Sartre thinks that if my personal identity depends on the perceptions of others, then who I am is degraded in such a way that I am only comfortable with myself when other people are looking at me. Each of us becomes, in effect, a reflection of other people so that nothing of the self actually remains.

Imagine what happens to our coffee pastime if Sartre is right. If the self does not really (authentically) exist, then there cannot be any true community. Any sense of "community" for Sartre would have to be based on faith in the goodness of humanity or in society's welfare[3] – which cafés attempt to promote – but Sartre thinks that neither humanity nor society's welfare are intrinsically good. Being a part of a group is no more valuable than any other activity for dark existentialism. Being in the military, voting for a specific political party, worshipping in a church, or playing in a city league softball team are all equal in value to, say, brushing one's teeth or washing the car. Special value for any act only comes if the person freely chooses to perform the act. (Of course, most people think that their actions are free. But, they forget that the reason they choose most of their actions is because other people are watching and judging them – not because they really want to choose that act.) Sartre wouldn't say that it is valuable when the neighborhood café donates its used grounds to the elementary school's organic garden. Instead, the value of the act comes from the free choice of the individuals participating in the project. Free choices have value, for Sartre, and so communities are valuable only for the choices their members make to join the group and for their individual actions within the group. To draw from the café, you and I can get together for coffee, but it isn't meaningful for us to drink coffee – but it might be valuable for me to make the choice to spend my time drinking coffee with you.

For Albert Camus, if the world were a café it would be as though everyone buys Folgers, either because they don't know about espresso drinks or they are afraid of what other people will think if they chose something different. Camus's existential thought is equally dark, then, and potentially negative, because it is grounded on the idea that all humans share the trait of feeling alienated from each other. Each of us is a stranger to our selves – we act as though we are free when we are not – and so each of us is a stranger to each other. The difference between most people and the existentialist is that the existentialist rebels against the social rituals that keep us as slaves (like those in religion, politics, and morality). Since these rituals are fundamentally absurd and meaningless, we can live freely if we dispense with them. Most people use social rituals to forget that each of us will die, but the existentialist recognizes that there is no escape from death and so there is no future except for what we choose for ourselves. At best, we can rescue value for our experiences by refusing to give into the pull of homogeneity and by choosing to be individuals.

Sartre and Camus agree that there cannot be true existential community, except in that we share a notion that being human means we are isolated from others. The two can be read differently, however, on the role coffee can play in how we respond to life's absurdity. Sartre at times seems to chide Camus for not choosing to place value on certain aspects of the existential human experience. In his comment on Camus's novel *The Stranger*, Sartre writes, "In this book, we reencounter one of the themes of surrealist terrorism ... No matter, for everything has the same value, whether it be writing *The Possessed* or drinking a cup of coffee. Camus does not demand of the reader that attentive solicitude that writers do who 'have sacrificed their lives to art'."[4] If Camus accepted a Sartrean sense of value, the freely chosen cup of coffee could have more value than an author's published novel, if the reason the author wrote the book was to fulfill a contractual obligation.

Interestingly, although the works of Sartre and Camus cannot easily explain the community that is generated by the coffee-drinking public, there is one voice among the traditional existential thinkers that suggests such a community is existentially possible, though difficult to come by. For Søren Kierkegaard, a main existential problem that hinders community is self-love, because when a person's focus is her own desires, she isolates herself from others. Proper love focuses on the needs of other people. Of course, Kierkegaard believes that it is only Christian love that can allow a person to properly love others, and so only Christian love can give meaning to life. In *Works of Love*, Kierkegaard writes,[5] "Fundamentally love to God is decisive; from this arises love to one's neighbor; but of this paganism was not aware. Men left God out; men considered erotic love and friendship to be love and shunned self-love.... Love God above all else and then love your neighbor and in your neighbor every man. Only by loving God above all else can you love your neighbor in the next man." What Kierkegaard thinks of as proper "love," then, cannot be separated from faith in God.

There has been a recent trend in the coffee world that mirrors Kierkegaard's view. The Christian coffeehouse has emerged not only as a business venture, but also as a way to communicate the notion of Christian love that Kierkegaard talks about and to facilitate a church-like community with its patrons. Often, the Christian café features only Christian artists and the groups that meet there are based in a local church. The Christian café, then, uses coffee as a vehicle to test the sense of love Kierkegaard thinks is possible only in a Christian setting.

So, if we are to look for an explanation of the community that many cafés without a religious bent attempt to create, the traditional existentialists will not be able to easily provide one. That does not mean, though, that existentialism as a philosophy (rather than as a theological arm) is divorced from community. Rather, we might be looking at the wrong sort of existentialism to frame the way we think about the coffee community. Existentialism that prescribes isolation for the individual simply cannot give a robust sense of community that is fostered by the café culture, since the coffee community is driven by helping the environment, the community, and (often) local artists and businesses. But there is a different kind of existentialism – one that is committed to the main tenets of existentialism but that also believes that our best chance at a meaningful life is to act collectively. By turning to this existentialism – a more optimistic existentialism – we see that the coffee community can serve as an example of a vibrant, meaningful, and altogether *existential* mode of living.

Coffee and Otherness: Community and Coffee

It isn't true, of course, that coffee *must* bring others into community, or that cafés are always enclaves for community gathering. (Gabriel Marcel would be quick to point out that we can sit next to each other and yet lack true presence with each other.) Any coffee drinker can tell stories about their worst café experience, or about the local retail chain they visit when they "just need some caffeine." But we need not look beyond economics to see that building communities is a way to foster the growth of a coffee business. Studies have found that cafés generate more funds when they create social gathering opportunities, rather than merely selling coffee as a commodity alone.[6] The experience of drinking coffee, and especially drinking coffee in a café, lends itself toward community building, and even in the United States – where in urban areas one never has to travel far without being away from a retail coffee shop – cafés have become symbols for gathering. The community knows that the café is a spot to come together, and the café often projects itself as a place to connect with others. Young and old, from all stations in life, people use the coffee shop and the experience of drinking coffee as a focal point of togetherness, and conversely, the café uses its status as a meeting spot to promote opportunities to tie people to their community (whether as a donation location, to advertise other community groups, or to highlight and coordinate community social efforts).

From the standpoint of the optimistic existentialist, there are aspects of the coffee-drinking experience that uniquely lend themselves to the development of community. First is that drinking coffee draws people together in meaningful ways. It is not a surprise that many of the experiences we have are really ways to connect with people – playing canasta, taking a class, the hot sale at Home Depot, or watching Robert Downey, Jr.'s latest exploits on the big screen. But the coffee-drinking experience brings people together for the sake of building community, perhaps even doing so in a way that differs from other types of drinking. We are social beings, but we can go about many of our daily activities without being involved in a community of others, and those activities are no better – or worse – off for the lack of engagement. But coffee drinking is different. Quiet cups of coffee can be treasured just as gregariously shared java, but whether it is the warmth, the bite, the aroma, or the ritual of coffee drinking, the experience of coffee is enhanced by the participation of others in the activity. Whether in grief or in celebration, joining with others to

JILL HERNANDEZ

drink coffee creates a feeling of something shared in a way that is different than an activity without coffee.

A number of thinkers can provide an existential basis, or "ground," for this coffee community. Karl Jaspers argued that the "interlinkage" of human beings allows each person to escape isolation and, ultimately, despair. It is true that we are, at our most basic level, bodies. When we realize that we ultimately will die, we can lose hope. Experiences, however, that intentionally bring people together – like that of sharing a cup of coffee – can lead us out of despair and hopelessness. Sharing coffee connects us to others by showing us more clearly that we have a duty to meet the needs of others, and to be ready to communicate with others. This connection, for Jaspers, is thought of as "encounter." In meaningful encounters, the bond that exists between those who encounter each other in community can be stronger than those forged out of social necessity. The beauty of Jaspers's encounter is perhaps best seen in the neighborly cup of coffee. The neighborly coffee visit is not something that must be done, but the fact that it is done allows people to make connections and meet needs. Coffee provides an opportunity for us to listen and then to respond. And, even more, for Jaspers, without those encounters, individuals can never truly know themselves. Those who participate in encounter "strike flame out of one another by the intimacy of their communication. They are the origin of the loftiest soaring movement which is as yet possible in the world. They alone constitute true human beings."[7]

Community for Jaspers, then, not only is possible but is also the tool through which a meaningful existential life can be had. The café, a gathering locale, fosters the type of community that Jaspers is looking for, especially when the café can produce encounter through encouraging communication and action in the community. If the coffee shop is merely a place where business is transacted, then it is useless as a venue for people to connect and to have community. Just as people can be objectified, the intimacy of the café (and so, whether the experience of sharing coffee can be significant existentially) depends on whether community is encouraged there. For Jaspers, the individual – if he connects with other individuals – can slough off the anguish that comes through living as though he is isolated. A community of coffee drinkers who are loyal to each other, then, can be an example of a group that, together, successfully lives.

Martin Buber would be careful to emphasize that a coffee community is possible only if those who participate in the coffee community treat each person in it as a "Thou" rather than an "It." Imagine that you enter your favorite café, happy for the repose the afternoon there will bring. When you approach the counter, the barista does not look at you, does not talk to you, even though she takes your money and you end up getting the correct drink. You wait for a table, finally get one (a single, next to the wall, closest to the restrooms), and not one person interacts with you when you are there. You would not be wrong to think that no one would miss you if you were not there, and that your presence (and not just your order) did not factor into anyone's thought process or decision-making. There, on that particular day, you were treated as though you were nothing except a *thing* – an "It" to be used and discarded without acknowledgment.

Being treated as a thing, rather than as a person, creates pain that can cause us to be disconnected from ourselves and from others. Pain can be an obstacle to living meaningfully. When we are treated as an It, as a mere thing, we cannot learn what it means to exist beyond how other people can use us. When that happens, we have no value except when we are being used. When we discover that the source of our pain comes from being treated as an object, we can connect to others in a way that was not otherwise possible. Buber writes, "Only then does his own pain in its ultimate depth light a way into the suffering of the world. Only participation in the being of present life discloses the meaning in the ground of one's own being."[8] An effective coffee community can help us break out of being treated only as an It. Cafés typically offer many opportunities for this to happen – from something as simple as calling out their patrons' names rather than their drinks, to something as grand as organizing a gift drive for local children during the holidays. My café uses a "neighborhood board" that locals use to post needs of the community (recent examples are help with mowing a lawn, a Tuesday toddlers book club, a pancake breakfast for a cancer patient in need, and a call for families to host international students at home). Such a venue allows people to be more than customers, and it connects others, mostly because it helps us to treat others as significant apart from what they do for us.

Buber would think of these activities as examples of his "dialogical principle" (which is when individuals might not understand true being, but still share in meaningful experiences with each other), and they provide examples of an existential ground of community. Buber's existential principle offers a way to have hope through the communities that can be fostered through the tradition of gathering for coffee. Just as cafés provide a chance to meet the needs of different people in the community

JILL HERNANDEZ

and to be reminded that we are not alone, Buber would say that meaningful existential life comes through being inclusive and through breaking out of the anguish that can come from being human. Buber thinks that loneliness is a key trait of being human, but that participating in a community can assuage this loneliness in a way that can't happen if we are isolated, and so, in a very practical way, if sharing a cup of coffee leads people to open up with each other, then the community created by coffee community can help our existential need to be together.[9]

Buber's existentialism does pose risks to the coffee community as well. The dialogical principle metaphorically bares its teeth to the hometown art and poetry nights of the local café, because those experiences present us with the possibility that we will attempt to connect with someone who does not want to connect with us. And since Buber's community also requires that we meet the needs of others who are different than we are, the coffee community must avoid the pitfall of elitism. If we must share each other's burdens to have meaningful community, then we must also meet the needs of diverse others.

Although we run the risk of more pain by sharing in the lives of others, if we take Buber seriously and treat others as a "Thou," we can create hope for those in our community. Being hopeful existentially is not simply wishful thinking. Existential hope isn't akin to hoping that I win the lottery, that the rain will hold off a few more hours, or that I will finish my paper in time. Instead, existential hope is a collective response to freely make choices and to freely create possibilities for ourselves, and so for others. (The fair trade movement is a great example of this. When a collective group saw the need of coffee farmers to earn a living wage, they raised their voices and saw change in the world, and those in the fair trade movement continue to work to better the lives of people they do not even see. Their actions – inspired by their coffee habit and motivated in the coffee community – create possibilities for others.)

Hope as the ability to create possibilities has an important voice in the work of Gabriel Marcel. There are significant similarities in the existentialist thought of Buber and Marcel, although Marcel specifically builds the idea of existential health around the idea of community. Most people are stuck existentially, because they are alone and so they allow themselves to be treated as objects for others. (Marcel calls such a person the "problematic man" – someone whose value is tied to how they are used, such as a problem one might solve.) Marcel thinks the first step one should take is to reach out to someone other than the self. If I can be orientated, or directed, toward another person rather than to just be focused on myself, I can avoid becoming an object. And if I can come together with others who also want to avoid their own objectification, I am free to break out of my problematic state.

When I was pregnant with my oldest child, I began to experience firsthand what Marcel meant. Especially in my last trimester, I had difficulty sleeping, and my thoughts were focused no longer on me or my life; instead I became focused on another's. And one particular café played a role in helping me refocus. Sweet Eugene's roasts its own coffee and caters to the college art scene in College Station, Texas. It would open very early in those days and when I was sleepless, my husband would take me for a uniquely designed decaf Snickers latte. We would swap stories with the owners of Eugene's and their staff, and we would relax and plan for our baby. At a more reasonable hour, friends would join us before our day began. At Sweet Eugene's, we began to practice Marcel's notion of community. We were free individuals, involved in a community of intersubjective people who were vulnerable to each other's needs, and receptive to their experiences. The café enabled our community because it helped us to focus on others besides ourselves.

If a community can be committed to the same goals, the individuals that make up the community no longer will need to struggle as individuals. Marcel uses the example of a physical body to explain how he thinks of community. Joints and bones have totally distinct functions in the body. But, the joints of a skeleton are tied together and adapted to bones so that they both can perform effectively. In the same way, an individual can create meaning by being oriented, conjoined, and adapted toward beings other than herself.[10] The most significant possible goal for any person who seeks meaning is to be immersed in a community of others, because it is in such a community that one gets to actually experience hope.

Coffee, Community, and Hope

It is through the optimistic existentialists that we can understand community, and also see how the coffee community can actually function effectively existentially. The community of others can help individuals out of existential despair and loneliness. Kierkegaard, Jaspers, Buber, and Marcel suggest that it is only through joining together in community that each individual can triumph over the hopelessness of existence. We are individuals, together, working toward meaning.

  JILL HERNANDEZ

The community of coffee drinkers is a venue through which the existential notion of "hope" can happen. The local coffee shop has paid attention to what neighborhoods have known for years: Good coffee makes good neighbors – or, in an existential vein, good coffee draws people into a community which makes hope possible. Anecdotal exceptions aside, the café not only is a place that has become symbolic for gathering together, but it also has become a local center for social justice advocacy, a platform for various aesthetic experiences, and a voice for environmental awareness. People go to the café not just to get work done, but also to *be together*. Most coffee shops – even the local retail leaders – have become venues for displaying the art, music, and poetry of those who drink coffee there. Reciprocally, those who go to the café have encouraged the fair trade movement, greater recycling efforts, and organic farming.

"Community" through the experience of sharing coffee has become a way for people to become active in their particular communities. This activity is what is existentially important. We all share a problem of being limited by our bodies, and of being unable to communicate the specific limits that come from living within our individual bodies. But, if we reach out toward each other, and treat each other as more than mere objects or problems to be solved, we can be hopeful: Possibilities are present. Gathering with others so that we can be receptive to the needs, dreams, humor, and desires of others is the first step toward creating possibilities. Coffee gives us the space to do this, and it naturally draws others in. Coffee provides an existential ground for community – it gives us a moment of shared hope.

NOTES

1 Jean-Paul Sartre, *Being and Nothingness* (New York: Washington Square Press, 1993), p. 363.
2 See, especially, Youngme Moon and John Quelch, "Starbucks: Delivering Customer Service," *Harvard Business School Case* 9-504-016, July 10, 2006, which cites Starbucks' own internal distress over this critique of the Starbucks brand. For example, Moon and Quelch write that, despite Starbucks' overwhelming presence and convenience, there *is* a significant differentiation between Starbucks and the independent specialty coffeehouses (see Table A below). The number of respondents who strongly agreed with the statement, "Starbucks cares primarily about making money" was up from 53 percent in 2000 to 61 percent in 2001, while the number of respondents who strongly agreed with the statement, "Starbucks cares primarily about building more

stores" was up from 48 percent to 55 percent. Christine Day (senior vice president of administration for Starbucks) noted, "It's become apparent that we need to ask ourselves, 'Are we focusing on the right things? Are we clearly communicating our value and values to our customers, instead of just our growth plans?'" Day argued that the customer satisfaction gap could primarily be attributed to a *service gap* between Starbucks scores on key attributes and customer expectations. When Starbucks had polled its customers to determine what it could do to make them feel more like valued customers, "improvements to service" had been mentioned most frequently (12).

TABLE A   Qualitative Brand Meaning: Independents vs. Starbucks

Independents: • Social and inclusive • Diverse and intellectual • Artsy and funky • Liberal and free-spirited • Lingering encouraged • Particularly appealing to younger coffeehouse customers • Somewhat intimidating to older, more mainstream coffeehouse customers
Starbucks: • Everywhere – the trend • Good coffee on the run • Place to meet and move on • Convenience oriented; on the way to work • Accessible and consistent

3   Sartre, *Existentialism is a Humanism* (New Haven: Yale University Press, 2007), p. 36.
4   Ibid., pp. 80–81.
5   Søren Kierkegaard, *Works of Love* (Princeton: Princeton University Press, 1995), p. 62.
6   In a fascinating geographical research project, researchers found that even in Third World countries, villagers would travel farther to buy coffee at cafés where they could be with family and friends than the local café that was closest to them. Lawrence S. Grossman, "Consumer Behavior and the Village Trade Store: A Papua New Guinea Example," *Geografiska Annaler: Series B, Human Geography* 68, no. 1 (1986): 41–49.
7   Karl Jaspers, *Man in the Modern Age* (New York: Anchor Books, 1957), p. 211.
8   Martin Buber, "The Philosophical Anthropology of Max Scheler," *Philosophy and Phenomenological Research* 6, no. 2 (December 1945): 316.
9   Robert Wood, "The Dialogical Principle and the Mystery of Being," *International Journal for Philosophy of Religion* 45 (1999): 94.
10 Gabriel Marcel, *Mystery of Being*, vol. 1 (Washington, DC: Regnery Press, 1951), pp. 201–202.

PART 2

GROUNDS FOR DEBATE: COFFEE CULTURE

CHAPTER 6

SAGE ADVICE FROM BEN'S MOM

or: The Value of the Coffeehouse

In the coffeehouse, the outside world seems worlds removed. Shelves are filled with books and magazines for patrons to read. The walls are covered with postmodern paintings. Classical guitar music wafts through stereo speakers. It is the perfect place to wax philosophical till the wee hours.

Christopher Phillips[1]

It might happen in a bar or in the woods, over email or in a private notebook, but very often we do our philosophizing in coffeehouses. Caffeine proves an effective stimulant for the mind and a natural complement to the activity. The setting – armchairs and all – is conducive to our speculative ruminations. Anymore, but admittedly less and less, our time in coffeehouses is some of the only time we're free from the engagements of day-to-day life, free to read or write or think quietly, free to talk long and seriously with friends, free to be thoughtful and playful at once. When the TV is off, the phone isn't ringing, and the Internet isn't connecting, we're left with what's inside us and immediately in front of us. And, nervous as it can make one to be away from technology for very long, our need for such time and mental space is a partial motivation for how much time people spend in coffeehouses. Of course, just being alone or with a group of friends without distractions doesn't necessarily mean someone will do philosophy. Philosophy isn't the same as simply talking or thinking: "What distinguishes the Socratic method [or, philosophy] from mere nonsystematic inquiry is the sustained attempt to explore the ramifications of certain opinions and then offer compelling objections and alternatives."[2]

So not all, or even most, talk – even when it's about serious subjects – that goes on in coffeehouses is philosophy. But some of it is, and for many people, participating in a philosophical dialogue in a coffeehouse can be their main exposure to philosophy. Some of the people engaging in such conversations or focused inquiry, though, might be reluctant to call what they're doing *philosophy*. With sad regularity, philosophy gets dismissed as that required class from freshman year that no one (not even, necessarily, the professor) understood, or reduced to something that smart people do in, but never let out of, academia. In either characterization, philosophy is frightfully abstract and has little if anything to do with what people in coffeehouses find important. Nevertheless, spend much time in a coffeehouse and you will soon overhear discussions, often thoughtful, of politics, ethics, aesthetics, community, and religion. When people gather and have adequate time to converse, these topics end up being a significant part of what they care about – as well as a significant part of philosophy.

But still, this is philosophy generally – what about philosophy specifically? In the mid-1990s, in response to personal and professional crises of meaning, Christopher Phillips began to think contemporary American lives tended to lack in thoughtfulness and could benefit from philosophy. He decided to give up his career and promote the practice of philosophy. But instead of convincing people to go back to their bookshelves and dust off their freshman-year books or drop in on a public lecture (he didn't think people needed to know a lot *about* philosophy), Phillips asked them to talk to one another about whatever was on their minds, and to do so in a specific way; he thought what people needed was to *do* philosophy – regularly and actively. And so he began facilitating public meetings where community members could gather and have philosophical dialogues. Asked what this kind of meeting should be called, he proposed "Socrates Café."

SCOTT F. PARKER

Socrates Café

It's worth mentioning first that Socrates Cafés aren't always held in cafés. Frequently they're held in schools, prisons, community centers, or anywhere else a diverse population can "get together and exchange thoughtful ideas and experiences while embracing the central theme of Socratizing: the idea that we learn more when we question and question with others."[3] It just so happens that coffeehouses are particularly good places to Socratize.

Phillips has called Socrates Café a church for heretics, and this is a good way of thinking about it. It's like a church in that people are invited to gather and reflect on the most important – and often the most difficult – aspects of life. And it's heretical in that there's a built-in aversion to dogma. Every single idea and opinion is open to questioning. The idea being that questions are actually more insightful than answers because they reveal the provisional status of our conclusions – even those we're inclined to think immutable. It's humbling to engage in this process. At any moment, one's deepest assumptions about reality can be problematized beyond recovery. The closest thing you'll find to an accepted conclusion at a Socrates Café is confidence in the method itself. In Phillips's words: "And the one and only firm and lasting truth that has emerged from all the Socrates Café discussions I've taken part in is that it is not possible to examine, scrutinize, plumb, and mine a question too thoroughly and exhaustively. There is always more to discover. That is the essence, and magic, of what I have come to call 'Socratizing.'"[4] It's the trust in the Socratic method, founded on a deeper trust in rationality, that prevents Socrates Café from becoming a relativistic forum where people can just share their opinions and have them go unchallenged. As long as a group of Socrateses[5] believes in Truth and that rationality is the way to it, it doesn't matter if they never agree what is true – the question of what truth ultimately is is just the kind of thing that would make for a good conversation topic at a Socrates Café.

The name Socrates Café comes from Socrates (469–399 BCE), who famously wandered the agora of Athens engaging in philosophical dialogues with whomever would talk to him. Phillips quotes Gerasimos Xenophon Santas on Socrates' method: "Socrates is questioning all the time. He greets people with questions, he teaches and refutes them with questions, he leaves them with questions – he actually talks to them with questions."[6] There's no record of Socrates having ever written anything down. We know him through the writings of others, primarily Plato. One thing not writing has done for Socrates is allow him to be associated with his method of questioning more than with any specific positions he argued for. Subsequently, his method has come to be seen as such an ideal for philosophy that Socrates himself has become the archetypal philosopher. Philosophers with the historic misfortune of being born before him are now known, diminutively, as pre-Socratics. But to appeal to the larger-than-life authority of Socrates doesn't answer the question, *Why question?*

Phillips describes a Socrates Café meeting devoted to this very question.[7] But the real answer to anyone who asks such a question is that you just do. If you weren't the kind of person to whom it occurs to ask this – and some people are not – you wouldn't have. That's true but maybe not very helpful. For those who are not naturally inclined to philosophize, a better reason to question is required. The arguments Phillips implements in his exaltation of philosophy are bold and meant to be universal. All of us must examine our lives and make sure what we're doing is aligned with our values – and if it's not we must change our lives: "Life is not a dress rehearsal."[8] Philosophy, Phillips thinks, is also necessary to preserve democracy:

> I think the Socratic way of inquiring is a paradigm of communication that calls on all participants in a dialogue to participate fully, and in an egalitarian way. And it requires that participants help one another articulate and then examine their perspectives, as well as the implications for society of these perspectives, and the assumptions within these perspectives. This, I think, is a type of "free and full" communication that can help ensure a vibrant democracy that can evolve over time.[9]

And one more: Philosophy can be an antidote to societal degradation. It was partly in response to what he saw as an increasingly selfish and self-absorbed populace, one marked by "a growing sense of pessimistic fatalism and helplessness," that Phillips decided he "wanted to be a philosopher in the mold of Socrates."[10]

Café Philosophique

In starting the Socrates Café movement, Christopher Phillips was not without predecessors. Other philosophers have promoted public philosophical dialogues as a way of continuing in Socrates' tradition.

  SCOTT F. PARKER

In 1992, drawing inspiration from Jean-Paul Sartre's philosophical discussions at Paris's Café de Flore, and growing dissatisfied with his academic career, the French philosopher and Nietzsche scholar Marc Sautet (1947–1998) invited a small group to the Café des Phares on the Parisian Place de la Bastille for weekly philosophical conversations. As the meetings became more popular they took on the name Café Philosophique and spread over France, and eventually over Europe.[11] These cafés-philos, like Socrates Cafés, are open to the general public and provide an opportunity to seriously discuss philosophical ideas without needing to be familiar with the philosophical canon. As with Socrates Cafés, cafés-philos do not feature a lecturer who teaches the public; rather, they are led by a moderator who guides the discussion, allowing participants to speak from personal experience and reasoning without sacrificing the critical approach. Sautet also practiced his public philosophy by hosting online debates, keeping up a private philosophy consulting practice, leading tours to sites of philosophical interest, and writing the book Un Café pour Socrate to defend his "popularization."[12] Since Sautet's death, cafés-philos have continued to spread around the world.

Philosophy for Everyone

In promoting the idea that philosophy can and should be practiced by all, Phillips, like Sautet before him, has inserted himself into a larger argument about the place of philosophy in society. Another movement that is inspired by the idea that philosophy should be freed from the cloisters of academia and be allowed to play an active role in civic life can be seen in the popular philosophy books published over the past decade by Open Court, Wiley-Blackwell, and The University Press of Kentucky, of which this book is an example. These series began with William Irwin's Open Court book Seinfeld and Philosophy.[13] Irwin is now the series editor for The Blackwell Philosophy and Pop Culture Series, and its statement of purpose offers an accurate description of the larger movement: "A spoonful of sugar helps the medicine go down, and a healthy helping of popular culture clears the cobwebs from Kant. Philosophy has had a bad public relations problem for a few centuries now. This series aims to change that, showing that philosophy is relevant to your life."[14] Note that this movement is conceived as an attempt to bring philosophy from academia to the people, in a gesture not so much of turning away as opening up.

Which is not to say that these series want to promote philosophy at the cost of dumbing it down. The guidelines for the present series read, in part: "This series is meant to promote philosophical reflection on everyday activities, and the associated titles are developed for a public – albeit philosophically sophisticated – audience."[15]

And so Christopher Phillips's work and these books are bedfellows, and it would be ridiculous of me to denounce Socrates Café in these pages, sharing, as we do, such common goals. But there are challenges (in good, open-minded spirit) worth considering.[16] One is that in any particular Socrates Café meeting nothing of lasting import may be said. That is, no new good ideas that will add to the tradition of philosophy may be advanced. One thing you notice in reading *Socrates Café* is that very many of the discussions Phillips describes are uninspiring – they don't cover much ground that hasn't already been covered by people who have made their own attempts at philosophizing. But this shouldn't be surprising – it's because good new ideas are so rare that they're so valuable; if everyone could think like Nietzsche, he wouldn't be that impressive a thinker – and it's not even the point. While the ideas in Socrates Cafés aren't always inspiring, the fact of them very often is. People are working their minds, thinking through issues that are relevant and challenging to them. If you think that's easy and silly, I submit you haven't done enough of it. In a Socrates Café you do philosophy for the reason I think it should always be done: because it matters to you; it matters like hell. If along the way you come up with something great, well, then maybe we'll put your name next to Nietzsche's. In any case, nothing is lost in the practice, and so much is gained in living philosophy.

Furthermore, to deny the value of doing philosophy is to engage in it. To the challenge that philosophy is confused rambling or a waste of time, Phillips has a ready-made response: "Tell me your reasons. Tell me *why*." Even an objection to philosophy on the grounds that it is unproductive and can't locate truth (If truth does exist, how would you know when you've found it?) is guilty of a performative contradiction: The act of saying is in opposition to what's said. To raise the question of truth is to partake in philosophy and give implicit support to the lesson Phillips takes from Socrates: that it's the process of reflecting on, in this case, *truth* that is worthwhile, not what if anything we conclude about it. Philosophy's only real adversary isn't relativism or even cynicism (both of which require some amount of the kind of defense that precipitates philosophy) but thoughtlessness.

SCOTT F. PARKER

Sophistry

Philosophers often deceive themselves about their supposed love and pursuit of the truth – not to mention wisdom – when ignoring the centrality of such concerns as their reputation in the agora and their status in the profession. Plato's bully in the Republic, *Thrasymachus [who said the just is what is to the advantage of the stronger], has in fact remained as much of a presence in philosophy as Socrates, though he is rarely recognized as who he is.*

Robert C. Solomon[17]

A related objection to the kind of philosophy that goes on in a Socrates Café is that it isn't *real* philosophy, that something crucial is lost when philosophy is taken out of the hands of professionals. This is a bit different than saying someone isn't good at philosophy; this objection actually says some people can't do it at all. The fear is that without adequate training a person might get away with passing off sophistry (or something that smells even worse than sophistry[18]) as philosophy. There is always the danger that a Socratic dialogue could devolve into a self-help session, where participants seek to have their feelings validated rather than their ideas critiqued. It is largely up to the group – and this is why a designated facilitator can be so useful – to ensure that every statement is open to questioning and can only be held with sufficient reason and evidence.

But the objections to coffee-shop philosophy aren't really concerned with protecting people from sub-professional dialogues; they're concerned with protecting the discipline from outsiders – as if philosophy were so vulnerable that the possibility of someone doing it without specialized training threatens its foundation. Rest assured, any philosophical problem so technical as to require years of advanced study is safe from the average coffee-shop philosopher, who is concerned primarily with questions that relate to everyday life: how to live.

Besides, any philosopher who says that philosophy should be left to the professionals, while claiming to be one, is walking face first into a counter-argument that's almost as old as philosophy itself. In Plato's *Sophist*, the stranger offers seven definitions of a sophist in his dialogue with Theaetetus. Of these, five involve receiving payment for what should not be sold, for what the sophists would like to call *philosophy*. The sixth and seventh definitions call the sophist the cross-examiner of sham-wisdom[19] and someone who is not wise but uses speech to appear wise,[20] respectively.

Whether most professors are guilty of the latter two forms of sophistry is something to maybe ask your college-age friends, but a version involving remuneration is undeniable. We needn't agree with any of the first five definitions in full to be stimulated by them: You better believe that if a professor's livelihood depends on his being the expert in a room full of novices, he's not going to say otherwise.

By contrast, neither Socrates nor the stranger in Plato's *Sophist* made any money from their philosophizing. Likewise, neither was primarily interested in promoting doctrines. The stranger never gives the definition of sophistry to Theaetetus doctrinally. Rather, he works them out with Theaetetus's assistance. From this, we can see philosophy at work as a practice that homes in on truth over the course of a dialogue (even if it never actually gets a firm grip on it).[21]

The Socratic method allows all assumptions and arguments to be checked and systematically disputed;[22] it is without presentation; it is not displayed through speeches or lessons. The way of the sophist differs in that he has an agenda insofar as he seeks to prove his own arguments or secure his income. To sincerely follow the path of philosophy (wherever it leads) is to forego the temptation to manipulate for the sake of personal benefit, as the only goal is to find the truth, not to display one's intelligence.

Following Plato's stranger here, it's actually the professionals not the amateurs who debase philosophy. Christopher Phillips in this case is more like Socrates than are most professors. He makes no money off Socrates Café[23] and thinks of leading the meetings as his calling. Also, in facilitating dialogues, Phillips has nothing to give anyone, no agenda or perspective to pass along – except the value of the method itself. Phillips is fond of pointing out that he always learns as much as anyone else attending the dialogues.

Bernard R. Roy, who has led a *café-philo* in New York since 1998, argues in his essay "The Philosophical Value of Coffee-House Debates" that coffeehouse philosophy can be good not only for the practitioners, but for philosophy too:

> Doing philosophy is a little bit like scratching where it does not itch; thus, whether one is a professional philosopher or not, doing philosophy requires disinterested curiosity, and courage; and in general, the more "knowledge" one has about a subject, the more courage it will take to examine it. If ignorance breeds audacity, erudition brings about caution. Thus, anyone who dares to look into, and challenge his or her system of beliefs is doing

SCOTT F. PARKER

philosophy. In this sense philosophy is a kind of therapy for a way of life, for our common sense beliefs guide our lives. So understood, philosophy cannot be restricted to professional philosophers. Of course, in that sense, and at worst, the practice is likely to be wasteful, for the wheel may be reinvented many times; but no harm will ever be done, and occasionally some insights will contribute to the growth of philosophy.[24]

But there's no need to be as optimistic as Roy to appreciate the value in public philosophy. Even if public philosophy is not good philosophy to professional philosophers,[25] it's good philosophy to those doing it. It's challenging and helpful and exciting, and no one who values philosophy should object to anyone doing it in whatever way they can. Again, the primary purpose of philosophical dialogues is for the participant, so she may engage the Socratic maxim *the unexamined life is not worth living.*

The Examined Life

Philosophy begins in wonder.

Socrates

Philosophy may begin in wonder, but it doesn't stay there. To repeat a quote from Christopher Phillips: "What distinguishes the Socratic method [what I'm calling philosophy] from mere nonsystematic inquiry is the sustained attempt to explore the ramifications of certain opinions and then offer compelling objections and alternatives."[26] It moves from wonder toward something like Socrates' maxim that *the unexamined life is not worth living.* The maxim itself is a hyperbolic idea that no philosopher would really subscribe to. Much as I agree with John Stuart Mills's support of Socrates – "It is better to be a human being dissatisfied than a pig satisfied; better to be Socrates dissatisfied than a fool satisfied" – his conviction invites an obvious retort: according to whom? Bet the pig's OK with things. Bet the fool is, too. Those trapped in the cave in Plato's allegory don't have a basis of comparison to know what they're missing out on. But while, strictly speaking, the maxim isn't true, it is provocative if instead of arguing with it we engage it.

Robert Nozick (1938–2002) engages the Socratic injunction in his book *The Examined Life* and identifies the personal nature of the challenge: "I do not say with Socrates that the unexamined life is not worth living – that is unnecessarily harsh. However, when we guide our lives by our own pondered thoughts, it then is *our* life that we are living, not someone else's. In this sense, the unexamined life is not lived as fully."[27]

I want to return to what I earlier called philosophy's adversary: thought-lessness. As Nozick suggests, if we do not actively do philosophy, we become soldiers for the status quo: Our lives are not fully our own; they get stuck on the default settings of our environments and authorities (parents, religion, culture, society, etc.). But status quo can result from inner forces as well as outer ones. Living a life of habit or choosing a life of convenience can be sure signs of a lack of philosophizing. At its core, philosophy is about being conscious and not accepting anything in life because it's what others are doing or what you've done before. It means questioning, doubting, and being willing to be confused and uncertain. It's not easy. In fact, it's hard.

> Philosophical inquiry is no panacea or magic bullet for our problems and … it would be the height of dishonesty to portray philosophy in such a light. Indeed, has a problem ever been cured or solved that has not given rise to a host of new ones? But isn't that okay? Isn't that, in fact, wonderful? Isn't that part and parcel of the glorious and agonizing experience of being a human? To be sure, probing philosophical inquiry can enable us to develop new ways of seeing and experiencing and empathizing.[28]

If you allow yourself to think about difficult issues, you'll come to see what you know and what you don't know. And without fail, this will lead back to the question of how to live your life:

> No matter what question we discuss at Socrates Café, the dialogues, as Socrates says in Plato's *Republic*, are not about any chance question, but about the way one should live. So the discussions do not just enable us to better know who we are but lead us to acquire new tactics for living and thinking so we can work toward determining, and then becoming, who we want to be. By becoming more skilled in the art of questioning, you will discover new ways to ask the questions that have vexed and perplexed you the most. In turn you will discover new and more fruitful answers. And these new answers in turn will generate a whole new host of questions. And the cycle keeps repeating itself – not in a vicious circle, but in an ever-ascending and ever-expanding spiral that gives you a continually new and replenished outlook on life.[29]

The philosopher (and Maurice Riseling says, "Sooner or later, life makes philosophers of us all") never stops questioning and thinking, never thinks that the way he sees things is the final way they can be seen. He's on a never-ending journey in search of wisdom. And the only consolations along the way are increased honesty and humility. Examining life isn't about reaching conclusions – the most we can hope for a conclusion is to be like Socrates in knowing we are wise only insofar as we recognize how little we know – it's an ongoing process whose goal is to keep the process going. Philosophy continues in wonder.

Oblivion

Cogito ergo doleo.[30]

Nietzsche suggests that "if you wish to strive for peace of soul and pleasure, then believe; if you wish to be a devotee of truth, then inquire." In this vein, Charles Sanders Peirce ... wrote that in a sense the "sole rule of reason" is that "in order to learn you must desire to learn, and in so desiring not be satisfied with what you already incline to think." From this rule, Peirce said, there "follows one corollary which itself deserves to be inscribed upon every wall of the city of philosophy: Do not block the way of inquiry."

Christopher Phillips[31]

To think with any seriousness is to doubt. Thought is indistinguishable from doubt. To be alive is to be uncertain. I'll take doubt. The essayist argues with himself, and the essayist argues with the reader. The essay enacts doubt; it embodies it as a genre.

David Shields[32]

We've looked now at ways in which philosophy is accessible for all, and why it's worth pursuing, but in this section, using David Foster Wallace as an example, I want to turn to the burden of thinking philosophically and consider the alternative to philosophy: thoughtlessness, or *oblivion*. According to Joshua Roiland, the writer and philosopher David Foster Wallace "suffered from an absence of oblivion, whose active role, according to Nietzsche, is 'that of a concierge: to shut temporarily the doors and windows of consciousness; to protect us from the noise and agitation ... to introduce a little quiet into our consciousness.'"[33] Wallace, whose writing is characterized by obsessive detail and meticulous attention to consciousness, was unable to shut his consciousness down and enter oblivion, which led to a constant state of discomfort – he was a concomitant philosopher.[34] Wallace's narrator is never satisfied, always questioning; he is never capable of completely joining in with the cruise ship attendees – to take one example from his journalism[35] – he describes (and reluctantly finds himself among): "They have allowed oblivion to close the door on their consciousness and in exchange they are happy – or at least believe they are happy."[36] Comforting and attractive as oblivion is, for Wallace, "to get away from it all is abdicate a moral responsibility, to dire effect."[37]

Wallace's time on the cruise ship would have been more enjoyable if he could have turned his mind off and accepted his pampering thoughtlessly. In Nietzsche's words: "The concierge maintains order and etiquette in the household of the psyche; which immediately suggests that there can be no happiness, no serenity, no hope, no pride, no present, without oblivion."[38] But the question remains: Would it have been right for him to turn his mind off, if he could? That's a hard question. Certainly, in some cases it might be healthy for the philosopher's mind to take a break. But is the cruise ship one such place? Reading "A Supposedly Fun Thing I'll Never Do Again," the essay about Wallace's cruise, I think not. Besides environmental concerns about cruises, there's an enormous cultural issue that Wallace fingers: the desire for constant self-centered indulgence (a symptom of which a cruise is just one example, albeit possibly the zenith of examples) does deep psychological damage to people, whose easiest response becomes oblivion.[39] By entering so deeply into the questioning of, and critical thinking about, cruising, Wallace offers to save us from oblivion.[40]

Doing philosophy means rejecting such oblivion, and it means being unwilling to lie to yourself, and it means putting yourself under a certain amount of permanent stress. Your conclusions will always be provisional; you'll always be on the lookout for ways in which you might be lying to yourself, or ways in which you are in oblivion. It's not easy to be a philosopher, but it's worth the trouble.[41]

And when we take moment to reflect – if on our cruises we cease for a moment to have our egos pampered, our selves indulged – we'll find it's unavoidable. "Philosophy is the one academic discipline that tends to naturally emerge in everyone's life, in times of turmoil or traumatic change or simply in quiet moments of reflection."[42] To do philosophy is part of what it means to be human. "As an adult, Wallace taught and admired Kafka's literature. In 1998, he delivered a speech entitled

SCOTT F. PARKER

'Laughing With Kafka' to the PEN American Center. In that speech Wallace claimed that the central joke in Kafka's fiction is 'that the horrific struggle to establish a human self results in a self whose humanity is inseparable from that horrific struggle. That our endless and impossible journey toward home is in fact our home.'"[43]

Conclusion (Who is Ben's Mom?)

The whole problem with the world is that fools and fanatics are always so certain of themselves, and wiser people so full of doubts.

Bertrand Russell

Who is Ben's mom? In a word: She's a philosopher. In a few more words: She's the mother of a college friend of mine. After not seeing each other for several years, we had a few moments recently to catch up. She asked what I was up to. When I mentioned that I was editing a book on coffee and philosophy intended for a popular audience, she said, "That's great. It seems to me, more and more in our society, we're failing to do the work of thinking critically. You see it politically and culturally, especially in the media, where it seems like the news is pre-filtered by agenda to tell us what we already think. We need philosophy. How does it connect with coffee?"

"One way it's going to connect is through coffeehouses as community spaces where people can gather to do philosophy."

"That's interesting. I see that kind of thing in my neighborhood [in Seattle]. It's hard to imagine these days where people would meet for conversation if it weren't for coffeehouses. I once was in a Starbucks by my house when Howard Schultz walked in. I looked around and saw people from our community interacting in such a positive way that I decided to walk up to him and say thanks for creating this space for us."

So Ben's mom is a philosopher? Well, not in the way we usually mean philosopher. She's published no philosophy articles and taught no philosophy classes. But in the sense that Christopher Phillips says we're all Socrateses, in the sense that Socrates engaged private citizens in public places, in the sense that part of philosophy always involves a defense of philosophy – yes.

The coffeehouse is our agora. But while cafés offer community, they can of course not promise it. Howard Schultz can give Ben's mom a place to philosophize, but he cannot give her philosophy. Philosophy is a conversation that keeps going. And it keeps going only as long as Ben's mom and you and me keep it going, as long as we're willing to question and doubt and clarify and reject the seductive temptation of easy certainty.

NOTES

1 *Socrates Café* (New York: W. W. Norton, 2001), p. 152.
2 Ibid., p. 21.
3 http://www.philosopher.org/en/Socrates_Cafe.html.
4 Phillips, *Socrates Café*, p. 9.
5 And Phillips thinks we're all Socrateses, as long as we're "not afraid to keep asking questions even when everyone else wants to stop." Phillips, *Socrates Café*, p. 16.
6 Ibid., p. 26.
7 Ibid.
8 Ibid., p. 40.
9 Ibid., p. 49.
10 Ibid., p. 130.
11 http://www.nycafephilo.org/Cafe_Philo_Site/History.html.
12 Marc Sautet, *Un Café pour Socrate: comment la philosophie peut nous aider à comprendre le monde d'aujourd'hui* (Paris: R. Laffont, 1995).
13 William Irwin, *Seinfeld and Philosophy* (New York: Open Court, 1999).
14 http://www.wiley.com/WileyCDA/Section/id-324354.html.
15 http://www.allhoff.org/other/philosophy-for-everyone/.
16 Just as the criticisms of this kind of book are worth considering. For a fun one, see http://flowtv.org/?p=270.
17 *The Joy of Philosophy* (New York: Oxford University Press, 1999), p. 201.
18 See Harry G. Frankfurt, *On Bullshit* (Princeton: Princeton University Press, 2005); and Gary L. Hardcastle and George A. Reisch, *Bullshit and Philosophy* (New York: Open Court, 2006).
19 Plato, *Sophist: The Professor of Wisdom* (Newburyport, MA: Focus Publishing, R. Pullins Company, 1996), p. 34.
20 Ibid., p. 83.
21 Incidentally, a postmodern critique of the concept of *truth* is probably the most effective way to undermine the Socratic method. If there's nothing to go toward (or if there is, but reason fails to take us in its direction), philosophy becomes just what many of those college-age friends will tell you it is: *bullshit*.
22 The question of whether there is truth, whether there is anything driving philosophy, is itself up for philosophical grabs.

  SCOTT F. PARKER

23 Although his three books about Socrates Cafés do sell well.

24 http://www.nycafephilo.org/Cafe_Philo_Site/Coffe_house_debate.html.

25 And I'm by no means granting this point. For a compelling argument that professional philosophy is detrimentally lacking in the very thing that brings non-professionals out to Socrates Cafés or *cafés-philos* – passion – see Robert C. Solomon's excellent *The Joy of Philosophy*.

26 Phillips, *Socrates Café*, p. 21.

27 Robert Nozick, *The Examined Life* (New York: Simon & Schuster, 1989), p. 15.

28 Christopher Phillips, "Beware of the Sophist," http://www.metalepsis.org/gramma/saved/bots.htm.

29 Phillips, *Socrates Café*, p. 12.

30 I think, therefore I suffer.

31 *Socrates Café*, p. 51.

32 *Reality Hunger* (New York: Alfred A. Knopf, 2010), p. 139.

33 Joshua Roiland, "Getting Away From It All: The Literary Journalism of David Foster Wallace and Nietzsche's Concept of Oblivion," *Literary Journalism Studies* 1, no. 2 (2009): 91.

34 I want to stress that this discussion should be limited to the David Foster Wallace we encounter through his work. The biographical information about Wallace's life and death may support the reading of his inability to enter oblivion, but for the sake of the discussion we should limit ourselves to his narrator's resistance to oblivion. Roiland's article, after all, is about Wallace's literary journalism.

35 David Foster Wallace, "A Supposedly Fun Thing I'll Never Do Again," in *A Supposedly Fun Thing I'll Never Do Again* (Boston: Back Bay Books, 1998).

36 Roiland, "Getting Away," p. 92.

37 Ibid.

38 Ibid., pp. 92–93.

39 Another example of this sort of thing comes from Las Vegas. The city that offers the apotheosis of self-indulgence – the city that offers us whatever we want and invites us to pretend our indulgences won't have consequences – is the city where, more than in any other city in our country, we end up killing ourselves.

40 To provide another example from Wallace of what it means to be philosophically engaged with the world, I want to quote at length from his interview with Dave Eggers in *The Believer* (November, 2003). Note his call for serious thinking as a response to what passes as public discourse:

> 95 percent of political commentary, whether spoken or written, is now polluted by the very politics it's supposed to be about. Meaning it's becoming totally ideological and reductive … There's no more complex, messy, community-wide argument (or "dialogue"); political

discourse is now a formulaic matter of preaching to one's own choir and demonizing the opposition. Everything's relentlessly black-and-whitened. Since the truth is way, way more gray and complicated than any one ideology can capture, the whole thing seems to me not just stupid but stupefying. Watching O'Reilly v. Franken is watching bloodsport. How can any of this possibly help me, the average citizen, deliberate about whom to choose to decide my country's macroeconomic policy, or how even to conceive for myself what the policy's outlines should be, or how to minimize the chances of North Korea nuking the DMZ, and pulling us into a ghastly foreign war, or how to balance domestic security concerns with civil liberties? Questions like this are all massively complicated, and much of the complication is not sexy, and well over 90 percent of political commentary now simply abets the uncomplicatedly sexy delusions that one side is Right and Just and the other Wrong and Dangerous. Which is of course a pleasant delusion, in a way – as is the belief that every last person you're in conflict with is an asshole – but it's childish, and totally unconducive to hard thought, give and take, compromise, or the ability of grown-ups to function as any kind of community. (Copyright David Foster Wallace, 2003. Used by permission of the David Foster Wallace Literary Trust. Originally appeared in *The Believer*, November 2003.)

41 Although I can't make a statement like this without presenting an alternate take: "There is no doubt, for example, that philosophers have almost always deceived themselves, if not others, about the importance of philosophy, a fact made manifest only occasionally by some iconoclast such as Nietzsche or Wittgenstein or a Zen master like Dogen." Solomon, *The Joy of Philosophy*, p. 201.
42 Ibid., p. 221.
43 Roiland, "Getting Away," p. 98.

SCOTT F. PARKER

CHAPTER 7

THE COFFEEHOUSE AS A PUBLIC SPHERE
Brewing Social Change

Lately, as I sit and sip my cup of coffee in one of the chain coffee shops, I look around and think to myself: people come into a coffeehouse these days for one of two reasons. They're either looking for a restroom (if they're tourists), or WiFi (if they're not). How did this come about? After all, coffeehouses started out a few hundred years ago as subversive sites of political resistance. It is there that the rebels from the Boston Tea Party told the royal British government to wake up and smell the coffee. The coffeehouses were centers of intellectual critique, nests of insurgency and lively conversation.

Coffeehouses were central to what we call "the public sphere," the place in which people come together to discuss and to act as a community. Philosophers have long argued that the nature and structure of any society's public spheres are an indication of the nature and values of society itself. And so, it is timely to question the place of the coffeehouse in our midst. Can we reclaim our public sphere in the coffeehouse? Can we be the baristas of our unique social blend?

Coffee – Philosophy for Everyone: Grounds for Debate, First Edition. Edited by Scott F. Parker and Michael W. Austin, series editor Fritz Allhoff.
© 2011 John Wiley & Sons, Ltd except for editorial material and organization © 2011 Scott F. Parker and Michael W. Austin. Published 2011 by John Wiley & Sons, Ltd.

The Golden Age of the Coffeehouses

From the perspective of today's coffeehouses, with their elevator music and laptop congregations, it is hard to imagine that coffeehouses were the ground zero of the profoundest social revolutions. Pieces of this remarkable history have been highlighted (and consequently debated and contested) in the early work of the German philosopher Jürgen Habermas, *The Structural Transformation of the Public Sphere.*

The first coffeehouse in Europe is said to have debuted in London in 1652, with the first in Paris opening twenty years later. These first buds anticipated what Habermas called the "golden age of the coffeehouses" in France and Great Britain between 1680 and 1730. And indeed, the coffee trend was infectious. By the first decade of the eighteenth century over 3,000 new coffeehouses opened in London. They were the place in which the aristocracy and the emerging bourgeois merchants and professionals began to mingle and interact. They were socially accessible places which embraced the wider middle class, including craftsmen and shopkeepers, and served as a public place for discussion. The critical debate sparked by works of literature and art quickly extended to include economic and political issues. This phenomenon was so widespread that already in the 1670s the British government had to issue official statements that confronted the dangers "brewed" by the coffeehouse discussions. According to Habermas, the coffeehouses were considered seedbeds of political unrest. He cites one such statement by the British government:

> Men have assumed to themselves the liberty, not only in coffeehouses, but in other places and meetings, both public and private, to censure and defame the proceedings of the State, by speaking evil of things they understand not, and endeavoring to create and nourish an universal jealousy and dissatisfaction in the minds of all his Majestic good subjects.[1]

On December 29, 1675, King Charles II even issued a special "Proclamation for the Suppression of Coffee-Houses," claiming that they were places where plots against His Majesty were being concocted.

The public sphere, which before was constituted by the authority of the state, was transformed in the coffeehouses into a public sphere in which *private* people came together to form a *public.* This freshly brewed public sphere compelled public authority to receive its legitimacy from this newly formed coffee-drinking public. To understand the full impact

ASAF BAR-TURA

of the emergence of the coffeehouses, let me mention two of their main characteristics as a social institution. First, Habermas claims that those in attendance in these café discussions disregarded (or "bracketed") social status – economic, political, or other. Mind you, this *bracketing* of status did not mean they presupposed the *equality* of status. But the highest authority in the house was the force of the better argument, and people enjoyed "the parity of common humanity."

The second feature of the coffeehouse discussion was that it uncovered and criticized aspects of society that until then had not been questioned. The coffee consumers back then were concerned not only with how good their latte was, but more so with how just their society was.

The Coffeehouses that Roasted Revolution

Today, over 50 percent of Americans drink coffee daily and another 25 percent drink coffee occasionally. It is estimated that Americans consume 400 million cups of coffee every day, making the United States the leading consumer of coffee in the world. Yes, we are a nation of coffee drinkers. Why?

There is an old saying that Americans lost their taste for tea because they had a strange habit of mixing it in salt water. This of course refers to the famous Boston Tea Party of 1773, during which dozens of anti-British activists dumped hundreds of chests filled with tea into the waters of Boston Harbor. Thus, when the British sought to punish the colonies by unfair taxation on tea, coffee became not only the preferred drink but the patriotic one as well. In fact, coffee was declared the "national drink" by the Continental Congress to protest the British taxation on tea. It is no surprise that the Green Dragon Inn, Tavern and Coffeehouse, was a regular meeting place as the rebelling Bostonians plotted The Party. After all, what better way to express American patriotism than to plan the overthrow of the British in a coffeehouse!

Another known hotbed of political, business, and social activity leading up to the revolution was Charlton's Coffeehouse in Williamsburg, Virginia. One of the most dramatic encounters of the period took place on the porch of the Coffeehouse in 1765, when an angry crowd protesting against the Stamp Act confronted the collector appointed by the royal governor. The collector later resigned his position and the Act was repealed by the British Parliament the following year.

But even before the Stamp Act protests, some English conservatives derided the American coffeehouses as "seminaries of sedition." The London Coffeehouse, which opened in Philadelphia in 1754, was a busy political and commercial center of this kind. People would come to negotiate deals, attend auctions, discuss politics, read newspapers, and, oh yeah, drink coffee. Serving also as a *de facto* mercantile exchange, it was a breeding ground for business and revolution. It was such a busy place that by the early 1770s the London Coffeehouse could no longer satisfy the increasing business demands of the city. Therefore, the city's merchants built the Merchants Coffeehouse, later known as City Tavern.

The City Tavern soon became the political, social, and business center of the new United States. It was among the first places where the Declaration of Independence was read aloud to the public, and it was a common meeting site of the newly formed Continental Congress. Washington, Jefferson, Adams, and others frequented the establishment, claiming to enjoy "a feast of reason and a flow of soul."

Of course, not only in America did the coffeehouse become a center of radical politics and revolution. Coffee ignited controversy as soon as it landed on European soil. Opponents of this spreading phenomenon, especially in the Catholic Church, called the beverage the "drink of the devil" due to its introduction to Europe through Islamic countries. It is told that the controversy was so great that Pope Clement VIII was asked to intervene, and after tasting it, he gave it papal approval (to this day, however, followers of the Church of Jesus Christ of Latter Day Saints, commonly known as Mormons, abstain from drinking coffee).

Despite the controversy, in the big cities of England, Austria, France, Germany, and other countries, coffeehouses were quickly becoming centers of social activity and communication. Paris was to be known as the café society, as many intellectuals and sons of the Enlightenment frequented these exciting new establishments. The French philosopher and writer Voltaire is known to have drunk between fifty and a hundred cups a day! One famous spot in Paris was the Café de Foy, in which heated discussions took place. It is told that from this coffeehouse some French revolutionaries stormed the Bastille on July 14, 1789.

Coffeehouses have remained at the forefront of political struggle in the twentieth century as well, and this was certainly not limited to Europe or the United States. A fine example is the India Coffeehouse in Lahore (now in Pakistan). Before the division of the Indian sub-continent into India and Pakistan in 1947, the region was bubbling with political activity under British rule, and in the midst stood, once again, the Coffeehouse.

The Pakistani historian and writer K. K. Aziz tells us that the India Coffeehouse was "for over 30 years the single most important and influential mental powerhouse which moulded the lives and minds of a whole generation."[2]

In Lahore, the India Coffeehouse and India Tea House, situated 150 yards apart, became the two most popular meeting places of the radical intellectuals. Aziz even writes that the Coffeehouse of Lahore "entertained more leftists than I found in the Communist Party office on McLeod Road."[3] They sipped their coffee and engaged in profound and contentious conversations. Aziz humorously writes that "the British were tea-drinkers, so were the Russians and the Chinese. But the leftists chose to issue their exhortations over a cup of coffee."[4]

Coffeehouses or Coffee Shops?

Not everyone conceives of the historical role of coffeehouses as liberators of the public sphere. The feminist philosopher Nancy Fraser criticized Habermas's depiction. She argues that while being an open space of political debate for some, the coffeehouses continued to exclude others, most importantly women. For Fraser the coffeehouses were a new form of political domination. She says that while being formally inclusive, these public spheres in fact excluded many.[5]

But even if we agree with Fraser's critical analysis, it still seems that today's coffeehouses are no longer the center of social and political activities they once were. The café scene is dominated by big multinational corporations. Coffee is big business, so big that it is one of the most traded commodities in the world. For many, the café is merely a shop, where you buy the product and leave. Paper cups have replaced more delicate forms of delivering the beverage, and lonely do-it-yourself counters holding milk and sugar have replaced the light-hearted conversation with the waiter. The variety of options of artificial sweeteners stands out as the uniformity of the artificial décor rests silently in the background. The diversity of beverage options far overshadows any possible diversity of thought and ideas. Between the Grande-Soy-Chai Latte and the Tall-Wet-Decaf Cappuccino, Starbucks dazzles its clients ("guests") with over 50,000 different beverage variations in an average location.

You might say that, as mentioned earlier, coffeehouses were always the site of commercial exchange and business dealings, a vibrant environment of interaction. But that is perhaps the point. Rather than being a site of interaction, contemporary coffeehouses have become a place of common isolation. A place to be alone together. People sitting in front of their laptop, staring into cyberspace, armed with earphones in case anyone invaded their little nirvana of detachment.

So, is it a house or a shop? Is it a public sphere, or a private one? It seems that the technology of the twenty-first century makes the line between public and private ambivalent, or at the very least different from the one about which Habermas writes in the twentieth century. Facebook, YouTube, and other social media have famously made the distinction between public and private a daunting task. Sitting on a couch in a coffee shop these days, with wireless Internet and telephone connections at the tip of our fingers, we can feel right at home, or at work. Literally.

The Third Place

We feel that we are in the business of human connection and humanity, creating communities and a third place between home and work.
Howard Schultz, Chairman and CEO of Starbucks
(Interview on "60 Minutes," June 2006)

Many, including Howard Schultz, speak of today's coffeehouses as *a third place*, referring to social surroundings that are separate from the two usual social environments of home and the workplace. This concept was first coined by Ray Oldenburg in his book *The Great Good Place*.[6] Oldenburg's idea was that third places are important for civic engagement, for a healthy democracy, and for providing a sense of place in the hectic and often overwhelming modern world. These places could be coffeehouses, but also community gardens, a main street, and even the post office.

For Oldenburg, the first place (home) and second place (work) are relatively isolated environments, especially when living in the suburbs. In contrast, third places can create regular and habitual associations, and can serve as social and psychological support systems. They are places to establish social ties and form a community.

As technology advanced, it enabled more people to "telecommute" and work from home. The first and second places have merged for many. Finding the home office to be a lonely environment, today's coffeehouse offers the opportunity to work in a public space. All of us have probably had the experience of sitting down for coffee in a café only to find out that not many are relaxing, or engaging in conversation. Students are studying, researching, and writing on their laptops (and checking their Facebook, of course); others are holding job interviews, or business meetings; some are sending e-mails or talking on their smart phones; heck, I've seen people paying their bills and going over their bank statements (sorry, couldn't help but notice).

Chain coffeehouses like Starbucks, Caribou, and others are willing enablers of this trend. They create an environment that, though striving to be a third place, nonetheless incorporates motifs of the home and the workplace. In one section of the café you may find comfortable chairs, a rug, sometimes a fireplace. The restrooms are "down the hall and to your right." You even have access to electricity if you need to recharge your cell phone or laptop battery. You can sit there for thirty minutes or all day. You can buy one drink or even none at all. No questions asked. Some bring their own lunch with them. The coffeehouse wants to be a home away from home. In another section of the café you have the usual, homogeneous tables and chairs, along with all the utilities you need to open your own private café office.

Yes, the chain cafés are filled with nomadic workers and vagabond students, but many still have a personal connection to the coffeehouse of their choice. Even though Starbucks has over 15,000 locations in dozens of countries, many customers have a personal relationship to a certain location. As loyal Starbucks consumers visit Starbucks approximately a dozen times a month, they see a particular location as "their Starbucks." The chain intentionally makes each location a bit different from the others, trying to give it the feel of a neighborhood coffeehouse, while still retaining the idea that anyone walking in will know what they can expect to find.

Today's coffeehouse, aspiring to be a third place, is designed to be a safe haven from the stresses of our daily lives. It sometimes feels like people are nicer, and more trustworthy in this environment. For example, who hasn't encountered the "laptop-restroom dilemma"? You are sitting working on your laptop, your belongings spread out on the table. And then, alas, you need to use the restroom (why is the air conditioning on in January?). The dilemma begins: *Do I pack up my things, put them all in my bag, and carry everything with me? The place looks packed. What if I don't find a table when I get back? Especially a nice table like this, next to the window and a power outlet...* A second option is to make a run for it, hoping to find everything intact when you get back. Really? Would you leave your laptop for five seconds (let alone five minutes) at a bus stop, or on a bench at the park? A third option is to ask someone to keep an eye on it for you. Weird. Why would you trust a complete stranger to look after your belongings so that other complete strangers don't steal them from you? This brings about the unrecognized science of scouting for the person you can trust to look after your stuff. If they have a laptop themselves, they are probably a better candidate. Another indication is if they seem like they plan to be here a while (with books and papers spread out on the table).

Most people opt for options two or three. I mean, really, do you pack your stuff every time you go to the bathroom at home, or at work? In the same way, the café is supposed to be a place that provides piece of mind. As one video produced by Starbucks says, it is "where the stresses of daily life evaporate like steam from a Grande Latte."

Where Did the Discussion Go?

Going back to Oldenburg, he thought that third places would be places where people come to be together, to converse, communicate, associate, and deliberate. They are vital to any dynamic democratic society. But is that what we have in today's coffeehouses? Indeed, people come there to *not be alone*, but they don't really come to be *together*. They come to a place where they can be around other people, without actually having to do anything with them.

Moreover, since many cafés have become pseudo libraries, taken over by the laptop generation, it makes you feel as if you should be quiet. God forbid you would actually talk while all these people are trying to study or work. Vocal discussion itself is implicitly discouraged, let alone a discussion involving multiple parties.

People in coffeehouses nowadays create a private space within the public space. By using technological devices, such as phones and computers, or by using simple things, like a book or a newspaper, customers define the boundaries of their private space through what they do. They seem to have such a sense of ownership over their spot that often you will see people cleaning their table, wiping it off before they leave, as if to say, "It'll be nice to have it clean and ready when I come back tomorrow."

Remember, Habermas pointed out that the main characteristic of the emerging public sphere in the coffeehouses was that private people came

  ASAF BAR-TURA

together *to form a public*. More than any other kind of relation (economic or other), it was defined by conversational ("discursive") relations between people. For many philosophers of the public sphere, it is the common and public engagement in discussion, and then in action, that constitutes a sphere as public. Hannah Arendt, in her book *On Revolution*, wrote: "Power comes into being only if and when men join themselves together for the purpose of action, and it will disappear when, for whatever reason, they disperse and desert one another."[7] Revolutions and social change don't take place where people come to be alone.

When you think about it, the cookie cutter cafés, where everything is more or less the same anywhere you go, are comfortably numbing (as Pink Floyd puts it). In the chain coffee shops you know in advance what to expect, where everything is, and what's on the menu. There are no surprises, no reason to rethink your preferences, no need to cope with uncertainty. You can walk up to the barista and order your Venti-Extra-Hot-Half 2%-Half Skim-No-Whipped-Cream-Caramel-Macchiato without giving it a second thought. The environment is easy, familiar, and, well, ordinary. Not only are you absolved from talking, but you are absolved from thinking as well.

Arendt's words, written decades ago in her book *The Human Condition*, are perhaps prophetic: "Thoughtlessness – the headless recklessness or hopeless confusion or complacent repetition of 'truths,' which have become trivial and empty – seems to me among the outstanding characteristics of our time. What I propose, therefore, is very simple: it is nothing more than to think what we are doing."[8]

Finally, we must ask ourselves why the shift to this kind of silencing third place has emerged. The fact that new technology enables it is not a sufficient answer. Why do we feel the need to flee the home and the workplace like never before? Why are they so stressful that all we want to do is be alone and feel together (with complete strangers)? Why do we substitute the intimacy of close relationships for the alienation of common solitude? Perhaps it is a symptom of broader social ills: Americans increasingly work more (much more than Europeans in terms of hours per day and days per year) and take fewer vacations. We are increasingly more stressed at work, and more anxious about balancing work–home demands.

The conclusion we reach may be that the social woes we face *should* drive us to the coffeehouse. But not so that we can sip our coffee alone, in self-created private enclaves within the public café. Not so that we can get away from others, but rather to congregate with others. To meet, discuss, and ultimately act to collaboratively mend our society. We must reclaim the legacy of the coffeehouse as a true public sphere.

Brewing Social Change

In order to promote a vibrant, critical, and democratic public sphere, we must conceive of cafés as coffee*houses* rather than coffee *shops*. As a place where ideas are developed and exchanged, not mere commodities. In an age of suburban sprawls and Facebook walls, the art of public gathering must be rekindled and refined. While it is a movement that should spread globally, it must be realized locally. It should build community, celebrate diversity, and spark a flame around which we can gather and converse.

But what would that look like in our day? Have we not gone too far beyond the days of the Charlton Coffeehouse and the City Tavern to come back to such a tradition? These are all important questions, and like any question of relevance to the public sphere, the ultimate answers will be given by the public, in its actions or lack thereof. What I can offer here is a glimpse into some exciting local initiatives that are brewing in the coffeehouses of my community, Chicago.

First is an initiative called Café Society. Coordinated by a non-profit called the Illinois Humanities Council, Café Society is a network of weekly gatherings in regular coffeehouses, where families, friends, neighbors, and citizens come together to discuss current events and other important political and social issues. The idea behind this initiative is that by engaging in the meaningful exchange of ideas and perspectives, these conversations enliven the core of our democracy and empower the public to participate. The initiative even provides tools and support for people who have no regular meeting in their neighborhood and would like to start one.

A second example is a grassroots project called Discussions over Coffee, coordinated by the Jewish–Muslim Community Building Initiative. The initiative was started by a local non-profit called Jewish Council on Urban Affairs in response to the 9/11 attacks, and has become a force that brings together the Jewish and Muslim communities in Chicago to seek mutual understanding and collaborative social change. The Discussions over Coffee, which take place in local coffeehouses, bring together people of diverse backgrounds to study and discuss what Jewish and Muslim traditions teach about issues that concern us today, including social justice, the environment, and more.

Through such initiatives, in which ordinary people engage in extraordinary discussions, coffeehouses are once again centers of activity, critical debate, and social change. But wait a minute, you may question, Why should this great activity be done in a coffeehouse? There are a few reasons why coffeehouses can play an important role in community building, promoting discussion, and encouraging participation in the public sphere. First, they provide a neutral and inviting setting where all can feel equally comfortable. It is not someone's home, or place of worship. It's a fun place to hang out, with food and drinks available. The casual atmosphere also levels the field, a field otherwise defined by social and economic status. In fact, as the coffeehouses spread across London in the seventeenth century, those who frequented them were referred to as "levelers" (same as the name of a political party at the time). The levelers celebrated the decay of the old feudal order with its rigid social ranks. Another advantage is that coffeehouses are open to all, and are accessible. They can become a center for a neighborhood's social activity, and you can incidentally run into people that you haven't seen or talked to in a while. It leaves open opportunities for the unexpected and unintended.

And finally, of course, the coffeehouse setting offers us the one thing that a good conversation cannot do without: coffee.

NOTES

1 Jürgen Habermas, *The Structural Transformation of the Public Sphere* (Cambridge, MA: MIT Press, 1991), p. 59.
2 Khursheed Kamal Aziz, *The Coffee House of Lahore: A Memoir 1942–57* (Lahore, Pakistan: Sang-e-Meel Publications, 2008), p. 22.
3 Ibid.
4 Ibid., p. 21.
5 Nancy Fraser, "Rethinking the Public Sphere: A Contribution to the Critique of Actually Existing Democracy," in C. Calhoun (ed.) *Habermas and the Public Sphere* (Cambridge, MA: MIT Press), p. 113.
6 Ray Oldenburg, *The Great Good Place: Cafes, Coffee Shops, Book Stores, Bars, Hair Salons and Other Hangouts at the Heart of a Community* (New York: Marolow and Company, 1999).
7 Hannah Arendt, *On Revolution* (New York: Viking Press, 1963), p. 175.
8 Hannah Arendt, *The Human Condition* (Chicago: University of Chicago Press, 1958), p. 5.

CHAPTER 8

CAFÉ NOIR

Anxiety, Existence, and the Coffeehouse

Coffee or Tea?

People are always telling me to drink tea. Tea is fine – if I'm sick. But tea just isn't coffee, meaning tea can't be substituted for coffee to the same effect. Not everyone understands this. Coffee is the drink that best expresses our peculiar (post-)modern predicament. It's not just that we need the caffeine to fuel us through the over-long work-weeks demanded by our greedy capitalist culture, though we do need it for this reason. And it's not just that the coffee industry is an example of a complex, global economic reality that implicates us all in the exploitation of the world's poor agricultural laborers and the glut of Western appetitiveness, though it is such an example. No, our obsession with coffee speaks to a deeper need to peer into the dark, bitter cup of our modern anxiety, of our experience of isolation, and ultimately, our confrontation with death.

Tea, on the other hand, reflects decorum, calm, health, order, and prosperity. When tea was first introduced to Europeans in the 1600s, it was touted for its medicinal properties and health benefits, and it remains a healthy alternative (to coffee) in the minds of many contemporary

Coffee – Philosophy for Everyone: Grounds for Debate, First Edition. Edited by Scott F. Parker and Michael W. Austin, series editor Fritz Allhoff.

Americans. When sick, we are urged to have some tea, and when well, we are encouraged to promote our health with tea. Tea is the beverage of well-being. Tea also retains its ancient association with ceremony. Tea consumption is a matter of sometimes elaborate and precise rituals involving the selection, preparation, serving, pouring, and drinking of tea. Whether in rituals from the Orient or the Occident, when people come together to drink tea, they impose a period of order and civility – a frame in which social statuses are observed and conversational exchanges are modulated – upon an otherwise disorderly and unruly social world. Whether this is a social fact – whether people today actually enact such rituals or seek to introduce or maintain social order and status when they drink tea – is not so important as the cultural representation of tea drinking. Despite the greater popularity of coffee in the West, little girls still play at giving prim *tea* parties, not coffees. "Ladies" still have teas and luncheons, not coffee and lunch. And one can still partake of British-style afternoon tea in five-star hotels and restaurants, complete with decadent accompaniments of dainty sandwiches, pastries, and clotted cream. Contemporary teashops often replicate a Chinese or Japanese aesthetic, marketing not just a beverage but also an associated experience of tranquility, clarity, and rejuvenation that comprises, in the American popular consciousness, the heart of Asian wisdom. The artful packaging and careful presentation of teas and tea accouterments suggest that drinking tea provides an occasion to slow down, to attend to the present and to the others who share your pot. It is not just that there is a ritual way to drink tea – drinking tea is a ritual; *it is an occasion in itself*. Whether one imagines a Victorian tearoom with lace doilies and foppish gentlemen or a Japanese teahouse with nimble geishas, tea is a time for careful gestures and careful conversation.

The cultural representation of coffee is, by contrast, decidedly déclassé. Whereas there is *tea time* – connoting the luxury of reserved time – there are *coffee breaks*, mere interruptions of work. Coffee goes to work, whether in a steel-handled thermos to the construction site or in a paper cup from McDonald's to the drone's cubicle or in the ubiquitous cardboard-sleeved Starbuck's cup to, well, any job at all. Despite the fancified coffee menu – flavored syrups, whipped cream, this-u-*ccino* and that-a-*latte* – the proliferation of Starbucks speaks to our bourgeois dissatisfactions: How can we make it through the wearying workday? Java provides a respite and a jolt. What are we to do with our money? The middle class has just enough expendable income to be able to blow it on $5 coffee drinks. Where can we go to get away from the monotony of work and the isolation of home? Pitiably, in contemporary America, public space is consumer space, and the coffee shop offers the chance to get out without spending too much. What pleasures are left us in our over-scheduled commuter lives? We have time for a coffee break, even if it's in the car. And that caramel-drizzled coffee concoction is a small-priced decadence that reminds us that one of the reasons for living is pleasure.

It is not just about the caffeine, for coffee and tea have comparable amounts of caffeine. Coffee drinking has a darker side, perhaps reflected in a host's question upon offering a cup – "How do you take it?" – as if coffee were a bitter, unpleasant medicine one must take or as if it were a test of character, something to be endured: Will you take it hard? Take it like a man?[1] Take it standing up? There is even a faint suspicion … too much sugar and cream and you are not a real coffee drinker. Coffee, black: There is realism in that.

The realism in coffee drinking is the kind that acknowledges the hard-edged limitations of life, which is one reason why the cultural representation of coffee drinking coincides with the actual practices of coffee drinkers. Real life is replete with trouble and the chaos that comes from being one human among a multitude of others equally real (and hence equally confused, desperate, unpredictable, and changeable). Coffee drinking often involves urgency and hurry – leaving stains on our clothes and papers, spills in the car – desperation and loneliness. Coffee drinking eschews ritual and formality as elitist and anti-realist: Careful gestures and careful conversations may attempt to impose a civilizing order that stabilizes social statuses and contains the chaos, but they do not succeed. Even the most seemingly tranquil of social exchanges over tea may harbor, just beneath the surface, every kind of deceit, cunning, disappointment, rankling, and withholding. Coffee is without such pretense; it is, comparatively, plainspoken. Another reason why the cultural representation of coffee drinking more closely fits the real practices of coffee drinking might be that Americans began drinking coffee in repudiation of import taxes on British tea. Remember the Boston Tea Party? Arguably, to this day, coffee consumption symbolizes revolt against institutional authority and aristocracy. Coffee is the drink of the proletariat.

The American Coffeehouse

True, in the cultural imagination, the coffeehouse represents a place of artistic and intellectual vibrancy, and artists and intellectuals are hardly the emblems of the proletariat or the heroes of the American working class. There are two important things to observe here. First, insofar as this idea of the lively coffeehouse is part of our representation of coffee drinking, it is an inheritance from European culture, from the coffeehouses of Paris, Vienna, Rome. Let's face it, Europeans have long had a greater appetite for the arts and greater appreciation of the intelligentsia. The Starbucks phenomenon made the coffeehouse an American experience, but in doing so, it remade the idea of the coffeehouse to suit the American psyche: It coupled corporate uniformity with consumer choice (grande or venti? vanilla or caramel? two pumps or four? hot or iced?) to make an old product seem endlessly new yet unfailingly consistent. The chain coffeehouse, where every armchair and every CD, not to mention every cup of joe, has met pre-established corporate standards applied just the same in Seattle as in Tampa, produces a place that is a non-place, a location (in any strip mall or shopping plaza) without locality. The chain-store is antithetical to the sort of disruptive, creative energy of artists and intellectuals that inhabits the cultural imaginary of the (European) coffeehouse. The American diner, once the authentic locale of coffee drinking, was not the equivalent – not in practice and not in the cultural imagination – of the European coffeehouse, being a somewhat lonely and desolate place that meets the needs of people in-between places or between shifts, and it is, sadly, almost extinct. So despite the tremendous success of Starbucks in America, we ought not draw the conclusion that Americans flock to coffeehouses in order to participate in a percolating intellectual and creative social milieu.

But perhaps a finer point is needed, for Americans may indeed be seeking something at coffeehouses that they are not finding there. They may be searching for a public space where social intercourse is possible without the excesses of consumerism, a place where social engagement is not centered on entertainment or purchasing. Perhaps the popularity of coffeehouses can be explained in part by a growing restlessness in the American spirit that signals a fundamental dissatisfaction with the materialist, consumerist, hegemonic culture and a desire for meaningful social, intellectual, and artistic expression. I'll have more to say about this, and about the distance between the coffeehouse of the cultural imagination and the contemporary chain-store simulacrum, shortly.

But there is a second thing to observe about the apparent tension between my claim about the realism of coffee, the drink of the working class, and my claim that the coffeehouse of the intelligentsia is what persists in the cultural imagination. It is that the picture of the coffeehouse as the gathering place for artists, intellectuals, and emerging politicos is still a picture of workers, for the energy and excitement of the atmosphere is characterized in part by the idea that there is work to be done – creative work, intellectual work, political work. It is a picture of striving, not complacency; of urgency, not rest; of intensity and focus, not idleness. Though the work may be more mental than manual, it is still a kind of work. Moreover, the cognoscenti of the coffeehouse are as likely to be self-taught underdogs and bohemian upstarts as established literati.

What do Americans find in the social milieu of the chain coffeehouse? Public anonymity. (This, despite baristas' practice of asking your name and writing it on your cup, which is partly a matter of efficiency, keeping track of orders.) Public anonymity is not a new or modern phenomenon, though the extent to which it organizes our experience and pervades our lives is. The experience of public anonymity is of being precisely yourself yet occupying a social space in which you are no one to anyone else present; you can do whatever you like, be however you like, and be seen doing and being this way and yet appear only as an anonymous other. No more integral to the social scene than the furniture, you are replaceable by any other patron. The non-place of the chain-store coffeehouse thus allows us to be non-persons, in a sense. We are private right out in public, and our devices facilitate this self-containment and public erasure – cell phones, smart phones, laptops, iPods allow us to engage in a social world that is happening elsewhere. It would seem we have better places to "be" than where we are – online, for example.

People in chain coffeehouses are busy, but this does not mean they are active, let alone interacting with those whom they encounter. They are checking email, studying for a test, reviewing documents, contacting clients, confiding in journals, playing video games, surfing the Internet, catching up on work, or chatting online. The coffeehouse can be a meeting place – a prearranged spot to meet a friend or colleague or client or associate – and conversations do occur; social exchanges do take place. But they have the curious quality of being transportable – they could occur just the same in any other non-place – and inconsequential with respect to the immediate social space – none of the anonymous others is affected. In this sense, it is a place where nothing happens.[2]

Why then have such places been so profitable? Why do we frequent them? This is the real question. For we could more cheaply and as easily make coffee at home or at the office and retain our privacy, catch up on our work and email. The draw, I think, *is* to the image of the coffeehouse as a hub of social intercourse, where real dialogue can take place. People stop in at coffeehouses and linger because they need society and conversation. For decades, large social forces in American life have forced a retreat into social isolation. These forces include single-family housing, suburban sprawl, bureaucratization, insufficient public funding of arts, education, and parks, long commutes and inadequate public transportation, lack of child-friendly public spaces and activities, and excessive media consumption (cable television, the Internet). People need to get out of their cubicles and away from their living room TVs and be with other people. People are lonely.

But the chain coffeehouse proves not to offer more than a simulacrum of the desired social milieu. Part of the problem lies with chains – uniformity is antithetical to individuality and locality, the things that give a place its interest and vitality. And part of the problem is with the patrons, who, given a quiet moment to themselves immediately dive back into cyberspace or who revolt at the idea of sharing a table with a stranger (an American norm that has a much lesser grip on European life). Or perhaps it is no problem at all. Perhaps the scene of the contemporary chain coffeehouse – people sitting alone or in small groups of two or three, each engaged in his or her own private activity, virtually unaware of the others who surround him or her – is the culmination of the political liberalism that undergirds American society. In over-emphasizing individual liberty, we have abandoned sociality. We share space, but only in the sense of partitioning it.[3]

But still there is that hunger for sociality, to be among others, in the hope of lessening our isolation, alienation, and loneliness. The ancient Greek philosopher Aristotle observed that we humans are social animals, but said nothing about isolation, alienation, or loneliness. His concern was to show the importance of our sociality to understanding the good life for human beings. Human beings can only flourish or lead happy lives (attain what in the Greek is termed *eudaimonia*) when they live in a properly ordered society and develop traits of character that allow for proper social relations and that foster friendship.[4] That citizens of the ancient Athenian democracy were already embedded in these social relations Aristotle could take for granted. A couple of millennia later, we cannot.

If the neuroses of the day are any indication – we are beset by anxiety and depression – what we experience as an omnipresent backdrop to our lives is not a reliable social world in which we each know our place and part but a precarious, shifting, attenuated connection to discrete or compartmentalized social settings. Ours is a highly mobile and transient society in which frequent changes in job, career, residence, or spouse destabilize social relations. Nuclear families mean dwindling kinship connections and social resources. Moreover, social relations are separable: Family, friends, neighbors, and coworkers may never mix or even meet. And religious, ethnic, linguistic, and cultural pluralism and freedom can leave one feeling vertigo before the many possible conceptions and instantiations of the good life.[5] Given the difficulties of finding and sustaining substantial social relations, whether among family or friends, it is no wonder we are susceptible to depression and to feelings of loneliness or alienation. And given the wide freedom of choice with respect to our individual identities and commitments, it is no wonder we sometimes step back from our lives and behold them as rather curious and contingent things, and in that peculiar position of stepping outside ourselves – seeing our lives float free of us – it would be remarkable if we did not feel disoriented and acutely anxious.

Individual Choice, Social Meaning

What we want to feel is a kind of confidence, confidence in the lives we are leading. Such confidence is a feeling of assurance that this life adds up, that it is meaningful, that it is heading in the right direction.[6] It is only such confidence (or else a slavish blindness) that can sustain us in recognition of our mortality. Without it, we are simply careening toward an inevitable death, and the ride is incoherent, nihilistic. But this confidence cannot come, not directly, from the individual's sheer choice. Though we are prone to all sorts of self-deception, this is one we cannot pull off: We cannot convince ourselves that our choices about how to live and who to be are meaningful or worthwhile by simple individualist fiat. Though we may be rightfully proud of our ability to make such choices, and in some cases to make them in opposition to significant social forces or in the face of substantial social disapproval, we cannot deceive ourselves that what legitimates our choices is simply our having made them.

Ungrounded choice works tolerably well for some things. Can't decide between the mocha-cappuccino and the caramel latte? Pay close attention to what you do in such situations. What you will do is (a) find *some* basis for choice, however slight, and go with it (perhaps the cappuccino has fewer calories, you think, though this has never mattered to you before) or (b) hand the decision over to someone else (*you choose*, you say to your companion) or (c) flip a coin or (d) act on impulse, choosing

BROOK J. SADLER

spontaneously. If you do (a), you produce a reason to ground your choice. If you do (b), you decide to let someone else take up the task of choosing, which means two reasons are in play – yours insofar as you think there is reason to let someone else choose for you – and the other person's reason when she decided you will have the cappuccino. In contrast, (c) is an ungrounded choice,[7] but notice how rarely we resort to it, even for trivial matters. In adopting (c), we attempt to bypass reason, determining action arbitrarily.

The last possibility, (d), is harder to account for. Sometimes, after fruitless deliberation, one simply blurts out, "I'll have the cappuccino," with no immediate understanding of why that is one's choice. Such impulsive or spontaneous choices may or may not count as unreasoned or ungrounded depending on your theory of reasons and your view of the will. If your theory of reasons ties them to first-personal, self-aware deliberation, then impulsive choice of this kind is ungrounded or unreasoned since the agent reaches no deliberative conclusion and experiences the choice as seemingly coming from nowhere. If, on the other hand, you think appeal to reasons can be made unconsciously, then even impulsive choices may be grounded in real, rational considerations, though the agent herself may be incapable of articulating them. The German philosopher Friedrich Nietzsche suggested that all action was impulsive in the sense of (d), since even when we engage in self-aware deliberation, we cannot give a clear accounting for why certain reasons and not others prove propulsive. Our ultimate reasons for choice, for our deliberative conclusions, or for acting as we do, are simply the last ones to occur before action; they are no more rational than any others for coming last in a temporal sequence of considerations.[8] Now, I think Nietzsche is correct about the phenomenology of this, which is often easiest to see in retrospect. Looking back at a decision made, we often cannot say for sure which reasons were conclusive or why the conclusive ones beat out the others. But even if the phenomenology is correct, it would be a mistake to conclude that we can get along without adopting the deliberative perspective from which we attempt to ground our decisions in reasons.[9] For rational creatures like us, we cannot simply turn off the reason-giving apparatus and still act.

But any time that we provide some basis for our choice, as in (a), we conceive of something as a reason that supports the choice. For example, if I tell you I am choosing the cappuccino because it has fewer calories, you will see my choice as justified, in the sense that you will understand why I chose as I did, even if you think the number of calories in a coffee drink is not the best reason upon which to decide what to drink and even if you believe that it is false that the cappuccino has fewer calories than the latte. What matters is that you can recognize that calorie-count is a possible and possibly relevant reason for choice here. The deeper point is that even if I'm alone, even if I never disclose to anyone my confrontation with coffee-drink decisions or the grounds upon which I make my choice, I nonetheless appeal to considerations that could be made public to others.

Imagine that you ask me why I am getting the cappuccino, and I reply, "Because today is the equinox." You will surely be puzzled, and probably ask for further explanation, some accounting of how the position of the sun relative to the equator has anything to do with the choice between a latte and a cappuccino. If I can provide no intelligible explanation linking the two, you will conclude that what I offer as a reason for my choice is no reason at all. You will not reach quite the same conclusion if I provide an explanation that makes sense but involves several key, false claims. In that case, you'll see clearly why *I* thought the equinox a good reason to choose the cappuccino, but believe that I was mistaken to think so. Again, the important point is that the same thing is true even if there is no one else around to witness your choice or inquire about your reasons behind it and never will be. For the equinox to serve as a reason for my choice, I have to be able to give an intelligible accounting of the link between it and cappuccino. And it's being intelligible *to me* means that it would be intelligible to others.[10] Thus, implicit in my generating such an intelligible account of the reasons behind my choices, I rely upon a language and a set of understandings that are socially generated, not just upon my own fiat.[11] Though I may desire to be a bold individual and to make my own decisions, my own decisions are not grounded simply by the fact that I have made them.

We require a larger sense that our life choices are justified, not arbitrary, that they could be seen by others as reasonable or good. In other words, though we are free, individually, to choose how we live, if such choices are to be sustained as meaningful in a way that puts to rest our anxiety, it must be possible for others to see them as meaningful. At least implicitly, there must be some standard – recognizable by at least some rational others – by which one's individual choice is justified. Or if "standard" sounds too concrete or too narrow, as though there is some single rule to be followed, let us say instead that there must be some common *understanding* that can be called upon in the light of which one's individual choice can be seen to be meaningful.

Nietzsche famously advocated that we reject the moral values we have inherited from Christianity and from much of the Western philosophical

BROOK J. SADLER

canon. He was highly suspicious of our collective, historically inculcated understandings. He believed that central values such as humility, pity, and charity, as well as some fairly basic concepts such as evil and free will, had denigrated humanity – both human culture and our potential as individuals. These values, he claimed, made people servile, obeisant, intellectually weak, and mediocre, favoring herd-like conformity rather than bold individuality and strength.[12] In their stead, he suggested we become the creators of values, that we seize our individuality and amplify it in whatever direction we decide. Nietzsche's rejection of traditional moral values and concepts has much to recommend it, and he presents his ideas in great detail and with great conviction. Notoriously, Nietzsche's positive suggestions for how to proceed after throwing off the yoke of traditional values are vague at best. However, this vagueness is perfectly consistent with his central claims since creative individuality cannot be taught, though it can be gestured at; and anyone who stands in need of such instruction has not the strength of mind or character to be an individual. (The view is decidedly elitist in this respect.)

Part of Nietzsche's genius lies in his emphasis on the importance of individual choice and laying bare the falseness of many of the limitations imposed by society. He, perhaps more than anyone else, articulated in the late nineteenth century what would grow exponentially in the twentieth and early twenty-first centuries – the confrontation between the individual and society manifest both in an expanding field of individual choice and the ever-more entrenched hegemony of an increasingly homogenized culture. (He would be very pleased to hear he was thought prophetic![13]) The contrast with Aristotle's worldview, in which sociality is fundamental, and individuality is conceived always in relation to established social roles, is sharp. So, too, are the contrasting characteristic attitudes. Aristotle brims with confidence: There is a social order and the good life, *eudaimonia*, is both comprehensible and attainable. Consequently, Aristotle need never mention social anxiety, alienation, or loneliness. Nietzsche's optimism about the coming age of individuals appears wan by comparison to his brooding and grim reflections; the superior *übermensch* may be on his way, but today's individual is simply alienated, free to reject social norms and values at will, but alone in her freedom. (It pleases *me* to use the feminine pronoun there, knowing Nietzsche would have scorned it!) Consequently, Nietzsche (both his writing and his life) is drenched in dour observations and surly tones of disappointment and estrangement. What I have suggested above is that there is a fundamental mistake in thinking – as *perhaps* Nietzsche did – that individual choice is in itself justifying without reference, however implicit, to a social world in which others, real or imagined, confirm the intelligibility of one's reasons and choices.

When we turn our attention from trivial decisions about coffee drinks to choices about how to live and who to be, we see that the need for society runs quite deep and is heightened in an age of anxiety.[14] Lacking confidence in the direction of our lives, we may develop a generalized sense of anxiety, an unshakeable feeling that things don't make sense, or won't hold still, or may fall apart at any minute.[15] The real social world is not nearly so fragile – social norms are deeply entrenched and social roles and positions typically change slowly – and likely won't fall apart, but that jittery feeling is nonetheless real and substantial: Without the necessary social reinforcements, small doubts can grow into a corrosive skepticism; momentary feelings of alienation can seep deeper and deeper into consciousness; loneliness can overtake one as quietly as a cloud casting its large shadow over the ground.

The contemporary chain coffeehouse is a symbol in this existentialist era. We are drawn to the promise of sociality, to a place where people engage each other in lively discourse and thereby establish common meanings that impart to our choices that needed sense of intelligibility, justification, and meaningfulness. We have a nostalgia for the coffeehouse experience because we have a nostalgia for real, embodied, face-to-face social intercourse and the enlarged sense of aesthetic, intellectual, political, and creative possibility it brings. But when we arrive at the chain-store coffeehouse, we find only dull corporate uniformity, the false choices of a homogenized culture, and an invisible and virtually impenetrable curtain drawn between ourselves and the others who occupy the same physical place. We remain encapsulated in a shallow privacy and individualism, even as we long to overcome the anxiety, alienation, and loneliness this encapsulated existence generates. Coffee is an emblem of our existential predicament, of our struggle to make sense of our lives and to carry on with our work, while the coffeehouse is a reminder that the meanings that permeate our lone existence are always a function of our social nature.[16]

NOTES

1   Arguably, the cultural representations of tea and coffee are gendered in various respects. Note the associations with female propriety in the girls' tea parties, the ladies' teas, and the geishas' serving of tea. Perhaps the masculinity

BROOK J. SADLER

of coffee, if it has such a gendered representation, is a function of coffee's association with work.

2 A casual interview with some chain coffeehouse employees produced this bit in response to my question as to what, if anything, happens at that location: "Well, for example, one day some guy came in and ordered twelve cups of coffee." That is what passes as a noteworthy event.

3 Maybe we have gotten to the point where we prefer things this way, but I don't think so. Social "space" can be created in online "communities," but people still want to get out of their homes and offices and come into a physical space with present, embodied others.

4 See the *Nicomachean Ethics*, trans. Terence Irwin (Indianapolis: Hackett, 1999) for Aristotle's view of *eudaimonia* and its relationship to a proper upbringing, society, and friendship.

5 Alasdair MacIntyre discusses the problem of the arbitrariness of individuals' identities and commitments in his *After Virtue* (Notre Dame: University of Notre Dame Press, 1984). See especially chs. 14 and 15.

6 Bernard Williams, in *Ethics and the Limits of Philosophy* (Cambridge, MA: Harvard University Press, 1985), pp. 170–173, discusses a similar notion of confidence.

7 Flipping a coin is not an ungrounded choice if you have made an antecedent decision to flip a coin to decide certain sorts of practical problems. For example, one might realize that one always wastes a lot of time over such coffee shop decisions and adopt the Coin-Flip Principle as an expedient way to deal with such indecision. If one adopts such a principle, it then serves as the decisive *reason* in the cases to which it applies, making the choice of cappuccino or latte fall under (a): the *reason* for the latte today is that the coin came up heads. The adoption of such a principle for a limited set of cases does not require the agent to abnegate her autonomy; for the ground of her choice for that set of cases is whatever spurred her to adopt the principle, in this case a concern with expediency in the coffee shop. However, the adoption of a *quite general* principle of decision that left choice to the outcome of a coin toss (or any other perfectly arbitrary or random method) would indeed represent an abnegation of individual autonomy, since it would no longer be tied to a particular justifying reason for the adoption of such a principle, linking it to the situational demands of a limited set of cases.

8 This point can be located in or assembled from many passages in Nietzsche's corpus. For example, see Friedrich Nietzsche, *Human, All Too Human*, trans. R. J. Hollingdale (Cambridge: Cambridge University Press, 1996), no. 39.

9 I am not convinced that Nietzsche makes this mistake, even though he rails against the notion of free will. As Kant demonstrates, the idea of free will is necessary from the perspective of practical reason: In order for a rational being to act, one must adopt a perspective from which one's reason is thought to be determinative of action. See his *Groundwork for the Metaphysics of Morals*,

trans. Thomas E. Hill, Jr. and Arnulf Zweig (Oxford: Oxford University Press, 2002) and the *Critique of Practical Reason*, trans. Mary Gregor (Cambridge: Cambridge University Press, 1997).

10 The sense in which it *would* be intelligible to others is a bit tricky to specify: It would be intelligible to others who were appropriately disposed to hear it (not being, for instance, in the grips of a prejudice against anything and everything that I have to say) and who were appropriately positioned to hear it (being, for example, speakers of the same language and participants in a sufficiently common culture or language-game). It is possible that there are in fact no such others, in which case there is no one for whom it *could* be intelligible.

11 Philosophers will recognize in this passage traces of Wittgenstein's so-called Private Language Argument and also of Korsgaard's extension of that argument into the realm of practical reason. See Ludwig Wittgenstein, *Philosophical Investigations*, trans. G. E. M. Anscombe (Englewood Cliffs, NJ: Prentice-Hall, 1958) and Christine Korsgaard, *The Sources of Normativity* (Cambridge: Cambridge University Press, 1996).

12 These ideas can be found in his *Beyond Good and Evil*, trans. Walter Kaufmann (New York: Vintage Books, 1989) and *On the Genealogy of Morals*, trans. Walter Kaufmann (New York: Vintage Books, 1989).

13 Nietzsche's texts are peppered with self-aggrandizing claims about his own prophetic wisdom as well as fables about the coming of a new era, a new kind of man, and a new kind of philosopher.

14 See W. H. Auden's 1947 poem "The Age of Anxiety."

15 Another poetic source for our modern feeling of anxiety is W. B. Yeats's (1921) "The Second Coming."

16 I would like to thank the proprietors of Café Kili, an independently owned, family-run coffeehouse with excellent coffee and a remarkably friendly and vibrant atmosphere, where I have spent many hours thinking, reading, writing, and talking. I am also thankful to those friends who often join me for coffee, whether at Kili or at one of those other non-places.

BROOK J. SADLER

CHAPTER 9

THE PHILOSOPHER'S BREW

The Philosopher's Coffee Buzz

The relationship between coffee drinking and doing philosophy has rarely been explored seriously. While philosophers and non-philosophers alike have often debated what it means to do philosophy, that is, to philosophize about theoretical or abstract topics concerning a variety of everyday questions, the link between coffee consumption and doing philosophy has frequently been overlooked. Philosophical investigations commonly take on a variety of forms, such as metaphysical speculations about the existence of God(s), moral questions addressing hot button social issues like abortion or capital punishment, as well as more technical pursuits like the logical study of argument forms. Additionally, philosophical practice may be found in a variety of contexts, such as the academic formality of classroom settings, philosophical exchanges during professional conferences, informal discussions entertaining philosophical concepts at a dinner party, an afternoon walk in the park, or while simply conversing in a local coffee shop. The different forms and contexts available for doing philosophy give rise

Coffee – Philosophy for Everyone: Grounds for Debate, First Edition. Edited by Scott F. Parker and Michael W. Austin, series editor Fritz Allhoff.
© 2011 John Wiley & Sons, Ltd except for editorial material and organization © 2011 Scott F. Parker and Michael W. Austin. Published 2011 by John Wiley & Sons, Ltd.

to a wide range of experiences. With each encounter, different levels of philosophical engagement and mastery are achieved; some of these are more effective than others for doing well or performing well, philosophically speaking. This chapter explores doing philosophy under the influence of coffee drinking in a variety of everyday contexts. What's more, it examines the prospects in which philosophical work thrives and improves as a result of coffee consumption. It will be shown that philosophical results stemming from circumstances where non-coffee beverages are consumed lack some of the distinction found in similar circumstances where coffee is drunk.

Preliminary Proposal: Coffee's Philosophical Advantages

When one is involved in philosophical reflection, coffee drinking offers an advantage in aiding the philosophical thought process to an extent unmatched by the consumption of other beverages. While alcohol, tea, and caffeinated drinks in general are also consumed by anyone interested in pursuing everyday philosophical questions, coffee offers a critical cognitive effect that seems lacking with competing beverages, especially ones that contain alcohol, caffeine, or some combination thereof. In the case of alcohol's effect on doing philosophy, it is well recognized that philosophical conversations commonly take place with the help of all sorts of libations. Ever since Plato's *Symposium*, written more than two thousand years ago, the image of philosophers (and other dinner party guests) debating the topics of the day over an amphora of wine has been firmly entrenched. The longstanding tradition of alcohol consumption and philosophical discussion depicted in the *Symposium* survives to this day in a variety of ways. Philosophical conversations have long been known to take place in bars or other settings where alcohol is served. The context in which philosophical reflection arises as a result of alcohol consumption differs from one in which coffee drinking dominates. Apart from the difference in context, philosophical results likewise differ. In this case, philosophical results achieved are mediocre at best, for they do not measure up to the philosophical seeds that sprout under the influence of coffee drinking. It may be said that alcohol consumption dulls the senses or reduces inhibition, thereby enabling drinkers to utter thoughts with little hesitation, trepidation, or much advanced forethought. At times, it may seem like drunken participants are well on their way toward reaching some philosophically fruitful destination. Indeed, it may initially seem as if inebriated stupors are more conducive to achieving a unique mental disposition that entertains abstract philosophical thought. After all, laidback drunken conversations often delve into interesting or provocative topics, and all too often they branch out into unchartered territory, encouraging participants to follow the conversation wherever it may lead. It seems like conversationalists are making good progress toward abstract excursions that uninhibited philosophical exploration invites. No doubt in some cases philosophical progress is made, but the general atmosphere that frames drunken conversations is one marked by specific time limits and a general lack of direction or seriousness. The thought process that takes place in the midst of a drinking bout is often improvisational, carefree, or humorous, enabling drinkers to uphold or reject ideas all too quickly. Lacking the sobriety and mental clarity to analyze intricate details of the topic at hand, drunken discussants quickly abandon one position in favor of another. And as soon as the booze wears off, so do their ardent convictions, especially since discussants may have forgotten what the ado was all about. Moreover, drunken conversationalists have the tendency to become contentious or volatile, thereby taking significant leaps away from the focused demands that routinely inform and animate sustained philosophical discussions. While caffeinated philosophical exchanges may likewise escalate into heated disputes, an overdose of coffee is not generally associated with a tendency for increased violence – there's a reason barroom brawls are much more common than coffeeshop brawls.

Apart from the common everyday practice of doing philosophy under the influence of alcohol, professional thinkers and those new to philosophy have often relied on other beverages to induce philosophical states. Drinks such as tea, energy drinks, soda, and carbonated beverages more generally top the list. In each case, alternative contexts are present and different experiences are had, as the variety of possible encounters amplifies with an increased combination of available stimulants. Apart from the popularity of alcohol and coffee, tea is perhaps the next most widely used beverage for doing philosophy. Tea, or *Camellia sinensis*, has been drunk by Chinese sages for thousands of years. Tea drinking originated in the Far East and is by now believed to be the most widely consumed beverage in the world (apart from water). Philosophers and thinkers of all stripes regularly use tea while engaging in philosophical work. It is difficult to group together all tea experiences into one unified category since there are hundreds of tea varieties yielding an abundance of different cognitive results. And if one focuses on caffeine content alone, some brands of tea contain more caffeine than coffee per serving.[1] But the mental or cognitive difference is not found in caffeine content alone: Coffee beans are an entirely different product than tea leaves. Tea has long been used for medicinal purposes, and it has a longstanding reputation for inducing soothing, nurturing, and calming qualities not commonly associated with coffee drinking. This does not mean that tea consumption is ineffective in helping to bring about worthwhile philosophical journeys – the large variety of teas available makes this a very likely possibility – but only that it is more difficult to achieve these results in the use of tea (or solely by the use of tea).

Heavily caffeinated beverages like energy drinks are often used to temporarily boost energy, increase endurance, or improve athletic performance. The jittery caffeine (and sugary) jolt one experiences here is similar to one had by taking an over-the-counter anti-sleep aid. The purpose of these and like substances is to provide a quick "pick me up" commonly sought after by those working long hours or graveyard shifts, or, in the case of soda or energy drinks, an immediate performance enhancer (as a direct result of taking in high doses of caffeine and sugar at once). The caffeine fix here is not associated with any social mechanisms that distinguish settings in which coffee, tea, or alcohol are consumed. Conversational settings are not a common feature of "pick me ups." In other words, soda, awake pills, and energy drinks routinely lack the social contexts and cultural characteristics that accompany alcohol, coffee, or tea drinking. Of course, this does not mean that social drinks cannot be used in isolation, but only that they are more frequently used in the context of social gatherings, thereby instilling a social dimension absent in environments where modern stimulants such as soda, energy drinks, or anti-sleep pills are used. Similarly, it is well recognized that soda, energy drinks, and anti-sleeping pills can also be placed within a specific social context, such as drinking soda while conversing with your coworkers at lunchtime. Put simply, the overall claim here is solitary stimulants are often used (and sometimes abused) apart from the need to place them within social contexts, as their regular use customarily fulfills non-social objectives.

Like alcohol consumption, tea drinking commonly takes place in social contexts where the act invites forging of interpersonal bonds and random discussions. Throughout the ages, coffee and tea drinking evolved into well-established cultural rituals. In the non-Western world especially, most routine social interactions such as casual gatherings or even business transactions customarily involve tea or coffee drinking. In most countries of the Middle East and the Far East, the first thing a guest will be served is tea, and sometimes coffee. In cultural artifacts such as paintings and other artworks across the Arabic-speaking world, the presence of a coffee pot in a work of art symbolizes hospitality, goodwill, and welcoming pleasantries.[2] The social and cultural associations that accompany coffee and tea drinking are missing in contexts whereby solitary consumption is the norm, and this particular social ingredient is partly responsible for encouraging interpersonal, conversational, and theoretical explorations. For instance, a well-entrenched cultural practice among Turkish, Persian, and Arabic traditions of the Middle East is coffee cup fortune telling. The custom involves flipping the demitasse (an espresso-sized cup called *finjan* in Arabic) upside down to rest on its saucer after it has been drunk. The coffee sediments drain over the inside of the small cup forming a variety of symbols, patterns, or images. After an hour or so of conversation, someone in the group skilled at *tasseography* (a fortune-telling method based on interpreting visual forms in coffee sediments) reads the fortunes of everyone in the group. The tasseographer may read everyone else's cup except her own, since reading one's own fortune is considered bad luck. During these sessions, the discussions that unfold range from merely superstitious entertainment to sophisticated metaphysical deliberations that sink deep into philosophical waters. The point here is simply to illustrate the crucial, firmly established, and far-reaching social dimensions of coffee drinking which have historically imbued the act with imaginative philosophical possibilities. In sum, the advantages of coffee consumption for doing philosophy are far greater than any advantages offered by competing beverages we have been considering.

Analysis: What Has Coffee Got to Do with Philosophy?

Up to now, little has been said about what it means to do philosophy. The argument has assumed that coffee improves cognitive abilities typically associated with doing philosophy. However, it helps to describe the sense in which philosophical work is meant to be improved as a result of coffee consumption. With the use of coffee, critical thinking abilities are sharpened, attention to detail is enhanced, mental alertness is maintained, and short-term memory is quickly activated. Many of these skills are precisely the ones needed and commonly used when one engages in philosophical dialogue or reflection. While the general claim here is that drinking coffee aids in strengthening the critical thought processes needed to do philosophy well, the argument does not advance a narrow or elitist hypothesis about a particular way of doing philosophy. The far-reaching and expansive global history of philosophy has shown that the full scope and range of philosophy, as a field of study or practice, is seemingly boundless. Of course, this does not mean that anything falls in the camp such that it has no distinguishing features of its own – simply put, if anything and everything is taken for philosophy, then nothing is.[3] Within the lengthy history of Western philosophy itself, there has generally been little or no agreement on establishing a unified method for doing philosophy. The analytic–continental rift that developed and intensified throughout the twentieth century was due partly to disagreements about how philosophy ought to be done, or how best to do philosophy. The discord concerned two dominant traditions in the Western canon, each claiming to have the best or most effective theoretical tools for practicing philosophy.[4]

Attempts at finding the most appropriate method for doing philosophy are not entirely new. Throughout the history of Western thought, one commonly finds philosophers in disagreement on many issues apart from how to do philosophy best, including debates about precisely what it means to do philosophy, how best to achieve its results, and of course, what it is ultimately good for. Notable disagreements such as Aristotle's rejection of Plato's theory of the forms or "epistemological" disagreements as those that took place between the so-called rationalists and empiricists in the history of early modern philosophy of the seventeenth century, for the most part, have yet to be settled. They exemplify some of the basic types of disagreements within Western philosophy. However, keeping in mind that philosophy is a multicultural and ancient practice, we find an overwhelming variety of non-Western traditions predating ancient Greek thought (China and India are obvious examples of this) that challenge any notion of unification within this broad and expansive global practice. A thorough investigation of both classic and contemporary approaches invites us to reassess what it means to do philosophy. For its part, this chapter has not been concerned with settling such matters. Rather, the focus has been on establishing a link between coffee consumption and the accompanying improved ability for doing philosophy well. Whether this means an improved ability at discussing philosophical subjects with friends or colleagues at a social function,

BASSAM ROMAYA

or simply improving the capacity for thinking through complex ideas philosophical texts are notorious for introducing, coffee aids in clarifying some of these conceptual obscurities and helps to fine-tune many of the communicative skills often used in expressing or conveying philosophical concepts. Be it reading, writing, or partaking in a classic Socratic dialogue attempting to uncover the nature of moral terms or other concepts (e.g., piety, virtue, courage, love, knowledge, justice, and so on), coffee saves the day when one is faced with conceptual conundrums and intellectual quandaries frequently encountered while doing philosophy.

Topical and Historic Considerations: Coffee's Advantages Beyond Philosophy

Indeed, it might be legitimately claimed that there is no unified or standard way philosophical work must be done, nor is there a reliable or independent criterion by which competing philosophical traditions are to be judged. In other words, in a sea of pluralistic possibilities for taking on philosophical questions, there is no foolproof method to use in every instance so as to achieve excellence in philosophy. Of course, this does not mean that anything goes, only that there will be more than one way of doing philosophy and doing philosophy well, by drinking coffee. For one thing, it is quite difficult to define what philosophy is, and much more difficult to characterize what "good" philosophy is. Philosophers regularly disagree on what kinds of pursuits may be considered philosophy, and they also disagree on what makes for good philosophy – sometimes this is even more difficult than figuring out what qualifies as philosophy. Historic disagreements on how to classify and evaluate philosophical work in this varied and far-reaching practice are not unique to this field. An analogy may be made with other ancient human practices that have busied people the world over. For instance, in fine arts, it continues to be a hotly debated topic as to what exactly counts as a work of art – that is, the attempt to articulate the relevant features which constitute an artwork (the definitional sense) and what criterion one might possibly use for judging excellence in art (the evaluative sense). Despite these complications, some sense of assessment is nonetheless warranted at times. For instance, the Sunday painter may be grouped together in the same category as the coffee shop philosopher, since both practitioners possess elementary skills of more complex pursuits that could be engaged with a greater degree of dedication, and improved over an extended period of time. What might be observed about coffee's contribution to philosophical work may equally be extended in the pursuit of other expressive or imaginative practices. Simply put, the argument detailed herein could be applied to a variety of contexts apart from doing philosophy. An analogous argument might be made in drawing a link between coffee consumption and art making (especially in the case of the plastic and literary arts). Just as coffee aids in doing philosophy, it is also equally useful for undertaking and plugging away at other creative pursuits like drawing, painting, expository writing, or sculpting, and, of course, more mundane activities like preparing a PowerPoint presentation for an upcoming business meeting. The point is, while coffee helps to improve the philosophical process overall, coffee is also well known for producing beneficial impacts in a variety of professional, recreational, or creative pursuits. There's a reason beat poets of the mid-twentieth century were known to congregate in coffee shops, just as European philosophers (especially French philosophers) had done during the Enlightenment. Many philosophical treatises and painterly masterpieces have been created as a result of drinking several healthy doses of coffee. Historically speaking, coffee drinking has been associated with social rebellion and political mobility, leading the drink to be banned at various times throughout its relatively short history (compared with alcohol and tea, both of which share millennial histories). Apart from its usefulness in generating the philosophical process, it is not difficult to imagine these links at play in the cases mentioned and perhaps in other human practices we have yet to consider. The history of coffee reveals both commonplace and obscure instances of utilization. While coffee consumption is enjoyed every morning in any corporate cubicle around the globe, a few centuries ago coffee was not so widely used, nor did it have the secular reputation it holds today. It was associated with religious practice (Islam in particular), partly due to its ceremonial use and origins in the form of a brewed drink throughout the southern tier of the Arabian Peninsula (or the region today known as Yemen). Ascetic Sufi monks would drink coffee before taking part in the ceremonial *sema* (as described by the Turkish Mevleve order) or religious ritual featuring whirling dervishes. In our times, the ubiquitous and habitual use of coffee enables us to easily overlook its profound historic significance, versatility, rarity, and mystique.

Critical Perspectives: Challenges to the Coffee-Charged Philosophy Thesis

It may be argued that despite the many possibilities available for practicing philosophy, coffee drinking in itself does not necessarily help to sharpen or develop any specific mental or cognitive skills needed to do philosophy well. According to this line of reasoning, some may argue that it is nonetheless possible to perform well, philosophically speaking, without coffee consumption, especially since there is no particular way philosophy must be done in order to achieve any worthwhile results. More to the point, since there is no standard way in which to embark upon a fruitful philosophical investigation, coffee consumption stands to benefit at most only some, not all, kinds of philosophical endeavors. So, it is likely that one could still do good philosophy without the need for drinking coffee. In this instance the objection exploits the diversity within philosophical approaches, such that given their vast dissimilarities and broad possibilities, it stands to reason that coffee drinking benefits only a specific type of philosophical pursuit, one that relies exclusively on rigorous thought and cognitive acuity, but not necessarily all forms of philosophical inquiry. Notwithstanding the varieties and alternative possibilities, all traditions primarily rely on the much-needed ability for using critical thought, deep reflection, and mental acumen, despite any particular conclusions reached or differences among varied traditions. There are some things that all philosophical speculations seem to have in common, and that is to wonder, ponder, and question uncritical assumptions about a variety of events in the world we inhabit; they involve a sustained effort at striving to uncover the ultimate constituents of reality – a process which repeatedly concerns itself with the task of asking questions as well as questioning answers.

Another point of departure may seek to dissect the contributive role of social contexts that sets apart coffee-induced philosophical settings from other pursuits in which coffee is absent, but the social context nonetheless present. Since social contexts supply the relevant features that generate an inquisitive or conversational framework conducive to doing philosophy (and doing philosophy well), it may be argued that social contexts are all that one needs to improve the ability for doing philosophy. No doubt social interaction is an important feature for mastering the conversational skills necessary to relay and evaluate philosophical concepts or arguments, but the general claim here is that social contexts enhance, though they do not replace, or substitute for, the propensity for improved mental clarity aided by coffee consumption.

Apart from questioning the links established by social contexts and doing philosophy, another line of argument may be pursued in considering variations upon the coffee theme itself. To put the matter plainly, some may object that while drinking coffee may facilitate or improve the philosophical thought process, it does nothing to address the link between coffee consumption in other forms and the tendency for improving one's capacity to do philosophy as a result of taking in non-imbibed forms of coffee, that is, solid foods that contain coffee. For instance, consider variations such as chocolate-covered coffee beans, coffee-flavored ice cream, a slice of coffee cake, and other coffee-flavored foods. It is reasonable to wonder what the philosophical effects are in circumstances where non-brewed or non-liquefied forms of the coffee plant are consumed. I surmise that in these cases and similar combinations, cognitive faculties are not enhanced to the extent that they are when roasted coffee beans are ground, brewed, and imbibed. Moreover, accompanying additives in the coffee-flavored foods suppress or deflect the potent intellectual effects of coffee in hot liquid form. Additionally, in many coffee-flavored foods, artificial flavors are often used, not real coffee beans. These types of synthetic chemicals have no observable impact on improving the ability to do philosophy well – especially since these foods often lack any traces of the coffee bean itself.

Combinations featuring coffee and alcohol, or concoctions involving coffee and psychedelic, psychotropic, or hallucinogenic drugs, are also ineffective in achieving the pragmatic intellectual clarity that an unadulterated cup of coffee has to offer in the form of immediate brain fuel. In considering non-brewed or non-liquefied forms of coffee, as well as other combinations apart from plain coffee drinking, we move beyond the specific relationship established here, one which simply focuses on a simple cup (or pot) of coffee and the joy of thinking intensely and philosophically about a variety of everyday issues. No doubt much could be said about the relationship between nicotine and philosophy, marijuana and philosophy, or the prospect for doing philosophy under the influence of recreational drugs more generally (with or without the use of coffee in any of these scenarios). Surely these are questions worth pursuing, though I'm only concerned with coffee and philosophy.

BASSAM ROMAYA

Afterthoughts: The Worldly Advantages of Coffee

This chapter has set out to explore the relationship between coffee drinking and doing philosophy. That is, engaging in philosophical inquiry while enjoying a healthy dose of coffee in the form of a hot liquid beverage. While there is no practical way to account for all of the possibilities and manifestations in which philosophical work arises, coffee helps aspiring thoughts come to the fore in any instance where critical reflection plays a central role. Whether the focus is on exploring concepts unique within traditional philosophy or in pursuing expressive or creative human activities that demand speedy analysis, deep thought, and cognitive clarity, coffee is the drink of choice to facilitate the necessary skills for doing well in all kinds of pursuits. Needless to mention, the associated complexities that arise in taking on philosophical topics will not be immediately resolved with a sip of coffee, but the drink will help to awaken and fine-tune the mental skills needed to take on these and similar complexities. Additionally, the links established here equally apply to other human pursuits, especially ones that demand a creative or expressive disposition for performing them well, as coffee sharpens many cognitive processes valued in other activities outside of philosophy. The varied social, cultural, religious, intellectual, occupational, and artistic contexts in which coffee has traditionally been used reveal a fascinating history of important contributions that humans have made as a result of incorporating coffee drinking into their lives. World civilizations have been enriched by the unique, iconic, and unparalleled role played by coffee throughout its history. Enriching philosophy is but one example of the many advantages of coffee drinking.

NOTES

1 For our purposes here, we are only addressing caffeinated tea leaves and caffeinated coffee beans, leaving aside any complications that arise from considering herbal teas, decaffeinated coffee, and other contemporary concoctions.
2 Nada M. Shabout, *Modern Arab Art: Formation of Arab Aesthetics* (Gainesville: University Press of Florida, 2007), p. 9.
3 Etymologically speaking, there is some tacit consensus (among philosophers at least) about the origins of the term *philosophy* and there is some agreement as to what type of pursuits it is generally concerned with (e.g., epistemology,

metaphysics, ethics, logic, and aesthetics). But things get a bit sticky once we consider specializations within the field or attempt to articulate what philosophy means exactly on an international and historic level.

4 *Continental philosophy* usually refers to philosophical traditions that grew out of France, Germany, and mainland Europe throughout the twentieth century. By contrast, what came to be known as *analytic philosophy* was a product of the English-speaking traditions that dominated philosophical work in Britain and America around the same time. The analytic approach usually incorporates scientific or mathematical technicality (hence the term *analytic*) absent in the multilingual styles and literary techniques commonly found in the continental tradition.

BASSAM ROMAYA

PART 3

THE WONDERFUL AROMA
OF BEAN: COFFEE AESTHETICS

CHAPTER 10

THREE CUPS

The Anatomy of a Wasted Afternoon

Cup 1: Macchiato

I have secured the optimum space for myself in this café, positioned so I can look out onto the street – the alternating sunshine and rain, the buses pulling up, the streams of passersby returning to work after their lunch breaks. It is twelve thirty on a Monday and I am shirking my own work, with a cup of coffee in one hand and a *pain au chocolat* in the other. I should be in my office, not here.

The coffee is a macchiato. I have been told that in Italy the macchiato is drunk almost exclusively by the old women it resembles – small, dark, and fierce, with a white head. I drink macchiatos without sugar. The *pain au chocolat* is fresh and still warm. I take a bite, then return the pastry to the plate.

I have chosen my seat carefully. I am not too close to the window, because I want to examine all the other customers: Those who, like me, are shirking work, and those who have no need to work or are bored with work or work strange hours or who have retired from work. But also I am not so far into the depths of the café that I cannot make out the precise expressions on the faces of those passing by outside. This, after all, is one of the pleasures of spending a Monday afternoon in a café, and so it is essential for the café to have large, unsmeared windows. As for the chair, it is not perfect. It is comfortable, an armchair in faux leather, not luxurious, but with the appearance of luxury. Still, it is certainly more comfortable than perching on the tall stools by the counter. These stools are fine for half an hour – about the minimum time that it takes to drink a coffee – but I am here for the long term. I have no engagements other than a class to teach later in the afternoon, I do not have my mobile telephone on me. Nobody at all knows I am here, and nobody who is here knows who I am – an admirable set of circumstances, ideal for writing and thinking.

The only complaint I have with regard to the chair is that the arms are a little high, and I am here to write. Ideally, if one is to write, the arms must be free so that the elbows can swing as and where they will, rather than confined, as they currently are, close to the body. No matter. It will suffice.

Already more than ten minutes have passed since I have sat down, and I have not touched my drink. I pause to have a sip. As I have said, the minimum time to drink a coffee is thirty minutes – ten minutes to wait for the coffee to cool to optimum temperature (I shun those coffee houses that serve their coffee already tepid), ten minutes for the drinking, and ten minutes for staring into the empty cup and either toying with the vague existential questions that flit through one's head, or sighing deeply and repeatedly at the thought of leaving this haven and resuming one's day. There is no maximum time, and no reasonable café owner will complain if their customers spend one, two, or even three hours drinking a single cup of coffee. This, at times, can simply be how long it takes, and anybody who understands coffee should understand this. I have at least two hours, three if I stretch, until I need to catch the bus back to my class. I can afford to take my time.

Through the window I see a man in his fifties, bearded and badly dressed, as all artists should be. He is carrying a music score, handwritten and then photocopied, and he has paused to examine it closely through the thick lenses of his glasses, hunching over the manuscript as he stands in the street. It is spotting with rain, just a little, and the wind is catching the corners of the score, making it difficult for him to read. He frowns, looks more closely, and then seems to give up, tucking it under his arm again and continuing on his way. I imagine that he is humming.

I reach into my bag and take out my philosophy book. It is a collection of essays by the philosopher of ethics Emmanuel Levinas. I have been interested in Levinas's work for a long time. He is a philosopher I find provocative, fascinating, and maddening in equal measure. This book, *Nine Talmudic Readings*, is a selection of his essays on the subject of Judaism. It is not one of his better-known works. Levinas was a Lithuanian Jew who became a naturalized French citizen. He was interned by the Nazis in World War II, at which time he drafted his first major philosophy book, *Existence and Existents*. After the war, he went on to become one of France's foremost philosophers.

I flip through the book more or less at random. There are many different ways of reading philosophy books. Sometimes you need to gallop through them Napoleonically, as the philosopher Franz Rosenzweig (incidentally, one of Levinas's greatest influences) suggests. Kant, for example, on first acquaintance, requires a kind of Napoleonic swagger if you are to make any headway at all. But sometimes you want to work through systematically from the first page to the last, taking notes as you go. Leibniz's *Monadology* is like this, if only because it is so short that by the time you have galloped in on one side, you have already galloped out on the other. And sometimes you want to browse through with no clear sense of direction, seeing what your eye ends up alighting on, seeing what new thoughts are provoked. Wittgenstein's *Philosophical Investigations* is, it seems to me, this kind of book.

Nine Talmudic Readings is a browsing book, or today I am in a browsing mood. I take another sip of coffee and flip through the book until my eyes fall upon a passage that seems particularly relevant to my present circumstance. It is, that is to say, a passage about the dangers of spending one's Monday afternoon lurking in a coffee shop. "The café," Levinas writes,

is a place of casual social intercourse, without mutual responsibility. One goes in not needing to. One sits down without being tired. One drinks without being thirsty. All because one does not want to stay in one's room. You know that all evils occur as a result of our incapacity to stay alone in our room. The café is not a place. It is a non-place for a non-society, for a society without solidarity, without tomorrow, without commitment, without common interests, a game society. The café, house of games, is the point through which game penetrates life and dissolves it. Society without yesterday or tomorrow, without responsibility, without seriousness – distraction, dissolution.

At the movies, a common theme is presented on the screen; in the theatre, a common theme is presented on the stage. In the café, there are no themes. Here you are, each at your own little table with your cup or your glass. You relax completely to the point of not being obligated to anyone or anything;

and it is because it is possible to go and relax in a café that one tolerates the horrors and injustices of a world without a soul.[1]

The first time I read this, I do so quickly. Then I decide it requires a further reading, this time more slowly. I take a sip of coffee before the third reading. Then I put the book down.

This is, I conclude, fairly alarming stuff. Levinas knew first hand more of the horrors and injustices of the world than a great many philosophers ever do; and so, if only for reasons that are not strictly speaking philosophical, when he writes about horror and injustice one cannot but take note. But is this idle afternoon (not entirely idle, note, for I am reading philosophy, which counts for something) really such an evil? I look around me and find myself asking: Is this *really* something that makes possible our tolerance of the horrors and injustices of a world? And, besides, am I as free of obligations as Levinas thinks, even here in the café with my mobile phone turned off? Is there no solidarity between us, we idle coffee drinkers who share the knowledge that others are hard at work? And do all evils truly occur – the quote, I suspect, comes from Pascal's *Pensées*, but because I am in a coffee shop, not a library, I cannot be entirely sure – because of our inability to stay at home in our rooms?

I put the book down and finish my macchiato. These are serious questions. If I am going to be able to respond to them at all, I'll need some kind of method. So, following hesitantly in Levinas's footsteps, I decide to attempt a kind of phenomenology – which is to say, very broadly, not an argument from first principles but instead a close attention to the question *what is it like?* Phenomenology could be seen as an exploration of the texture of experience. And so I resolve to attempt a phenomenology of this afternoon spent here in the café drinking coffee.

It's hard work, phenomenology. I think I'll be needing another cup.

Cup 2: Turkish Coffee

I am fortunate that my local café serves Turkish coffee. Not only this, but they serve it in beautiful blue and white cups, and if you are lucky they place a single piece of *lokum*, a soft, sugar-dusted cube of Turkish delight, on the side of the saucer.

There is an art to drinking Turkish coffee. The coffee comes already sweetened, and you drink it as it comes. The grains lurk at the bottom of the cup, so if you change your mind and add sugar later you will disturb the coffee. While drinking, if you slurp too quickly you swallow the grains. The true experts can manage to siphon off just enough of the liquid to leave sludge of such optimal viscosity that they can turn their cups upside down and read their futures in the grains that are left behind. I have little skill in predicting the future, and am somewhat skeptical of those who claim such abilities; but I am impressed by anyone who can reduce the sludge of grains to this exact consistency.

I go to the counter and order. The waitress says she will bring it to the table. "By the way, what are you writing?" she asks. I tell her I'm writing about coffee. She looks a little surprised. "Philosophy," I clarify. "Philosophy about coffee."

"Ah," she says, as if to say that the fact that I am doing *philosophy* explains everything – my presence here in the café on a Monday afternoon when I should be at work, my feverish activity, and the strange, distracted look in my eye.

I return to my seat and open my book again. I'm puzzling over it so deeply that I hardly notice the coffee arrive. I nod in thanks. Right, I think, let's take this from the beginning. Did I come in without needing to? That is undeniable: There are plenty of things I need to do this afternoon, but drinking coffee is not one of them. Am I drinking without thirst, eating without hunger, sitting down without fatigue? These claims, too, are hard to contest. I am certainly not tired (last night I slept exceedingly well), but all the same I came to sit down. I am not hungry or thirsty (I had a good breakfast), but I have just finished a *pain au chocolat* and am now working through my Turkish coffee, and a piece of *lokum*.

Suddenly, little waves of guilt begin to ripple over me. Shouldn't I be in my office? I have tax forms to fill in, bills to pay, essays to mark. Shouldn't I do the responsible thing? Then it occurs to me that what I'm doing here is *hiding*. I don't want to be discovered. I'm relishing my solitude. Isn't Pascal – if it is indeed Pascal – right in suggesting that the root of all evil (unfinished tax forms, unpaid bills, unmarked essays…) lies here, in my restless inability to stay in my own room? And even if I am not, to my knowledge, currently indulging in a great many sins of commission, the more I think about it, the greater the catalogue of sins of omission grows.

Except, I remind myself, my office is probably not much like Pascal's room. Pascal, unless I'm very much mistaken, did not have a new e-mail popping up every few moments. He did not have students and colleagues knocking on the door. He did not have the unbounded distraction of the Internet on his desktop computer. He did not have to fill in endless forms demanded by bureaucrats and administrators. He did not have a telephone that squatted on his desk like a malevolent toad, threatening to croak at any moment and wrench him away from whatever he was working on. How easy, after all, is it to be alone in one's own room? One's own room is the least solitary of places. To find a measure of solitude it is necessary to flee for somewhere else.

Nevertheless, the solitude of the coffee shop is a curious *kind* of solitude. I am not alone in the way Pascal would have been alone in his room. It is a kind of solitude alongside others. But it is also a particular kind of solitude alongside others. Going to a cinema on one's own, it is sometimes claimed, is a melancholy activity; eating in a restaurant alone renders one the object of suspicion and speculation. But solitude in a café is acceptable. Or, more than acceptable, it is a kind of solitude on display. *Look*, the solitary reader seems to be saying, *I am reading my book! I am writing in my notebook! I am perusing the newspaper! Please, do not disturb!* And in this way the solitude of the coffee shop is one of the most public kinds of solitude. It is not a solitude that excludes others. As one sits there, reading or writing or drinking coffee, one can share a kind of camaraderie with the other solitary drinkers. This is not a non-society, or a society without solidarity, as Levinas might fear. There is a kind of courtesy between us, we Monday afternoon shirkers and lurkers. We respect one other's solitude. We take care not to intrude, as if we are each of us the guardian of one another's solitude. We do not raise our voices. We are in this together, sipping our coffees and reading our books.

Not everyone in the coffee shop is alone, however. Two women close by the window are having a serious conversation. There is a table where three others are speaking animated Spanish. And I'm not sure, looking round, that this is only casual social intercourse without responsibility. After all, great decisions are made in cafés. The French and American revolutions were, they say, born in the coffeehouses. Bonds of love are forged and broken. Novels, poems, and essays on philosophy are written. It is often said that at philosophy conferences the best philosophy goes on in the bar and not in the lecture hall; and while I would agree that the lecture hall is a particularly dismal place for any kind of creative thought, when I recall the most stimulating conversations, the ones that have moved me most and provoked the most thought, they are not those that have taken place in bars but those that have occurred in coffeehouses to which I have retreated with my fellow philosophers.

However, whether we are alone or with others, it is clear that we are in some sense taking refuge from the world outside; and perhaps it is the very fact that we are taking refuge that makes Levinas so suspicious, because to the extent that we are taking refuge, we are shutting ourselves off from the demands that are upon us, we are closing ourselves off from the needs of others. Could Levinas be right that the function of the café is, strictly speaking, not so much to refresh the body as to offer escape from those things that can sometimes seem intolerable, a kind of evasion of our responsibilities? It is clear the café is also (unless we are the kind of philosophers like Sartre – toward whom it is hard not to see Levinas's essay accusingly pointing – who spend our lives in the cafés, who treat them as our second homes) a place of only *temporary* respite. Tax forms, like death, cannot be hidden from forever. We coffee drinkers know this: We know that the demands upon us are by no means diminished as we sip upon our drinks; we know that we will have to return to the fray. But perhaps some respite is *necessary* if we are to be able to respond to the demands that are laid upon us at all. There is much in the world that is intolerable. It is good to attempt to redress those things that we are capable of redressing. Yet if we find ourselves thinking life itself is intolerable, it becomes difficult to see how we might be able to respond to the demands upon us with grace. I have always thought ethics cannot be a matter of furrowing the brow and gritting one's teeth. Perhaps our responsibility to others is also a responsibility to maintain and to keep alive this grace, this sense of life as something worth living.

This, it seems to me, is a thought worth pursuing, but when I glance at my watch I realize that I really should get back to work. Then, looking outside the window, I see that it has started to rain. Two lovers run past, laughing, hand in hand, almost knocking over a man in a suit who scowls at the weather as if he might have the power to transform it. My cup is now empty, and I have no desire to go outside. A convoy of city buses roars past the window. I take off my watch and put it in my pocket. To hell with it, there's philosophy to be done. I go up to the bar and order another drink.

Cup 3: Decaffeinated Cappuccino

As I queue at the bar I take another look around at my fellow drinkers. From the back of the café I can hear one woman's voice, a little harsh but undoubtedly cheerful, cutting through the hubbub. At the table just by the door a love affair seems to be ending: The two protagonists face away from each other, her thumb rubbing the side of her cup, his face tight with worry. Three men are reading newspapers in Arabic, passing the occasional comment. There are two or three solitary readers. One seems to be reading Nietzsche. I think I recognize the cover of the book, but I can't quite be sure, and I don't want to stare.

"Still here?" asks the waitress.

I smile and shrug.

"Another Turkish coffee?"

"I think I'll have a decaf cappuccino," I say. I've had enough coffee, after all. Three cups might tip me over the edge, or cause me to wake at two in the morning in a kind of existential cold sweat. Levinas himself describes these cold sweats in *Existence and Existents*, these moments of insomnia; but I once read somewhere that if you habitually drink too much coffee in the day and in the night wake in a state of dreadful philosophical perplexity, then the first thing to ask yourself is not "what is wrong with the universe?" but "shouldn't I lower my caffeine intake?" And while certain philosophers might turn their noses up at decaffeinated coffee as somehow *inauthentic* (one cannot imagine Sartre drinking decaf, after all), advice such as this, it seems to me, goes beyond philosophy into the realm of wisdom. The two, I think, are not the same. There are many friends I have who would shrink in horror at the thought that they might be philosophers, but whose wisdom I admire; and I have encountered not a few philosophers who have been able to talk into the depths of the night about the most abstruse matters, but who have been manifestly lacking in ordinary, everyday wisdom. If one has to choose, then wisdom, in general, is preferable to philosophy.

"I'll bring it over," she says. "Have you got the day off?"

"Not really. I'm just killing time," I say.

I am killing time: the ultimate waste, the one thing that you can squander without any hope of being able to recoup it. Once it is gone it is gone. And yet, as I wait for my third drink, I realize that killing time is a strangely satisfying experience. We are told endlessly that time is money, but this is simply not true. It is a ruse to hide that which unsettles us most about time, the fact that it cannot be hoarded. It cannot be stored up. There is no interest gained upon reserves. This may be why idling is, in the end, so satisfying. It undermines our facile sense of the economics of time. It goes against the grain, a guilty pleasure. It allows a sense of pleasure to return into our lives of endless obligation.

The waitress brings over the coffee. "Enjoy," she says.

The café is filled with customers. I try to watch them without staring. The café, it occurs to me, is a hiatus for all except those who work there.

And perhaps this is what makes the pleasure of the café so intense; and this is why Levinas may simply be too severe. It is not possible to turn away entirely from the trouble and horrors of existence, however many hours one spends in a café. But it is useful, perhaps, for the troubles (or the horrors, if horrors there be) to be interrupted from time to time, for there to be a break, a pause. Then for a while you are detached from all projects and plans and proposals, from the most burdensome of your obligations; and being detached you are free to play with possibilities in a way you are not free elsewhere. Here, again, I find myself both agreeing and disagreeing with Levinas. In a sense, the café *is* a house of games, it allows the kind of playfulness that comes from our responsibilities being in abeyance. Why not flee the responsibilities that are crowding in upon you, at least for an hour or two? Who could be so hard, so straightfor-wardly *unkind*, as to deny their fellow human beings this little respite? The horrors and sufferings of the world will continue perfectly well with-out our fretting over them. Tolerable or not, tolerated or not, misery and suffering and horror roll on endlessly. They have never ceased, and never will. Do we not have a responsibility to respond to these sufferings crea-tively? Doesn't the fact of our responsibility demand that we find places of respite in which we can play with new possibilities, in which we can find new ways of responding? One must not sleep, Levinas says else-where. One must philosophize. While the world continues to suffer, we must remain ever-vigilant, we must respond to these sufferings, there is no time to waste. But I'm on decaf now, because I know from bitter expe-rience that while vigilance may be good and useful, it is also necessary to sleep – and not just to sleep, but to idle, to daydream, to linger in the sun scratching yourself, to doze.

Long ago, in ancient Greece, Epicurus and his followers, those peaceful souls, withdrew from the hurlyburly of everyday life into simple pleasures – a pot of cheese, some good wine, a quiet garden, a few friends – and for this they were vilified. And yet what the critics overlook is the fact that the Garden of the Epicureans (of which the coffee shop could be seen as the heir) is not a denial of the sufferings of the world but a response to these sufferings.

I reread the passage from the essay by Levinas. "You relax completely to the point of not being obligated to anyone or anything; and it is because it is possible to go and relax in a café that one tolerates the horrors and injus-tices of a world without a soul." Toleration is a forked concept: It is good, on the one hand, that we do not tolerate horror and injustice, that – where we can, when we have the capacity, when we believe that our actions may improve things – we maintain both the capacity and the willingness to respond; but it is also good that we learn to find ways of living in a world with good cheer, even if every day we hear of terrible acts and events; it is also good that we learn not only to tolerate this world in which such things are possible but to appreciate it too. The best response to the intolerable is not grim duty but instead a kind of invention, the opening up of new possibilities. And without standing back, without respite, without open spaces where thought, invention, and creativity can flourish, I find it hard to see what hope can remain within the world.

Putting Levinas's stern injunctions to one side, but not entirely forgetful of the horrors of the world, and granted a little time when the obligations upon me are in abeyance, I am grateful that such spaces exist. If the Epicurean Garden is not a disavowal of responsibility but the thing that allows us the creativity, the capacity for invention, that we need to respond at all, then what the world with its many troubles needs is not fewer of these spaces but more of them. I stretch myself and flick back through this notebook. My mind is out to graze now. It is raining hard outside, and the people outside are hunched against the cold and the wet. Inside it smells of damp clothes and coffee. I have before me three empty cups. I reach into my bag to take out my watch and realize that it is later than I thought. My left hand – my writing hand – aches a little, and my thoughts are somewhat buoyant with the caffeine, my right foot betraying signs of jitteriness. I smile at the lightness of my body and stare out the window a little longer. The rain is not going to ease off any time soon. It doesn't matter. And anyway, I simply can't justify a fourth cup. There are, after all, limits.

I rise to my feet and pull on my coat. Momentarily, I am overcome with a kind of inertia and I sit down again to stretch out this glorious hiatus a little longer. But it cannot be put off. I have a class to teach. I am ready now. On the other side of the café a man is photographing himself with a mobile telephone and studying the results with careful attention. I wonder what he is up to, but decide that it is, when it comes down to it, not my affair. Then I gaze for a few moments into my empty cup, get to my feet again, and head to the bar, where I pay the bill.

Outside the door of the café, I hesitate in the streaming rain. It is two thirty in the afternoon. The buses continue to roar past. I have a pleasant buzz from the caffeine. The day has taken on a different shape and feel. I recall how when I took refuge in the coffeehouse I was at the end of my tether, unwilling to engage with the world and its many obligations. How

WILL BUCKINGHAM

different it now seems. I have things to do, tax forms to complete, classes to teach, innumerable demands upon me. This is what the critics of the Epicurean Garden forget: The garden needs tending. *One must cultivate one's garden.* Voltaire, I think. But I'm in the middle of the street, not a library, so I can't be entirely sure.

No matter. I have things to be getting on with, and when it comes to the responsibilities pressing upon me, checking the veracity of quotes from Voltaire is fairly low on the list. I turn down the street and make my way through the crowds and the rain toward the bus stop.

NOTE

1 Emmanuel Levinas and Annette Aronowicz, *Nine Talmudic Readings* (Bloomington: Indiana University Press, 1994), pp. 111–112.

CHAPTER 11

IS STARBUCKS REALLY BETTER THAN RED BRAND X?

Sitting in front of me (and soon to be consumed) are three packages, each containing a different version of coffee. All three offer the same natural active ingredient, caffeine; and none has any added ingredients.

The first package is a plastic jar whose coffee I will call Classic Red Brand X. It is the most common product from one of the most familiar American coffee brands, for decades a familiar presence on grocery store shelves in its shiny red can (now a dullish plastic jar), and an appropriate representative of the inexpensive blended and pre-ground coffees that until recently dominated America's expectation of coffee.

The second is a bag. It is made of stiff, shiny material, white in color with the familiar green Starbucks seal near the top and the words "Guatemala Antigua" next to the seal. At the bottom of the bag is a stylized representation apparently depicting a Guatemalan woman with a colorful basket poised atop her head. The mountain ranges and volcanoes surrounding the Antigua valley of Guatemala, where this coffee was grown, are suggested in the background. Elsewhere on the bag

Coffee – Philosophy for Everyone: Grounds for Debate, First Edition. Edited by Scott F. Parker and Michael W. Austin, series editor Fritz Allhoff.
© 2011 John Wiley & Sons, Ltd except for editorial material and organization © 2011 Scott F. Parker and Michael W. Austin. Published 2011 by John Wiley & Sons, Ltd.

are paragraphs of accurate, if somewhat romanticized, text about Latin American coffees and the Antigua coffee-growing region.

The third package also is a bag, slightly smaller than the Starbucks bag, but constructed of the same stiff, shiny material. This bag bears a somewhat less colorful and perhaps more fact-oriented label than the Starbucks Guatemala Antigua bag. It indicates that this coffee was roasted by the George Howell Terroir Coffee Company, is called "La Esmeralda" (the name of the farm that produced the unroasted coffee), and is from the Boquete region of Panama. Further label copy provides the interested consumer the altitude at which the coffee was grown and the botanical variety of coffee tree that produced it.

Here are the prices consumers were willing to pay in March 2010 for these three versions of coffee: Classic Red Brand X blend $5.75 per 11.3 ounces, or an equivalent of $8.14 per pound; Starbucks Guatemala Antigua $10.95 per pound; and the Terroir Coffee Esmeralda Panama $49.95 per 8 ounces, or an equivalent of $99.90 per pound.

If we assume that price is a way of defining value, then it appears our culture values the Starbucks Guatemala Antigua about 35 percent more than the Classic Red Brand X and the Esmeralda Panama an astounding 900 percent more than the Starbucks.

What about non-monetary valuations? We can safely say those few of us who make a living evaluating coffees value the contents of these three packages in the same order as the prices suggest, though perhaps not to the same degree. In tasting competitions, for example, the Esmeralda has come out in first place in thirteen major internationally juried competitions when competing against a range of other coffees. And it has recorded the highest score ever awarded in an internationally juried coffee competition: 95.26 points out of 100.[1]

The Esmeralda is a coffee consisting of beans from one farm; in fact, one small part of one farm; the Red Brand X blend consists of unnamed coffees from different countries and regions; and the raw coffee making up the Starbucks Guatemala Antigua is not identified with sufficient specificity to qualify it for entry in a juried coffee competition. Nevertheless, *Coffee Review*, an online publication with thirteen years of history evaluating retail coffees (and of which I am the editor), has rated the Esmeralda (roasted by a variety of companies) twenty-two times for an average of ninety-four points out of one hundred, the Starbucks Guatemala Antigua or a similar Starbucks Guatemala coffee three times at an average of eighty-seven points, and the Classic Red Brand X blend five times at an average of seventy-six points.

Finally, by way of what scientists call anecdotal evidence, I can safely vouch that coffee professionals and informed aficionados would, unanimously I think, rate these three coffees in the same order: Esmeralda the best, Starbucks Guatemala Antigua excellent, and Classic Red Brand X in the basement.

The Tree and the Bean

So much for the cultural evidence. What happens if we consider these preferences from a distance, from what we might call a detached or *philosophical* perspective? Can we unequivocally confirm that the Esmeralda is the best of the three, Classic Red Brand X blend the worst (or least good), with the Starbucks Guatemala Antigua somewhere in the middle?

Well, as usual with philosophy, the answer is both yes and no.

(I need to interject here and say that I chose these three coffees as representative of entire *classes* of coffee products. The Classic Red Brand X represents mass-market supermarket blended and pre-ground coffees; the Starbucks Guatemala Antigua stands for the many whole bean coffees sold by country of origin by both Starbucks and its large- and medium-sized competitors; and the Esmeralda represents only the most spectacularly honored and expensive of those single-farm coffees of the world that are evaluated and doted on like fine wines. These three coffees are points on a continuum; the companies involved sell coffees at a range of styles and price points. Red Brand X offers several different coffees in different styles; Starbucks offers an enormous changing array of coffees of different styles and origins, ranging from very fancy limited edition coffees to supermarket offerings that compete directly with some of the Red Brand X line. Perhaps most importantly, there are many very distinguished fine coffees from single farms or cooperatives that are almost as admired as the Esmeralda but which cost $15 or $20 per pound rather than $100.)

Returning to the philosophical examination of whether we can universally claim superiority for the Starbucks Guatemala Antigua over the Classic Red Brand X blend and the superiority of the Terroir Esmeralda over both, let's start with the perhaps least contentious approach to this question, which is how the coffee industry itself would assign value to the unroasted coffees contained in these three products.

The first industry criterion relates to the kind of trees that produce the coffee. We'll start with species. There are many species of coffee trees but only two of commercial importance: *Coffea arabica* ("Arabica" for short) and *Coffea canephora* (commonly called "Robusta"). As even coffee neophytes know, coffees from trees of the Arabica species are universally considered better than coffees from trees of the Robusta species. Why? A cynical economist's answer might be that Robusta trees are easier to grow and produce more coffee per tree, making Robusta coffees potentially less scarce than Arabica coffees, hence cheaper. But the coffee industry and most of its experts would assert, with considerable conviction, that most Arabica coffees, treated right, taste dramatically better than Robusta coffees. We will plunge into the thickets of taste preferences shortly, but for now let's simply acknowledge the prevalence of this "Arabica tastes better" assumption.

Now, as you doubtless surmised, the coffee in the Classic Red Brand X container is made up of a large percentage of coffees of the Robusta species, with Arabica coffees making up the remainder of the blend. However, both the Starbucks Guatemala Antigua and the Esmeralda are made up *entirely* of coffees of the Arabica species, making them, according to the species criterion, better than Classic Red Brand X.

Fine, but then why is the Esmeralda so grandly expensive and fawned upon when both it and the relatively modestly priced Starbucks Guatemala Antigua consist entirely of coffees of the Arabica species? To answer this question, we need to go farther into the trees, as it were. Even though there are only two commercially important species of coffee, there are many botanical varieties or cultivars of Robusta and Arabica, just as there are numerous varieties of wine grape (cabernet sauvignon, merlot, chardonnay, etc.). The Esmeralda happens to be made up of coffee from a special variety of Arabica tree called Geisha or Gesha that we believe originated in Ethiopia but has naturalized on a certain hillside of a certain farm in Panama and has proven to produce a very unique coffee, in terms of both the appearance of its green bean and, more importantly, how the final beverage tastes. Again, the cynic might argue that this coffee is valuable mainly because it is so rare, but most coffee industry experts, at least those who deal with coffee in the refined javasphere of fine or *specialty* coffee, would claim the Esmeralda not only tastes different from other varieties of Arabica but also tastes *better*. (We'll get to an examination of the validity of this claim in the next section.) The varieties of Arabica that make up the Starbucks Guatemala Antigua are not specified, but most likely the coffee is composed of a mix of traditional varieties commonly grown in Latin America, varieties that are respected but hardly as striking in flavor as the Esmeralda Gesha.

A second industry criterion for assigning value to coffee is how carefully it has been transformed from the moist, fragile seed of a tiny fruit into an unroasted coffee bean stable enough to be transported and stored until roasting without great loss of flavor. This transformation requires a set of complex acts involving harvesting the coffee fruit from the trees, stripping the fruit from the seeds (or beans), and drying them. These acts can be performed with cavalier carelessness, obsessive attentiveness, or somewhere between. Again, as you may have guessed, the green beans that went into the Classic Red Brand X container, especially those from trees of the Robusta species, most likely were not treated well. A significant percentage of the contents of the container probably consists of Robusta coffees that were stripped from trees and dried, fruit and all, in deep layers in which some of the fruit fermented, some developed mold, and some even flat-out rotted. All of these flavors – ferment, mildew, and a sort of composty half-rotted flavor – are imparted to at least some of the beans. Now it so happens that the blenders and coffee buyers for the companies that produce the Classic Red Brand X class of coffees are superb at what they do, and through a combination of simple technology (rewetting and scrubbing the beans, for example) and skillful blending and careful roasting, manage to eliminate all but a faint whiff of all those ostensibly objectionable flavors. But what's left? For that question let's wait until we get to the taste consideration; we're almost there.

As for Starbucks, the coffees in the Guatemala Antigua undoubtedly were harvested with considerable care, and the fruit was removed before it could do much, if any, fermenting or molding. The beans were dried carefully enough to avoid inducing mildew and were sorted and cleaned with some care. So, by this second more or less objective criterion, the Starbucks Guatemala Antigua is again better than the Classic Red Brand X blend. And the stratospherically priced Esmeralda? Here the picking, fruit removal, and drying were even more careful; in fact, they were performed with something close to obsession.

The Taste Test

So much for the coffee industry and the way it assigns value. Let's actually taste the coffees.

In the Classic Red Brand X blend I register a heavy, rather syrupy mouthfeel and a bittersweet (more bitter than sweet) taste. I also register a woody nut sensation, a faint suggestion of unsweetened "baker's" chocolate, and – yes – a very faint but discernible rotten, compost-like note.

The Starbucks Guatemala Antigua has a satisfying mouthfeel, though perhaps just a bit less full than the Classic Red Brand X. The basic taste is also bittersweet but clearly leans more to the sweet side than does the Classic Red Brand X. Rather than a flatly woody sensation, there is a hint of livelier aromatic wood, suggesting cedar perhaps. As with the Classic Red Brand X, I register chocolate, but it is a bit sweeter and less vegetal in the Starbucks. Finally, there is a hint of tartness, suggesting fresh ripe tomato perhaps. Not a hint of mildew or rot.

And the Esmeralda? The mouthfeel is a bit more syrupy than the Starbucks Antigua, though a tad lighter in weight than the mouthfeel of the Classic Red Brand X. But the basic tastes and aroma and flavor notes are much different. They are complex and intense. The sweetly tart sensation I registered in the Starbucks Guatemala Antigua is richer, livelier, more like ripe lemons than ripe tomatoes. The aromatic/flavor notes are many and densely layered. There are notes that suggest flowers (especially the heavily scented kind like honeysuckle that send out their aromas at dusk), baker's chocolate, lemon, orange, roasted nut, and nutmeg, among other possible associations.

So, OK, the Starbucks Guatemala is sweeter, more intense, and livelier than Classic Red Brand X, and the Terroir Esmeralda is more intense, livelier, and still more complex in flavor than the Starbucks. Does this *prove* that the Starbucks Guatemala Antigua is absolutely and universally better than Classic Red Brand X and the Terroir Esmeralda absolutely better than the Starbucks?

I don't think so. Once electrical impulses from our sensory receptors intersect with the learned world of language, culture, and personal history stored in our forebrains, there is no way that I know of to conclusively prove that any one of these three coffee experiences is in itself universally or absolutely better than the other two.

I imagine some of my fellow coffee experts crowding up at my side now, arguing to the contrary. They might in particular focus on what the coffee world calls *acidity*. Akin to the dry sensation in table wines, this is a complex and variable sensation created by the overlapping impact of various organic acids that presents itself to our senses as simultaneously tart and sweet. Acidity is generally considered a mark of superior coffees. Most Robustas, for example, display almost no acidity. Only Arabicas grown at relatively high altitudes display a robust and assertive acidity. Furthermore, any carelessness in harvesting or preparation of the green beans will distort the balance of the acidity and turn it sour and astringent (too much unripe fruit in the mix, for example) or bitter (mildew developed during drying).

On the basis of those observations, my fellow coffee experts might claim something like this: Everyone loves fresh-squeezed juice from perfectly ripe oranges with that perfect balance of sweet and sour, right? And that sensation is analogous to the balanced, sweetly tart acidity of the Esmeralda, right? Therefore, the acidity of the Esmeralda ought to be universally considered a better sensory characteristic than analogous sensations displayed by the other two coffees, particularly the almost acidity-less Classic Red Brand X blend.

This argument may sound persuasive, but there are those in our society who don't care for acidy beverages of any kind, including juice from the ripest oranges, and whose bodies furthermore provide nasty feedback when subjected to acidy beverages, even those as refined as the sweetly acidy Esmeralda. Certainly these individuals would be justified in claiming that Classic Red Brand X, with almost no acidity, and the Starbucks Guatemala, with less acidity, are better than the Esmeralda. Furthermore, entire communities of coffee drinkers – particularly in East Asia – generally dislike assertively acidy coffees. Similar exceptions can be cited for almost every characteristic that an expert might marshal in attempting to prove the universal superiority of elite coffees like the Esmeralda to the Starbucks Guatemala Antigua or the humble Classic Red Brand X.

The conclusive argument supporting the relativity of taste in coffee is the presence in the world of nation-sized communities of coffee drinkers who clearly enjoy some of the very characteristics that North American experts consider evidence of insultingly bad coffee.

Take the "rio-y" flavor note found in some carelessly dried Arabica coffees from Brazil, for example. The rio note, a kind of harsh medicinal sensation apparently created by certain molds, is universally shunned by all mainstream North American coffee blenders and roasters. Imagine the taste of a moldy shoe pulled out of a damp closet, perhaps with a dose of iodine sprinkled on it. Whenever I introduce coffee embodying even a muted version of this flavor note to American consumers, they not only notice it immediately but generally proclaim how repulsive it is.

However, this despised flavor note is greatly enjoyed by mainstream coffee-drinking communities in the Middle East and Central Europe. A coffee roaster of my acquaintance, who operates one of the most admired and successful coffee-roasting companies in the Middle East, buys only Brazil coffees with this flavor note for his popular blends. An expert in his

KENNETH DAVIDS

company might find the absence of the medicinal rio-y note in a blend as offensive as a North American might find its presence.

Finally, take coffee of the Robusta species. In fact, let's take coffee of the Robusta species that has been so unselectively harvested and sloppily dried that it shows distinct signs of ferment and mildew. Surprisingly, southern European roasting companies know exactly how to use these abused coffees in their espresso blends to produce a rich, brandied cherry chocolate sensation, albeit a brandied cherry chocolate sensation usually shadowed by faint (sometimes not so faint) hints of mildew and rot.

North American experts, of course, focus on the mildew and rot. They *do not* like blends containing such serendipitously tainted coffees. For them, the woody dullness of the Robusta species overlaid with hints of mildew and rot is a sensory insult no matter how well these characteristics can be coaxed into producing a sweet, brandied cherry chocolate sensation. Yet blends heavy with this dullish, fermented cherry chocolate character are the most popular style of espresso coffee in Europe.

So here we have a coffee type that violates both the "Arabica is better" rule *and* the purity of preparation rule, yet is enjoyed by a large swath of a population generally admired for its culinary sophistication.

A Way Out of Relativism

As a reminder, last I checked no one has claimed any coffee preferences for God, so we must make do with human beings to establish our universal hierarchy of coffee. Where does that leave us? Floating around in the boring relativity of the "I don't know, but I know what I like" school of coffee criticism?

I think there is a way out of relativism that is philosophically honorable and yet opens the way to legitimate evaluation of coffee. About three decades ago in the world of literary theory, a scholar named Stanley Fish (b. 1938) popularized the following set of ideas. Fish starts with the argument that everyone reads a piece of literature differently; in fact, there are as many different versions of Mark Twain's famous novel *Huckleberry Finn*, for example, as there are people who have read the book. Not only that, but there is a *new* version of *Huckleberry Finn* created every time the same individual reads the book again. The same might be said for music. There are as many different versions of the Beatles' song "Let It Be" as there are people who have listened to it and times they have listened, since different occasions always change our perception. The version we listened to half-drunk at a party will be different from the version we listen to when sober doing the dishes two weeks later, even if the artist and the recording are exactly the same. Our emotions, focus, body chemistry, and a lot of other things were different at the party than while doing the dishes.

Applying this idea to coffee, one could therefore argue that there are as many Terroir Coffee Esmeraldas and Classic Red Brand X blends as there are people who have tasted these coffees and moments when they have tasted them. All is relative from person to person, and even from moment to moment.

Nevertheless, Fish's argument continues, there exist in societies *interpretive communities* that use similar language and, often without realizing it, make similar assumptions about objects and experiences they define as related or the same. Literary critics, for example, are all members of a similar community of interpretation and, although their specific interpretations of *Huckleberry Finn* may be different, sometimes quite different, they operate inside a broad set of basic assumptions that are accepted as true by all of them. Hence, when they read *Huckleberry Finn* their experiences of the book overlap sufficiently that they can argue about it as though they really were all actually reading the same book at the same moment in the same state of mind.

Similarly, a dominant global community of interpretation exists around coffee, and it is this dominant global community of interpretation that could lead us to proclaim confidently that the Terroir Esmeralda is superior to the Starbucks Guatemala Antigua and the Starbucks Guatemala Antigua superior to the Classic Red Brand X blend. Other communities of interpretation for coffee exist that make somewhat different assumptions about coffee using somewhat different languages, but these communities don't make much fuss about their assumptions and tend to keep their heads down, busy producing coffees the consumer members of their communities enjoy while not rocking the boat of the dominant group of coffee experts. (I need to point out that the dominant community of coffee experts I am describing is a global community, including coffee professionals from all over the world, with a particularly rich representation from Latin American coffee-producing countries.)

What are the criteria for excellence applied by this community of expert tasters?

- Acidity is fundamentally good, so long as it is not harsh, overbearing, or astringent.

- Smoothly viscous or lightly syrupy/silky mouthfeel is better than thin, watery, or silty mouthfeel.
- Aromatic and flavor notes that are complex and intense are better than those that are simple or faded.
- Given that coffee is an inherently bitter beverage, natural sweetness is good, whereas too much bitterness is bad.
- Aromas and flavors that develop naturally from the coffee bean itself, like floral, fruit, citrus, honey, molasses, and chocolate (in coffee, fruit notes are often turned toward chocolate by the caramelizing of sugars during roasting), are better than flavors that come from mistakes made during fruit removal and drying, like fermented fruit, mustiness or moldiness, or rotten or medicinal flavors.
- A long, sweet, flavor-saturated aftertaste is better than a short, fast-fading, astringent or aromatically empty aftertaste.

Given these shared assumptions, if members of this interpretive community were given the Esmeralda, the green coffee that went into the Starbucks Guatemala Antigua, and the coffees that make up the Classic Red Brand X blend, I have little doubt that their evaluations would fall out as I have assumed throughout this chapter. Some members of the community might be almost shocked and bewildered by how intense and complex the Esmeralda is, and some might be more forgiving than others in regard to the Robustas incorporated in the Classic Red Brand X blend, but the order of preference and value assigned to the coffees would be about the same.

One could find other coffees that might provoke disagreement among the members of this dominant interpretive coffee community, even cause a bit of a battle, but the battle would be conducted using common language and understandings shared by the community. One disagreement that has been quietly smoldering within the dominant coffee community for some years, for example, concerns Robusta coffees. Should all coffees of the Robusta species, with their essentially low-acid, aromatically subdued character, be despised and given low ratings, or should there be languages and criteria for differentiating between *good* Robustas and *bad* Robustas, and should good Robustas be honored and offered to consumers on their own terms?

A much hotter battle is being fought between those tasters who feel that all coffees that have acquired a fermented fruit note during drying should be despised because this taint perverts the natural taste of the coffee bean and those other tasters (a minority at present) who admire this taint when it is not too intense. The pro-ferment school argues that many human beings enjoy the richly fruity, brandyish flavor of the better ferment-influenced coffees and that the coffee community should attempt to understand and ultimately honor this coffee type.

But regardless of how these skirmishes in the tasting trenches are resolved, we are left with a worldwide community of experts who, despite their relatively minor disagreements, pretty much assign values to the sensory character of coffees in similar ways, using roughly similar language and criteria.

Other Considerations

Of course there are other reasons besides the fundamental characteristics of the green coffees that could lead someone to consider one of these three coffees better than the others. Roast color, for example. The darker the roast color (in other words, the more *done* or *roasted* the coffee), the more likely floral/honey, nut, or fruit notes characteristic of fine Arabica coffees will be replaced by a caramel- or chocolate-like character together with flavors reminiscent of cedar or other aromatic woods. A darker roast also will mute the tart-sweet acidy sensation of medium-roasted Arabica coffee, turning it more bittersweet. At a still darker, almost black, roast color, often called "French roast" in the United States, scorched wood notes dominate and almost all taste and flavor nuance is likely to be burned out of the beans.

There is very little consensus among the dominant community of coffee experts about which level or darkness of roast is exactly best, apart from an almost universal dislike of extremely dark French roasts because they so drastically limit the flavor possibilities of the green coffee. Generally, members of the expert community argue that the roast level should be chosen to best develop the flavor characteristics of the green coffee, but exactly where on the roast spectrum that sweet spot is located for a specific coffee or blend of coffees still depends on the taste of the roaster and the expectations of the roaster's customers.

George Howell, the well-known coffee leader at Terroir Coffee, argues, as many of today's taste-leading roasters do, that a light-to-medium roast color best allows the full range of flavor to develop in a fine coffee. On the other hand, the roasters at Starbucks might argue that the darker roast style they applied to their Guatemala Antigua best develops the Antigua's tendency toward an attractive, dark chocolatey bittersweetness. Plus, of course, the Starbucks roasters need to satisfy an international army of habitués who expect their Starbucks coffees to taste richly bittersweet rather than brightly complex.

Classic Red Brand X is medium roasted for at least two reasons. For one, the Robusta and other inexpensive coffees that dominate such blends are so relatively flat and woody in flavor that a lighter roast is necessary to preserve whatever acidy liveliness they started with. The other reason is that the original and historical Red Brand X was a medium-roasted blend and the contemporary Classic version of the Red Brand X attempts to preserve that tradition and satisfy its clientele.

Still other criteria for goodness exist. Take freshness, for example. Green coffee held before roasting maintains its flavor rather well, but roasted coffee is a notoriously fragile product, best consumed anywhere from one to ten days after roasting unless protected from the atmosphere by special packaging. Here the Esmeralda and similar coffees from small, elite roasting companies appear to have an edge. Pre-ground coffees like the Classic Red Brand X typically have been allowed to sit for hours after grinding but before packaging because otherwise the carbon dioxide that floods off freshly roast and ground coffee might blow the top off the container. Such "degassing" is needed to allow the carbon dioxide to dissipate. On the other hand, the Starbucks Guatemala and Terroir Esmeralda were sealed almost immediately after roasting in foil bags that contain a valve that lets the carbon dioxide out while preventing staling oxygen from getting back in. Furthermore, both the Starbucks and Esmeralda I sampled are whole bean coffees, which means the natural package for the flavor oils, the bean itself, remains intact until the consumer grinds the coffee, an act that all of we tiresome experts hope happens at home at the kitchen counter just before the coffee is brewed.

Super elite coffees like the Esmeralda from small, top-end roasting companies like Terroir offer still another edge in freshness over everyday whole bean coffees like the Starbucks Guatemala Antigua: They typically are sold soon after roasting, rather than allowed to sit inside their protective packaging for a length of time undisclosed to consumers, often up to six months. Terroir's Esmeralda, for example, is not even roasted until it is ordered. Terroir exhibits roast dates for its finest coffees on its website, and customers put in their orders in advance of the roast date. Other elite coffees from small companies are not treated with quite such fastidiousness, but they do generally display a "roasted on" date on the packaging, so customers know at the time they buy the coffee whether it was roasted within the preceding two weeks or so, the period that the expert community generally considers optimum for freshness.

Try It Yourself!

Having come this far with me, some readers may feel in need of a cup of coffee. Perhaps three cups, one from each category of coffee discussed here. If you feel inclined to replicate my experiment, you needn't spend $49.95 for 8 ounces of Esmeralda from Terroir Coffee. The same basic generalizations apply to certain other very distinctive coffees from other parts of the world roasted by other coffee companies. The best Kenyan coffees, for example, usually display striking flavor characteristics that the expert community I describe admires; the same goes for the finest coffees from the Yirgacheffe region of Ethiopia. Splendid coffees are produced by many other regions of the world, like the Antigua region of Guatemala that produced the Starbucks sample, but they may be less distinctive or unique tasting than the Esmeraldas, the Kenyas, and the Yirgacheffes of the world, which are admired not only for their quality but also for their unusual and striking flavor.

So you can conduct this experiment yourself by purchasing the Classic version of the Red Brand X blend at your local supermarket, the Starbucks Guatemala Antigua at your local Starbucks, plus a medium-roasted Ethiopian Yirgacheffe coffee from Terroir or any number of other admired small roasting companies the connoisseur crowd in your area can probably point you to. But of course, they too are probably in cahoots with the dominant expert community, so don't take their word for it, or mine. Try the coffees yourself and remember that, philosophically speaking, you can't go wrong.

NOTE

1   100-point rating scales are an important component of the specialty coffee industry's apparatus of communication and coffee evaluation. Scores are assigned by professional coffee tasters, called "cuppers," following set tasting protocols and using forms that solicit numerical assessments of various sensory attributes of coffees based on a combination of intensity, freedom from taint, and pleasingness. Such forms and ratings are used in green coffee

competitions, by importers and sellers of green coffees, and in communications with aficionado consumers. A score of 80 or higher is usually taken as an indication that a coffee can be considered a "specialty," or fine, coffee. A score of 90 or higher is usually taken to indicate that the sample represents a particularly outstanding specialty coffee.

CHAPTER 12

THE FLAVOR OF CHOICE

Neoliberalism and the Espresso Aesthetic

Viva la revolución? Hmm … As you quaff your double-decaf-lite-soy-hazelnut frappuccino from your local cooperative coffeehouse, it ain't the ghosts of Marx or Che watching over you – it's more likely the specters of Hayek and Reagan. For a product as bound to cultural activism as it is to cognitive activity, coffee these days sure is laced with a dash of irony.

Of all the radical changes in the last twenty years in the way we consume and appreciate coffee, the most notable has been the growth in popularity of espresso-method coffee. The artistry and technique required to control the many variables that contribute to the perfect espresso have become central to the marketing of espresso and the café industry. Indeed, few products so perfectly illustrate the competing forces of the free market and artisanship.

This chapter traces the aesthetic of espresso from its origins as the *raison d'être* of the Italian *caffè* to its redefinition as a mass-consumed and chameleon-like beverage, and considers whether the qualities that make espresso the definitive coffee experience have been diminished in the name of profit. It also explores the increasingly professional practice of the barista, and the emergence of new skills and features, suggesting that the aesthetic ingredients so essential to the simple sophistication of espresso have been diluted so as to be virtually indistinguishable.

While couched in terms of the nuances and delights of espresso, this chapter ultimately questions the possibility of a neoliberal aesthetic. Neoliberalism has emerged as the over-arching "ism" applied to the theoretical shift that absorbed neoclassical *laissez-faire* economics, and was subsequently accompanied by a hybrid social conservatism often associated with the leadership of US President Ronald Reagan and British Prime Minister Margaret Thatcher in the 1980s. However, its contemporary dominance is limited not only to economic and political theory and practice; neoliberalism's dependence on *the individual* as its governor has enormous repercussions for the question of taste. How can one person's judgment of taste be superior to someone else's when everyone is his or her own governor? How then, against the heightened expectations and empowerment of the consumer, might we rediscover certain simple pleasures lost amidst the mechanics of the free-market economy? This chapter considers espresso as one such pleasure.

The Cultural State of the Coffeehouse

Since it started spreading around the world in the 1990s, Starbucks has been the bête noire *of posh boys with dreadlocks ... and organic-patronizing, barefoot commentators.*

Brendon O'Neill[1]

One need look no further than this editorial rant to see the contradictory forces that shape this topic. As the "posh boys with dreadlocks" retreated from the advancing market forces to the faux-*Sandinista* camaraderie of the coffeehouse, political observers swiftly honed their critical blades on the paradoxical nature of their position. The thousands of jobs lost when Starbucks succumbed to the economic downturn of 2009 registered a mere blip on the conscience of the posh boys, whose militancy forgave no engagement with the enemy. Nor was any heed granted the initiatives such companies introduced, despite Starbucks' Corporate Social Responsibility Fiscal 2007 Annual Report[2] being replete with commitments to ethical coffee sourcing, repairing imbalances in employment opportunity, and environmental sustainability targets.

The predicament both our corporate and radical citizens have found themselves in is cacophonous with the sounds of ideologies clashing. The cynical eye cast over the posh boys' agenda is as fierce when applied to the corporate warriors, whose desire to satiate the growing demand for environmental and social activism is seen by many as little more than the advancing wolves of capitalism dressed as ethical sheep. It is with candor, rather than irony, that many of the new wave of liberal economists acknowledged this. Among the most prominent of all, Milton Friedman stated: "Of course, in practice the doctrine of social responsibility is frequently a cloak for actions that are justified on other grounds rather than a reason for those actions."[3] Appalled neo-Marxists rallied, yet the power of advanced capitalism to absorb all in its path meant that even their iconography became fodder for the market. Witness, now, how Mao and Che peer impotently from department store T-shirts. All of which brings me to present here an alternative viewpoint – one concerning *the aesthetic* – which not only serves to illustrate the paradoxes more clearly but might also offer some resolution by way of our sensual engagement with espresso.

A Personal Encounter

First, I should explain my own experience with coffee (and, thus, my own position in this quandary). I spent some twenty years amidst the manifold machinations of the coffee industry before entering the far less vocationally sustainable machinations of the philosophy industry. I worked for ten years as barista in one of my hometown's best-loved and busiest cafés. I trained a conga line of liberal arts dropouts like myself in the espresso method, all the while perfecting a facial expression peculiar to the occupation; tormented existential angst meets (near-comatose) urbane aloofness. I donned a Janus mask to work for multinational coffee companies, advising countless (either inspired or deluded) souls as to how to make their fortunes from a humble bean. To my ultimate despair, every success story carried umpteen tales of woe, none more typical than that of the retired couple who had invested their life's savings in the wrong café, in the wrong place, at the wrong time. The inner-city suits and their deep mocha dollars evaporated in the sweet lavender of the couple's

ANDREW WEAR

old-world charm. The double-macchiato-on-polished-steel-and-granite brigade avoid hearty peach muffins and big ol' buckets of coffee like the plague; they like their coffee with minimalism – and a sneer.[4] I found myself participating in peculiar events – competitions – among baristas, all battling for supremacy of their artisanship. Upon winning one such competition I became aware of a cultural turn in espresso-method coffee making. The training, the advising, (the sneering), and even the sudden emergence of internationally recognized affiliations between baristas had somehow culminated to dilute the stylish simplicity that drew me to the method in the first place. The espresso aesthetic appeared lost!

A Few Steps Back

The oft-recalled tale of the Ethiopian goat herder and his caffeinated caprids has come to mark the origin of coffee as a digestible. As the green beans were roasted brown and trade routes funneled them into the Venetian waterways, the coffee culture we now speak of was born. Today, millions visit Venice's Caffè Florian, Italy's oldest operating *caffè*, to recline in its rococo splendor. Its garish coffee menu of thirty-three varieties belies its humble beginnings. Yet Florian remains a show-pony amidst the workhorses that day-in, day-out deliver the millions of espresso shots propping up Italian mornings. For the essence of Italy's coffee culture, picture not Florian's garishness; rather, conjure the image of oaken elbows on oaken counters, a copy of *La Repubblica* shuffled slapdash across the bar, a cigarette slow-burning in the ashtray, and a tiny white porcelain cup (atop a tiny white porcelain saucer) half-filled with a rich sienna liquor. A few opinionated barks at the day's headlines or gossip – perhaps some back from the barista – a few Euros tossed on the bar, and the patron is off for the day's duties.

The technical and social machinations of the espresso method as presented in this image are clearly idealized in an aestheticized Marxist model, since it describes a range of aesthetic conditions that call out humble purity and unity in commonality, breaking the socioeconomic ties that bind. Initially, Marx might not appear a likely port of call for theorizing the aesthetic; yet translation of his political and economic theory into aesthetic and cultural theory has been among the more passionately undertaken philosophical ventures in recent history, particularly in light of the hitherto unpredicted development of Soviet and then Sino industrialization that twisted Marx's *Communist Manifesto* into parody. Marx's critique of bourgeois despotism came to sound more like a description of the miserable clunking factories of Stalin's USSR or Mao's China:

> Modern Industry has converted the little workshop of the patriarchal master into the great factory of the industrial capitalist. Masses of labourers, crowded into the factory, are organised like soldiers. As privates of the industrial army they are placed under the command of a perfect hierarchy of officers and sergeants. Not only are they slaves of the bourgeois class, and of the bourgeois State; they are daily and hourly enslaved by the machine, by the overlooker, and, above all, by the individual bourgeois manufacturer himself. The more openly this despotism proclaims gain to be its end and aim, the more petty, the more hateful and the more embittering it is.[5]

The kitschy idealized imagery, usually prefigured upon man, woman, and child marching toward a utopian dawn (they always seem to be looking or heading somewhere beyond ...) is what many of us would associate with what might be described as the "communist aesthetic." Not so. This was mere propaganda to distract from the drabness of reality and, thus, not really representative at all. Others might argue that the much-maligned concrete gray monoliths of Cold War Chemnitz, Katowice, or Kiev are more true to the ideal. I would contend that the mechanisms of espresso production speak of the conditions of twentieth-century industrialized communism, with the product the concept of egalitarianism idealized in pure and simple liquid form. For be ye businessman or street sweeper – *it matters not, comrade!* – every morning *your* espresso will be the same as *his*! Even the political, historical, and industrial backdrop to this tale speaks volumes of the rise of espresso culture in Italy; Gaggia's production of the first piston-driven espresso machine in 1945 coincided with a resurgence in electoral support for Italy's communist and socialist parties, and almost all of the major coffee-importing and roasting companies have held on to their logos from this period. While there must have been rumblings in the boardrooms over the years, those Euro-Soviet fonts and designs are now dripping with nostalgic chic.[6]

We must be cautious, for the politicizing of this model does no favor when staking certain aesthetic claims. The mark of aesthetic perfection is the pure simplicity of espresso as a product, masking the complexity of its production. Behind each twenty-five milliliter measure is an expanse of labor, expertise, and technique. Putting aside the slew of ethical

ANDREW WEAR

consideration now coloring these variables, this little cup of coffee's perfection is determined by seven key factors: the source of the beans; the intensity of the roast; the balance of the blend; the precision of the grind; the fortitude of the espresso machine; the purity and temperature of the water used in its extraction; and the skill and finesse of its maker. If any one of these variables falls short, the espresso will be compromised.

The first clue to the arguments for realigning the contradictory forces producing the misshapen aesthetic of neoliberalism might be the free market's capacity to facilitate the smooth and successful running of these multiple variables. Let us not forget that beyond my idealized aesthetic of espresso's halcyon days, the countless tons of coffee imported into Italy (and subsequently, beyond) were, by and large, the result of the blood, sweat, and tears of impoverished colonies. Lambasting multinational corporations pays no heed to the increasing and benevolent push toward fair trade, organic, environmentally sustainable, and bird-friendly production of coffee – not to mention the countless advances in science and technology. As the case of the posh boys vs. Starbucks suggests, realigning the contradictory forces might not be so simple.

Aesthetics and Liberalism

The philosophical backdrop to this investigation is the troubled marriage of *the aesthetic*[7] with liberal ideals. To be more politically (sadly, not any less ambiguously) defined, we might call the couple *taste* and *liberalism*. To get to the bottom of the contemporary debate circling their "management," I now turn to, and conjure, our dear friend Immanuel Kant (1724–1804). Few challenge Kant's credentials as a philosopher, even though plenty of cruel folk have plenty of cruel things to say about him. For instance, some have mocked him for never leaving his hometown of Königsberg; others snicker unkindly while discussing his virginity; others feign nausea upon hearsay of a body odor not unlike poorly smoked sprats.[8] Regardless, Kant's philosophy has had such an immeasurably profound affect on philosophy that any attempt to abbreviate (even a fragment of) his inquiry is fraught with danger. So, as I don my disguise and flak jacket, I will consider Kant's role in this discussion.

Immanuel Kant was a little odd, sure, but he was a mighty mind. His published critiques were vast and comprehensive systems of knowledge and morality, and he remains virtually unparalleled for the sheer breadth of his inquiry. After his first two critiques – *Critique of Pure Reason* (1781) and *Critique of Practical Reason* (1788) – laid the groundwork for his philosophical systems, his third – *Critique of Judgement* (1790) – was (while an extension of the two earlier critiques) where he tackled aesthetics. In this third critique, Kant raised questions about, and sought to define, both our judgment of and the constitution of *beauty* and *pleasure*. This was not as simple a task as one might think, not least for the importance Kant placed on the hierarchy of judgment. That is, to consider something pleasurable because it is beautiful is, after all, Kant says, very different from considering something beautiful because it is pleasurable. Kant whittled away at these distinctions and the order of cognition therein, bringing forth that most intriguing of aesthetic notions: *the sublime*. Its entry into daily parlance as a descriptor for, say, a magnificent chocolate dessert falls short of capturing Kant's sentiment. Kant writes of the sensation we experience when encountering an occurrence or object so sensually and emotionally overwhelming as to be beyond our faculties of perception or expression. Kant's description of the sensation of supreme and boundless freedom this encounter invokes illustrates how fresh his work on aesthetics remains:

> Bold, overhanging, and, as it were, threatening rocks, thunderclouds piled up the vault of heaven, borne along with flashes and peals, volcanoes in all their violence of destruction, hurricanes leaving desolation in their track, the boundless ocean rising with rebellious force, the high waterfall of some mighty river, and the like, make our power of resistance of trifling moment in comparison with their might. But, provided our own position is secure, their aspect is all the more attractive for its fearfulness; and we readily call these objects sublime, because they raise the forces of the soul ... Sublimity, therefore, does not reside in any of the things of nature, but only in our own mind, in so far as we may become conscious of our superiority over nature within, and thus also over nature without us (as exerting influence upon us). Everything that provokes this feeling in us, including the *might* of nature which challenges our strength, is then, though improperly, called sublime, and it is only under presupposition of this idea within us, and in relation to it, that we are capable of attaining to the idea of the sublimity of that Being which inspires deep respect in us, not by the mere display of its might in nature, but more by the faculty which is planed in us of estimating that might without fear, and of regarding our estate as exalted above it.[9]

Poor Immanuel is often harshly judged for the "heavy gossamer"[10] that renders his work notoriously opaque; indeed, the richly subjective

  ANDREW WEAR

propositions of Kantian aesthetics veiled his reputation as a political philosopher. Questions of subjectivity, taste, and judgment troubled Kant then, and they trouble this inquiry now. Sometimes a simple switching of words helped. In *Critique of Judgement*, Kant offers the category of *aesthetic liberalism* to counter his original presentation of *liberal aestheticism*. As simple as it sounds, the ordering of the words is the key, kind of (but not strictly, of course) like the difference between a *tame* lion and lion *taming*. This isn't a historical precursor to political flip-floppery; this was defining language. Confused? Bear with me – it's critical to the whole argument:

> This latter category seems to depend on the unacknowledged invocation of liberal political principles, which are then predicated of the aesthetic "object" – e.g. its ability to hold together contradiction and coherence, or to admit a multiplicity of interpretations while preserving its identity as an irrefutable ground of truth.[11]

Okay, the "ground of truth" joke might be overly frivolous; nevertheless, this explanation of Kant's distinction activates the debate concerning the aesthetic qualities of espresso at the mercy of the free market. One of the major consequences of this "invocation of liberal political principles" was the invocation of liberal economic principles (namely, the free market). Thus we arrive at that point where the aesthetic enveloping espresso-method coffee is unable to withstand free-market forces any longer. The critical factor in this equation is, of course, the emergence of *the individual* as the defining force of aesthetic judgment. As the multiplicity of individuals rise to challenge the herd mentality of communitarian society and economy, contradiction challenges coherence. The customer is, we are told, "always right." Suddenly, *the singular* aesthetic becomes an impossible *many*.

The Power of the Consumer

One of the more enduring examples of this trend is the caffè Americano. This beverage has its origin in the American demand for a big, black cup o' drip-filtered joe when traveling in Italy. Trouble was, no such thing existed in Italy. After much confusion in translation and realization, a barista recreated this alien beverage with the tools at hand. First, a rich, *crema*-laden espresso was poured. Upon finding the vastest vessel available, the barista upturned the shot into it, before blasting it with a top-up of scalding hot water. The market adapted, the product was born, and the customer was content.

While the Italian *caffè* adapted to external pressures, Anglo-American culture took its own little piece of Italy home. Though espresso was available in the Italian enclaves in countries like the United States, Canada, and Australia, entrepreneurial types became hand-wringingly aware of both the natural charm of traditional Italian culture *and* the significant profit margins espresso-method coffee offered. The chain model swiftly entered the commercial mainstream. Coffee producers were already beneficiaries of market dynamics. Now, competitive marketing of a ready-formed "cultural package" fused with consumer demand saw cafés and their fare change from a gastronomic sub-heading to an industry in its own right. Cafés sprouted in shopping centers, urban villages, and apartment complexes, all competing for customers by offering wildly ambitious menus and flat-packed ambience. Before long this most simple of products was a signature – or a personality signifier, if you like – as portrayed in the memorable café scene in the 1991 film *L.A. Story*. In the scene, a waiter arrives at the table to take the coffee order:

Tom:	I'll have a decaf coffee.
Trudi:	I'll have a decaf espresso.
Morris Frost:	I'll have a double decaf cappuccino.
Ted:	Give me decaffeinated coffee ice cream.
Harris:	I'll have a half double decaffeinated half-caf, with a twist of lemon.
Trudi:	I'll have a twist of lemon.
Tom:	I'll have a twist of lemon.
Morris Frost:	I'll have a twist of lemon.
Cynthia:	I'll have a twist of lemon.[12]

One of the great ironies of this explosion of choice is the primacy of what this choice says about the consumer. While this necessarily incorporates aesthetic elements, many of the critical aesthetic qualities that determine espresso-method coffee – most notably flavor – have become secondary at best. If ordering a "half double decaffeinated half-caf, with a twist of lemon" is, as the scene above illustrates, a powerfully suggestive amalgam of, say, courage ("a double"), restraint ("decaffeinated"), and enigmatic edginess ("a twist of lemon") within a cup of coffee, then the aforementioned seven-stage constitution of the brew is barely important. More options simply dilute the original essence.

ANDREW WEAR

Signs are appearing to suggest this particular period of coffee culture may be nearing its end. From the baby-boutique-bean-brewers popping up daily in downtown alleys and pigeon holes to the genuine, old-school powerhouse cafés pumping out hundreds of consistently excellent coffees each day, the signs are there to suggest that some oases of aesthetic concern survive – indeed flourish – within the dynamics of the free market. The former might have the luxury of time to perfect a palm-frond, a puppy-dog, or a love-heart for your cappuccino's cap, and the latter might be a tad brusque in its manner and style, but both are a result of blessed access to a wealth of economic and cultural resource.

Three Capitalisms

Countless philosophers have pondered the all-consuming advance of capitalism into culture, and some have been more prophetic than others. At times, certain unholy unions within economic theory have produced bastard sons. Until they were forced to flee fascism, Germany produced a body of influential theorists who worked under the moniker of the Frankfurt School. Post-war, and from various locations in Europe, the United Kingdom, and the United States, these *critical theorists* resurrected Marxism through reference to Kant, Hegel, Nietzsche, and Freud, among others. Theodor Adorno, Walter Benjamin, and Herbert Marcuse dedicated their most admired works to defusing the threat capitalism posed to the auratic qualities of art and culture. Popular culture was deemed particularly noxious. However, it's no coincidence that the Frankfurt School fell out of favor about the same time Andy Warhol and Miles Davis were producing elegant, intelligent, and thought-provoking counters to the theorists' increasingly dated readings of consumer culture. In their wake, those irrepressible, hallowed survivors John Maynard Keynes (1883–1946) and Friedrich August von Hayek (1899–1992) came to – and continue to – inform the mainstream; timeless pillars of economic opposition. Neither Keynes nor Hayek were particularly fluent cultural theorists,[13] yet they sustained the fundamental divide between the economic policies of (well, heck, while I'm on a run with sweeping generalizations and caricatures …) the left and the right throughout the late twentieth century. Naturally, any implementation of their respective economic theories had cultural consequences; nevertheless, it took some time before philosophers again recognized *the aesthetic* as ubiquitous in consideration of the economy. Thus, from within this somewhat scatter-shot proposition concerning the troubled relationship between liberalism and aesthetics, I conjure one final perspective.

Pierre Bourdieu (1930–2002) presents a theory of *cultural capital* that serves to return my thoughts to the (im)possibility of synergy between liberalism and aesthetics, or, perhaps less poetically, *capitalism* and *culture*. Here, Bourdieu explains:

> Depending on the field in which it functions … capital can present itself in three fundamental guises: as economic capital, which is immediately and directly convertible into money and may be institutionalized in the forms of property rights; as cultural capital, which is convertible, on certain conditions, into economic capital and may be institutionalized in the forms of educational qualifications; and as social capital, made up of social obligations ("connections"), which is convertible, in certain conditions, into economic capital and may be institutionalized in the forms of a title of nobility.[14]

Now the *economic capital* Bourdieu speaks of is that pure and simple, no-strings-attached type we all understand. But the models of *cultural* and *social capital* are less easily defined. Put simply, Bourdieu reckons the fortunes of the mightily educated and socially networked few determine the ongoing survival of those avant-garde pursuits that regenerate popular culture before becoming themselves passé. What again brings espresso-method coffee to our attention is the aesthetic bridge it builds between Bourdieu's *capitalisms*. Bourdieu might be hesitant to coalesce so easily; for he is rather ardent in his delineation of the contours of *cultural inheritance*:

> A work of art has meaning and interest only for someone who possesses the cultural competence, that is, the code, into which it is encoded. The conscious or unconscious implementation of explicit or implicit schemes of perception and appreciation which constitutes pictorial or musical culture is the hidden condition for recognizing the styles characteristic of a period, a school or an author, and, more generally, for the familiarity with the internal logic of works that aesthetic enjoyment presupposes. A beholder who lacks the specific code feels lost in a chaos of sounds and rhythms, colours and lines, without rhyme or reason.[15]

That "aesthetic enjoyment" is commonly defined (not only by Bourdieu) according to a limited palette of sensual perception is troubling. The oft-neglected aesthetic enjoyment gained from taste, smell,

  ANDREW WEAR

and touch is less critical than is reasonable. Despite the heady claims of those who can afford fine champagne, beluga caviar, and Alba truffles, magnificent flavors may be savored by all, for little. Of course, so might the setting of the sun or the call of a lark. But espresso so purely represents such a vast system of human productivity and process. More importantly, unlike a glass of 2004 Domaine de la Romanée-Conti La Tâche Grand Cru, the finest espresso known to humankind should set you back only a few dollars.[16] Neglecting (or at best, misunderstanding) the aesthetic qualities imparted in the tasting of flavor speaks volumes for the emergence of the spectacle of espresso-coffee production. Whether it be a rustically styled or themed café, the swirling visions of latte artists, or simply a masterfully rehearsed sneer, spectacle has consumed some of the concern for flavor. Ironically, the hours of practice to develop and perfect the techniques a barista commits to the visual splendor of having the Sistine Chapel recreated atop your *caffè latte* are often many more than those committed to sourcing good beans, equipment, and knowledgeable staff. Some fusion of the two conditions is ideal, but when offering an income rarely above the minimum wage, the espresso *übermensch* can be hard to find. Sadly, my apron never functioned so well as a cape, and my aloofness was more often than not poorly disguised laziness. If pure chance guided me to glory in the heady world of competitive barista-ing, the rewards came to be measured in frustration.

My prize for victory was a superb, Italian-made espresso machine. Oh, how its bedazzling polished steel and sparkling Euro-Soviet logos impressed its credentials! This machine gave me some months of joy, producing potent *crema*-laden double-shots of espresso and tornadoes of silken milk. That is, until one day it simply ceased to function. *Guasto.* Phone calls searching for a repairman quickly went international, costing me nearly as much as the machine itself was worth. Finally, one morning, in a red-faced and caffeine-withdrawn fury, I unplugged the machine, and dropped it (still warm) into the garbage. In its place sits a tidy little Japanese model that has functioned perfectly and effortlessly ever since. Such truths have affected all sides of the industry. External competitors have forced Italian espresso machine makers to be better, and in the afterglow of the boom and bust of the 1980s and 1990s, corporate models are less uptight. Sure, we might have to endure visions of guys on six-figure incomes wearing Che Guevara T-shirts, but like all stories of survival, adaptation and cooperation have come to the rescue. Economic capital and cultural capital are increasingly shared – and when harmonious, we are all the better for it.

Complex and Lasting Beauty

I hope the beauty of this model of inquiry has been justly represented. I hope also to appeal to the understanding that there are many products that we might start to consider in aesthetic terms, not simply as objects of beauty, but as portals to philosophical realms. In this case, the industry that goes into making a single shot of espresso is what renders it such a brilliant model for aesthetic inquiry. Its minimal splendor and physiological effect (caffeine is, after all, a drug) is all the more profound when considering its 25 ml extraction as a representation of a labor chain of thousands that reaches from countless unregulated and impoverished workforces in some of the world's poorest countries to urban café baristas in some of the world's wealthiest countries. Perhaps cherishing this single shot of espresso is, in this light, little more than cruel indulgence. Then again, perhaps this single shot of espresso is a more humble and beautiful memorial to those who toil for its form than a double-decaf-lite-soy-hazelnut frappuccino.

NOTES

1 "Starbucks and the Socialism of Fools," *Spiked!* Online website. Available online at http://www.spiked-online.com/index.php?/site/article/5547/. The page also includes a range of links to other articles about the Starbucks closure and enlightening partisan perspectives.
2 Full details of the report available from Starbucks' website: http://www.starbucks.com/aboutus/csrreport/Coffee_Report_PDF_FY07.pdf.
3 Milton Friedman, "The Social Responsibility of Business is to Increase its Profits," *The New York Times Magazine*, September 13, 1970.
4 Essentially the result of an imbalance between aforementioned angst and aloofness, due to income not reflecting the unrecognized and (usually self-perceived) worldly brilliance of barista.
5 Karl Marx and Friedrich Engels, *The Communist Manifesto* (London and New York: Verso, 1998), p. 17. Originally published 1848.
6 Among countless others, the logos used by Caffè Torrisi, Lavazza, and Segafredo typify this aesthetic.
7 By *the aesthetic* it should be understood that we are thinking or operating within a *realm*, much as we might discuss *the social* or *the political* realm. For further description see Jenny Edkins, *Trauma and the Memory of Politics* (Cambridge: Cambridge University Press, 2003).
8 While none of the cruelty is deserved, two of these rumors are, indeed, true.

9   Immanuel Kant, *The Critique of Judgement*, trans. James Creed Meredith (Clarendon Press: Oxford, 1964), pp. 109–114.

10 Attributed to the mighty Johann Gottfried von Herder, who studied with Kant at the University of Königsberg, when describing Kant's style. Arsenij Gulyga, *Immanuel Kant: His Life and Thought*, trans. Marijan Despaltović (Boston: Birkhäuser, 1987), p. 315.

11 A. J. Cascardi, "Aesthetic Liberalism: Kant and the Ethics of Modernity," *Revue Internationale de Philosophie* no. 196 (1991): 12.

12 L.A. *Story*, dir. Mick Jackson; written by Steve Martin (Coralco Pictures, 1991).

13 Hayek's "theory of cultural evolution" was – while one of the theoretical pursuits he remained most proud of – little more than a Darwinian natural selection theory devised to prop up his economic theory. See Erik Angner, "The History of Hayek's Theory of Cultural Evolution," *Studies in History and Philosophy of Biological and Biomedical Sciences* 33, no. 4 (2002): 695–718.

14 Pierre Bourdieu, "The Forms of Capital," In J. Richardson (ed.) *Handbook of Theory and Research for the Sociology of Education* (New York: Greenwood, 1986), p. 242.

15 Pierre Bourdieu, *Distinction: A Social Critique of the Judgement of Taste* (London: Routledge and Kegan Paul, 1984), p. 2.

16 With the exception of *Kopi Luwak*, which is made from coffee beans eaten, partly digested, and then excreted by the Indonesian palm civet. On an official visit to Australia, Indonesian President Susilo Bambang Yudhoyono presented a gift of *Kopi Luwak* to Prime Minister Kevin Rudd. The President suggested that Rudd might make a "crapuccino" with the beans. At the current market rate, this crapuccino would cost about $52.

CHAPTER 13

STARBUCKS AND THE THIRD WAVE

Hating on Starbucks is now *de rigueur* for coffee snobs: "They burn their beans!" "They brought that abominable Via instant coffee to market!" (It's not that bad.) "They had the audacity to offer breakfast sandwiches in their stores!" But if, in a quiet moment, you ask a third waver to come clean and honestly assess the effect of Starbucks on their business, they'll have no choice but to say: "Without Starbucks, there would be no third wave."

It's true. The third wave[1] would not have been possible without the Starbucks juggernaut clearing the way. Let me explain with a story.

Recently I had the great pleasure to patronize a wonderful shop in Portland, Oregon, called Barista. It is a small, industrious place, crammed full with two espresso machines, three grinders, the coffees of various roasters, and a few sit-down bar seats. While Barista is justifiably renowned for its espressos, with three different offerings available each day, I came for the vacuum pots.

A vacuum pot is a double-chambered brewing device, where a heat source boils water in the lower chamber, forcing it through a cloth filter into the upper chamber. Here the water and grounds percolate. When the heat is removed, the brewed coffee returns to the lower chamber, resulting in a wonderfully clean cup of coffee. For this I paid the going rate of $9 for a 12 oz. cup of an Ethiopian Sidamo, and gladly tipped my skilled barista.

How did coffee, once the proletariat drink *par excellence*, good for keeping workers awake and revolutionaries feisty, become such a bourgeois beverage? On what planet is $9 an acceptable price for a cup of coffee? And how is it that I feel comfortable admitting such excess in print with only the slightest bit of shame? The answer is simple: Starbucks taught us to pay for quality coffee. Without the consumer education provided and paid for by Starbucks, places like Barista could not easily survive.

Starbucks has taught us much about what makes for good coffee, but in this chapter I will focus on two subjects. First, Starbucks has created a signature blend and roast, and taught consumers to expect boldness as the *de facto* standard for specialty coffee. This, coupled with the aura of artistry in the creation of beverages, is the aesthetic component of a Starbucks education. Second, and just as importantly, Starbucks has gone to great pains to craft an ethical narrative about its coffees. Commitment to fair trade and C.A.F.E. (Coffee and Farmer Equity) Practices, community involvement, and concern for the environment are forefront in their image.

The genius of Starbucks branding lies in this intertwining of aesthetics and ethics. When you buy a drink at Starbucks, you are told, not only do you get a delicious treat, but you do good in the world at the same time. Such was the success of this advertising scheme that the ubiquitous green-logoed cup was, for a time, one of the primary images of conspicuous consumption in America, a status symbol affordable to the masses.

In *Everything But the Coffee: Learning about America from Starbucks*,[2] Bryant Simon describes the relationship between Starbucks' branding and neoliberalism. The basic tenet of neoliberal economics is that fostering individual freedoms is the primary task of good governance. To achieve this end, government must limit its activity, creating institutional conditions for the maximization of free markets and private enterprise. With this comes an evacuation of governmental influence from the public sphere, so that private interests and corporations come to fulfill many of the tasks necessary to a properly functioning society. For better or for worse, this remains the dominant economic ideology of our day. All problems – public and private – are now understood to entail private solutions. If your child's school is bad, find a tutor. If municipal water tastes terrible, buy a Brita filter. If you need an army to fight a war, hire Blackwater.

It is in this context that the power of the Starbucks brand must be understood. What was a relatively cheap commodity crop has become a costly luxury, at once comforting and invigorating. Starbucks was able to effect this metamorphosis by refashioning both coffee and the coffeehouse. Instead of being a dingy place filled with beatniks and wannabe revolutionaries, Starbucks turned the coffeehouse into a "third place" that appealed simultaneously to laptop warriors, soccer moms, and status-seeking teens. Your cup of coffee, you are told, is brewed from the finest beans, ethically sourced, and artfully roasted. Even the consumables – the cups, napkins, sleeves – are emblazoned with evidence of their sustainability.[3] Doing business with Starbucks thus becomes the most painless sort of doing good in the neoliberal fantasy that the corporation is equally devoted to profit and social justice. Your toting a Starbucks product becomes a way to tell the world that you're trendy, socially responsible, and a bit of an aesthete.

The Starbucks Aesthetic

Starbucks' initial success had much to do with the creation of an easily identifiable aesthetic. This involved their trademark dark roast coffee, of course, but equally important was the positioning of the brand as being authentic, as offering "real coffee." When Howard Schultz took over Starbucks in 1987, he made it a point of honor to require extensive coffee knowledge of his workers. Baristas ground coffee in store, pulled espresso shots by hand, and partook in public cuppings, or coffee tastings. The performance of these rituals led to a well-educated workforce, as well as a palpable feeling of authenticity.

Such labor-intensive methods are, however, difficult to scale. Extensive training requires time and money, which may not be recouped given staff turnover. As Starbucks expanded at a nearly exponential rate, some of this authenticity had to be sacrificed in the name of simple logistics. Automated espresso machines were installed, cutting the time required to produce espresso-based drinks. No longer was coffee ground in store, but instead it was shipped pre-ground. These small changes proved damaging to the Starbucks mystique, and when coupled with the increased visibility of non-coffee beverages and merchandise, Starbucks' coffee cred began to slip.

The explosive growth of the frappuccino market represents an important mutation in Starbucks branding. It might seem odd that a company built upon the image of coffee authenticity would become so well known for what amounts to a coffee-flavored milkshake, except that the frappuccino is a prime example of retail therapy – the purchase of a good or service as a response to unhappiness – and its popularity coincided with a shift in Starbucks' branding from a company that specialized in coffee to one that catered to self-indulgence. In this context, a frappuccino makes a perfect "self-gift," a low-cost bit of consolatory consumption.

Self-gifting is best understood, in my view, against the backdrop of neo-liberal ideology. As Simon correctly notes, there is a reason that Oprah – the high-priestess of neoliberalism's self-help through consumption – would regularly proclaim her love of Starbucks on television. Self-gifting is an entirely rational choice given the logic of the free market. But such a habit gets expensive quickly. Given the realities of the American economy today, on what basis can self-gifting be understood as rational?

Self-gifting is a way of signaling one's worth in a world that seems to revolve around market fundamentalisms and the profit motive. Your purchase of a fancy drink is an investment in oneself, an affirmation of self-worth in an age of relentless consumerism. Solace takes on a dollar value. The market provides a tangible, affordable cup of affirmation. It is in this sense that self-gifting is fully rational – it observes the basic postulates of the free market in its practice.

Let me, before moving on, be very clear. I am not trying to effect a moral argument about self-gifting or conspicuous consumption. After all, I'm the guy who spent $9 on a cup of coffee! I am simply making two points. Much of the initial success of the Starbucks brand involved its careful crafting of an aesthetic, both in terms of the coffee itself and the feeling of authenticity in the shop. When this aesthetic changed, part of the Starbucks mystique was lost. Part of the response to this shift was a corporate decision to hawk non-coffee beverages and sundry mer-chandise in the store, banking on the brand's power to sell music, books, and so on. This decision was, again, rather astute in terms of understanding neoliberal purchasing, but the side-effect of this com-mercialization of the brand was a further loss of its authenticity. Such brand delegitimation opened much of the market space where third wave coffee would thrive.

Starbucks and Ethical Sourcing

Thus far I have been arguing for the role of aesthetics in the success of Starbucks' branding. Here I take up the ethical component of its brand. It is not only that you are being sold solace at Starbucks, but your purchase allows you to "make a difference" in the world, too. Because Starbucks demands that its suppliers engage in ethical practices, ranging from adherence to fair trade standards to the use of recycled materials in consumables, your purchase of its product indirectly subverts the inequalities of global capitalism and aids in the protection of the environment. Starbucks also makes sure that its initiatives in this area are well publicized. From in-store signage and fair trade logos to corporate outreach via public speaking and the Starbucks website, patrons are continually informed of the good their consumption can do.

Surely such initiatives are laudable. Indeed, one sign of their importance is the speed with which third wave coffee has taken up similar causes. But here again we run up against the problem of scale, common to both Starbucks and third wave roasters.[4] The explosive growth of the Starbucks brand, from the physical store to supermarket coffee, means that the company couldn't use all fair trade beans if it tried – there aren't enough in the world![5] According to Starbucks' own website, fair trade coffees made up approximately 10.6 percent of all coffee sold in 2009, while an additional 3.8 percent of coffee sold was certified organic. Now, to be fair, some 81 percent of coffee purchased by Starbucks in 2009 adhered to its internal set of "C.A.F.E. Practices," which subject the economic, ethical, and environmental practices of both buyer and supplier to third-party verification.[6] Notably absent from the materials promoting these practices, however, is the fact that such coffees are not necessarily organically produced. Additionally, specific requirements for producers are glossed over.

Again, my point is not to denigrate what I assume are good-faith efforts by Starbucks to balance its desire for social responsibility with the voracious need for profit. Starbucks is, as its website notes, the world's largest purchaser of fair trade coffees; for this, it should be commended. It is the disconnect between the image and the facts, however, that gives pause. That so many people are aware of these kinds of slippages between branding and reality is an important event in American consumerism, part of a broader cultural backlash against crass commercialism. That, despite this awareness, so many people continue to consume according to the winds of advertising remains troubling. One is reminded here of nothing less than Slavoj Žižek's understanding of how ideology operates under neoliberalism. The cynical function of ideology requires that "they [consumers or, more generally, political subjects] know that, in their activity, they are following an illusion, but still, they are doing it. For example, they know that their idea of Freedom is masking a particular form of exploitation, but they still continue to follow this idea of Freedom."[7]

From Starbucks to Stumptown

I have been arguing that the third wave of specialty coffee would not have been possible without Starbucks. Only by Starbucks' vigorous education of the masses, through the costly fashioning of an appreciation for a specific coffee aesthetic and image of corporate responsibility, could the third wave have come along and challenged its hegemony. Third wave coffee depends upon a consumer with a nuanced palate, a taste for social justice, and a fat wallet. Starbucks has done the hard work of creating just such a consumer. Now third wavers show their appreciation for this expenditure by stealing Starbucks' clientele.

They do so by following the Starbucks game plan to the letter – the emphasis on artisan, handcrafted coffee coupled with a commitment to a more ethical version of capitalism. While Starbucks was tinkering with breakfast sandwiches and private-label compact discs, third wave giants like Counter Culture, Intelligentsia, and Stumptown were sending staff out to coffee farms across the globe, laying the groundwork for what would become today's direct trade initiatives. While Starbucks was introducing automated espresso machines into its stores, third wave baristas were forming the Barista Guild, organizing regional training sessions, and competing in international barista contests.

Third wave coffee has, in effect, overtaken Starbucks among aficionados by becoming better versions of Starbucks. The drinks seem more authentic. The commitment to ethical practice is better publicized and often more transparent, with initiatives like Cup for Education[8] and Crop to Cup[9] becoming increasingly common components of business models. The commitment to certified coffees – from fair trade and organic to Rainforest Alliance and Slow Food – also signals customers as to the ethical standards of a roaster or shop.[10]

These same companies, however, face an increasingly important challenge. How can they learn the lessons of Starbucks' recent troubles while they expand their businesses? How, in other words, can they remain true to their ideals while expanding their businesses? Counter Culture has training centers in New York and Washington, DC, Intelligentsia has just opened shops and a roastery in California, and Stumptown, having moved some of its roasting into New York, is being described in the press as the "new Starbucks."[11] Can these third wave businesses succeed without cutting corners to improve profits? Can they maintain their brand prestige while expanding into new markets?

Here we encounter the most interesting question about third wave coffee. Can it endure its growth and increasing commodification? Does it scale? In the end, of course, all third wave companies are working within the capitalist system. They are profit-seeking enterprises. This, to my mind, is the key test of the third wave model – is it possible to be a capitalist and remain committed to some kind of ethics in business practices, or does success require preferring profit over people?

To further investigate this question, we must return to the two key elements of Starbucks' branding success – aesthetics and ethics – and see how they are refined in third wave branding. If it is possible for a company to succeed without succumbing to the most crass forms of profit seeking, this success will depend upon the careful negotiation of an aesthetic and ethical vision that moves product and spirit equally.

Fair Trade Revisited

The fair trade movement and ethical sourcing are deeply embedded in the third wave ethos. TransFair USA, one of the leading certifiers in the Americas, describes the certifying process as one that "empowers farmers and farm workers to lift themselves out of poverty by investing in their farms and communities, protecting the environment, and learning the business skills necessary to compete in the global marketplace."[12] The fair trade ideal is thus twofold: to simultaneously improve both the coffee itself and the livelihoods of producers by tying improved purchase price to social and environmental controls. But what does fair trade really do? How is it viewed by producers and purchasers? Is it ultimately fair?

In *Brewing Justice: Fair Trade Coffee, Sustainability, and Survival*, Daniel Jaffee offers a studied critique of the fair trade movement on the basis of multi-year fieldwork in Oaxaca, Mexico. One of Jaffee's key insights is that there are at least three competing visions for what fair trade is and should be.[13] To the three versions of fair trade described in Jaffee's book, I will add a fourth.

There are those who view fair trade as a way to address the problem of market *access*. On this view, fair trade counteracts economic barriers and injustices enforced on producers by facilitating market access. Because wealthy nations often float heavily subsidized commodities on the international market, artificially depressing prices in the process, the idea behind this version of fair trade involves the carving out of niche spaces in the market for certified goods and services.

There are also those who view fair trade in terms of market *reform*. Given the fundamental inequalities present in global economics, fair trade works to reform capitalism by giving producers a more direct, or less mediated, avenue for sales and marketing. The hegemony of capitalism is not contested here; rather, fair trade as market reform device works within capitalism to better the lives of producers.

Such a desire to work within the system is not part of the third vision described by Jaffee. On this view, fair trade is a way to work toward dismantling the abuses of capitalism. Such a *market-breaking* strategy views depressed global commodity prices as components of broader economic evils. The price protections built into fair trade agreements help to counteract the deleterious effects of neoliberalism on developing countries and the Global South.

For Jaffee, these competing visions for fair trade often result in differing tactical plans for activism. While some advocates define success in terms of the adoption of certified coffees by local shops, others would argue that such a narrowly defined project does nothing to undercut broader systemic evils. Moreover, there is an argument to be made that one of the underlying premises of fair trade – that justice can be effected within the framework of free markets – only further ensnares producers in the vagaries of the market. Evidence for this viewpoint can be found in the quotation from TransFair above, where the benefits of certification basically devolve to greater capital investments and increased market competitiveness.

From the perspective of the roaster/coffee salesperson, there is a fourth account of the fair trade movement to consider. This involves the *marketability* of certified coffee. One of the first things I learned in the roastery retail room was the marketing cache of certification. Some people would come in and ask specifically for fair trade or organic coffee; others, when presented with choices, would tend toward certified products. From the roaster's perspectives, fair trade is important, at least in part, because *it sells*. Any discussion of third wave coffee that does not acknowledge this is, in my opinion, obfuscatory.

Granting, then, the four differing accounts of the reasons for fair trade coffee, we must now tackle a much larger question. Is fair trade really fair? Jaffee concludes that fair trade is a "necessary but not sufficient"[14] step in the right direction, and I direct the reader to his book for the details. I do, however, want to investigate one of Jaffee's concerns more specifically, because it cuts to the heart of the debate over the fairness of fair trade. Certification is often overlooked in discussion of fair trade or organic coffees. Because of the transparency built into the certification process, it is easy to assume that everything is above board. Nevertheless, the stringent, sometimes arcane nature of the rules for compliance can disqualify otherwise qualified participants, and even small errors in documentation can lead to decertification.

The cost of certification is also problematic. Small farmers may not have the financial resources to pay for certification, even if they fulfill all other requirements. The same is true of organic certification, and such financial disenfranchisement is doubly tragic given that smaller farms are often organic by necessity – petrochemicals are prohibitively expensive for many producers. Because small farms may not be able to afford certification, even while fulfilling all other requirements in the process, they lose out on access to fair trade/organic markets and marketing.

There is, then, some reason to agree with the Mexican extension agent, quoted in Jaffee's book, when he describes certification as "ecological neo-colonialism."[15] Certification, by definition, entails the imposition of foreign regulations and what amounts to monetary tribute on indigenous producers. Because there are limited, if any, avenues for producers to contest the terms of certification, describing the process as a form of colonialism is not wholly unreasonable.

Some third wave companies, in light of the concerns addressed above, are moving toward alternative forms of ethical sourcing. So-called "relationship coffee" and direct trade are two avatars of this movement, designed to get around the remaining problems of the fair trade movement. Granting the real advantages of this alternative model for sourcing, the dual challenges of eco-colonialism and scale linger. If the standards set by the purchasing company are not met by the producers, even with the assistance of their corporate partners, sales will not go forward, or purchase price will be decreased. That the purchaser holds all of the cards in the relationship, setting terms and conditions, etc., only further reinforces the specter of colonialism.

The problem of scale also haunts the direct trade movement given the nature of the environmental controls built into most relationship agreements. Would organic practices work on large-scale industrial farms? The jury is still out on this matter.

If, in the end, fair trade is not a panacea, why is it so well promoted by producers and in marketing campaigns? The answer, in part, is that certification sells. Highlighting a commitment to ethical sourcing allows the consumer to feel as if her purchase is doing good in the world, as if the corporation cares about those upon whose backs its wealth is built. To its credit, Starbucks does seem to possess a corporate concern for responsible sourcing, is known for its decent treatment of employees, and evinces some level of environmental awareness. How much of this commitment is authentic, and how much is a form of greenwashing, is a question that ultimately admits of no clear answer. Such is the continued effectiveness of Starbucks' branding.

Third wave shops are equally guilty of having mixed motives regarding the fair trade movement. Ethical sourcing is surely a cornerstone of the third wave movement, and the various levels of direct trade represent some real advances over the limitations of fair trade certification. But we need to be clear on this matter. Direct trade does not only position a roaster as a good corporate citizen. It also gives that roaster exclusive access to a well-grown, delicious cup of coffee, and this exclusivity may result in sales within an increasingly discerning marketplace.

Fair trade represents an improvement upon the traditional coffee market. Certification has introduced some real changes for good. The problems of scale and eco-colonialism still haunt the movement, and until they can be fully exorcised, the promise of fair trade will not be fulfilled in its practice.

The Hermeneutics of Taste

The third wave did not just take over the ethical component of Starbucks' branding. It also co-opted the aesthetic dimension by promising consumers a better cup of coffee. More specifically, the third wave builds upon Starbucks' branding by refining customer palates, and by introducing a touch of elitism into its marketing. There is, without question, a certain snobbishness and hipster attitude built into the third wave, and for good reason: It sells.

My goal in this section is to puncture one of the primary myths of the third wave. I quote Nicholas Cho, former owner of Murky Coffee, to set the scene.

> So what of this "Third Wave?" In an admittedly esoteric way, I usually refer to the "Third Wave" as *letting the coffee speak for itself*. During the first two waves, we appreciated coffee for what it gives us: caffeine, a hot beverage to sip and enjoy a conversation over, a drink to modify with sweetener, dairy (or non-dairy) creamers, syrups, whipped cream, etc. The Third Wave is about enjoying coffee for **what it is**.[16]

The third wave lets "the coffee speak for itself"? Nonsense. What the third wave does, and does incredibly well, is create a narrative or hermeneutic for coffee, a set of expectations that a consumer comes to internalize and insist upon. Taste – for coffee, whiskey, fine clothes, whatever – is not innate, but must be taught. It is the *language* of third wave coffee, in particular, that requires apprenticeship. An example helps to make this clear.

I am currently drinking the last of an order of Intelligentsia's House Blend. The bag claims that "this medium-bodied blend offers subtle fruit notes with milk chocolate and caramel close behind. The balanced acidity finishes with notes of baked apples." If I were to ask a non-initiate to have a sip and describe what she tasted, her description would not in any way resemble Intelligentsia's. She might say that it was strong or bitter, or perhaps even bold. But "milk chocolate and caramel with baked apple on the finish"? Highly unlikely. Such a nuanced palate is made, not born. And it is made most directly through the ritual known as cupping.

Coffee cupping is the coffee industry's preferred method for sampling and testing various coffees, providing a standardized mechanism for evaluating coffees while minimizing participant bias. While cupping is a daily practice at most good roasteries, functioning as the first line of quality control, it also can function as a powerful teaching tool for coffee newcomers and enthusiasts.

How does cupping work? To begin, a series of small cups is placed around a table, where uniform scoops of coffee are saturated with near-boiling water for approximately three to four minutes.[17] Ted Lingle, former director of the Specialty Coffee Association of America, recommends a ratio of 7.25 grams of coffee to 150 milliliters of water,[18] but the specific ratio is less important (for non-professionals) than its consistent application across all samples.

As infusion continues, coffee grounds will rise to the tops of each cup, settling to the bottom as time goes on. A "cap," or crust, remains at the top of the cup, and the first task of the cupper is the breaking of this crust. The novice is instructed to take his spoon and gently stir the grounds into the cup, getting his nose close to the cup in the process and deeply inhaling the coffee aroma. Experienced cuppers will often gain important clues as to origin simply from the aromatic properties of the cup.

After the crust is broken and the surface of each cup is skimmed to remove loose grounds, the actual tasting takes place. Each participant takes a cupping spoon and brings a small portion to their mouths. The trick to a successful tasting is *the slurp* – slurping the sample allows for a broad coating of the mouth, and it also allows the sample to undergo aeration, maximizing the aromatic component of the taste experience. After the slurp comes *the spit*, familiar to anyone who has done any wine tasting. The process ends with the rinsing of one's spoon, and the transition to the next sample to be cupped.[19]

Let's examine what a cupper experiences in those few seconds between slurp and spit. A small amount of liquid is introduced into the mouth and rolled about, coating the tongue and the back of the throat. Perhaps the coffee has a distinctive mouthfeel, or perhaps some aspect of its flavor immediately manifests itself. The great mystery for most beginners is the specificity with which an experienced cupper can pinpoint some element of the taste experience. I remember vividly how perplexed I was when, at my first cupping, the lead instructor proclaimed that he got notes of plantain in one cup, and graham cracker in another. Plantain and graham cracker! To me, such descriptions smacked of unadulterated hucksterism – all I could taste was *coffee*. Part of me thought that they were simply having fun at my expense. Why couldn't I taste the plantain?

Now, of course, I know that there was nothing wrong with me. I had not begun to develop the necessary experience or vocabulary for such accuracy. As time progressed, and as I cupped more regularly with others, I began to pick up some of what they were talking about. I would ask others what notes they got from a particular cup, and compare my findings with theirs. Slowly, I began to connect words with specific flavors, and certain coffees with their defining characteristics. For all of this, I must confess that I have yet to taste the plantain or the graham cracker.

This example also helps to make clear the two interrelated aspects of the aesthetics of coffee. Coffee aficionados are not born, but made. More specifically, they become *initiates* through an educational process that reshapes their coffee understanding and perceptual experience. Once you have become accustomed to specialty coffee, there's no going back. What was once normal becomes abnormal and undrinkable. Such a perceptual shift depends upon the insertion of the consumer into a specific understanding of coffee, one that is not merely intellectual but infiltrates the most basic functioning of the sense organs.

The success of third wave is thus built upon the creation of a coffee *hermeneutic*. Here I borrow from the work of Martin Heidegger (1889– 1976) and Hans-Georg Gadamer (1900–2002), two of the pioneers of the contemporary philosophical movement known as hermeneutical phenomenology. In hermeneutics the goal is to account for the ways in which all modes of human understanding presuppose some kind of familiarity with the world by means of reflective consciousness or interpretation.

Heidegger, for example, believed that human beings are always-already thrown into a world that is pre-laden with meaning. The world is thick with received meaning, so that all of our experience is already shot through with historical and cultural norms, expectations, and so on. Even our most basic perceptual experience is pre-colored or "fore-seen" due to historical and cultural situatedness. That we experience the objects of the world as integral and important already implies for Heidegger the constitutive role played by such situatedness.[20]

We know that chairs are for sitting just by looking at them, and we know that cups are for drinking from. Such pre-knowledge does not operate on the level of conscious experience – we don't pause for a moment while looking at a chair in order to categorize it. Rather, our situatedness in a meaning-laden world means that chairs and cups are disclosed immediately in normal experience *as* chairs and cups. So long as the cups and the chairs remain in good working order, we need never problematize their use again. We expect them to hold liquid and support our bottoms, and we are shocked when they fail at either task.

Third wave coffee, in educating its customers through conversation and cupping, actively creates a hermeneutic for its product. What was once a black, bitter liquid becomes an aromatic delight filled with notes of plantain and graham cracker. It is not merely that we interpret the brute perception of the liquid differently – *the experience itself changes* in light of the new set of expectations and standards we bring to the cupping table. Our experience of coffee is no different in this regard than our experience of the chair. For a properly educated customer, specialty

JOHN HARTMANN

coffee becomes the new normal. The success of third wave coffee depends upon the continual creation of a hermeneutic and the initiation of its customer base into it.

At last we begin to understand the peculiar naïveté of the quote above, where Cho proclaims the primary goal of the third wave as "letting the coffee speak for itself" and "enjoying coffee for what it is." No human experience speaks for itself. No experience is immediately given without filter or condition. Instead, all of our experiences are mediated by time and place, history and culture. We approach each cup of coffee just as we experience a chair. Both are encountered in light of a set of non-thematic preconceptions and expectations, or what I have been describing as our hermeneutical situatedness.

Cho's quote is doubly curious given the emphasis placed by third wavers on customer education. Because customers do not tend to want to spend upwards of $20 for a pound of coffee without good reason, they must be taught to appreciate the nuances of specialty coffee. Much time and money are spent on educational outreach, websites, and cuppings. Why such expense and investment if the coffee speaks for itself?

Perhaps a better model for understanding the third wave emphasis upon customer education and the crafting of a coffee aesthetic is found in the ancient art of ventriloquism. The ventriloquist is an illusionist, creating the appearance of an inanimate object speaking through misdirection and the throwing of her voice. If coffee speaks for itself, as Cho maintains, it does so only through an act of ventriloquism. What we hear, and what we taste, when we encounter specialty coffee is not entirely attributable to the coffee – there is always someone behind the scenes, feeding our cup its lines.

Ethics and Aesthetics in Action: The Roast

Third wave coffee, I have argued, brands itself as a new kind of capitalist entity, as interested in altruistic causes as it is in corporate earnings. Such branding is, at least on the face of things, fundamentally at odds with the realities of the marketplace. The cardinal rule of any business is that it must move product if it is to survive. Talk about ethical sourcing and precision roasting is all well and good, but if the company fails to make money, no amount of branding will keep it in business. Why the apparent subterfuge?

This is, in part, a question of perspective. What appears to outsiders as altruism is almost certainly better understood as careful brand positioning. Nevertheless, we should not underestimate the novelty of companies like Intelligentsia. What we witness in third wave coffee are some of the most successful attempts yet at social entrepreneurship, where free enterprise is combined with social activism in the interest of amelioration. All of the decisions made by a third wave roaster – from purchasing beans to roasting to marketing – must serve the dual ends of profit and justice. While I do not want to contribute to the myth of the roaster as rock star or genius,[21] I cannot over-emphasize the difficulty in successfully navigating the Scylla and Charybdis of profiteering and simple do-gooding.

Here I want to briefly consider the ways in which the roaster must continually keep both the aesthetic and ethical elements of branding in mind if he or she is to succeed economically. From ordering beans, to the roast itself, to marketing and education, the roaster must always be mindful of the ways in which his or her decisions affect the bottom line.

We see this in something as simple as ordering green beans to roast. A roaster may rely on the advice of his broker, of course, and can cup samples sent by his importer. The most important factor in choosing which lot to buy is marketability, or the potential for steady sales. If costs are similar, I'd take some kind of certified bean over its non-certified twin for this very reason. Certification sells coffee because it positions your brand as socially conscious. That certification means a producer is paid a fair price for her product is an incidental side benefit. Subverting neoliberalism is nice, but in the end, there's payroll to meet every week.

Roasting is often seen by outsiders as some kind of mystical practice or high art. Here again, however, appearances do not resemble reality. Anyone can learn the rudiments of roasting in a day or two. A "paint by numbers" roast on a Diedrich roaster, for example, boils down to three tasks. The roast should hit two time/temperature targets (280°F at 4–6 minutes, 340°F at 8–10 minutes) without much intervention. In order to control the speed of the roast, the roaster should alter the airflow through the roasting drum. There are also audible clues (the first and second cracks) that inform the roaster as to the progression of the roast. Everything else – the charge temperature, roast level, etc. – is up to the discretion of the roaster.

Expertise is nevertheless necessary to wring the last bit of potential from green beans. For the expert roaster, the three tasks I've just described are not discrete events but components of an organic process guided by a knowledge of his or her clientele.[22] I have a friend, for example, who roasts just about everything in his shop very darkly because he thinks that's what his customers want. But the roaster, if he is striving for quality, cannot simply roast according to the whims of his customers – not everything that can be roasted dark should be!

The roaster must therefore effect a dialectic between customer education and catering to existing taste. Here, however, is where the third wave sometimes over-extends itself. Just as my friend really should try to lead his customers toward a more nuanced understanding of coffee through education, some third wavers move too far in the opposite direction and ignore customer demand. Flavored coffee is anathema to many in the specialty coffee world, but smart roasters will sell it – and lots of it – without hesitation.

Conclusion

Is it really possible for a company to do good *and* make money? This, I have argued, is the ultimate test of the third wave and for specialty coffee more generally. As we have seen, some companies are better at enacting this ideal than others. Starbucks has seen its branding discredited to some degree, despite its good-faith efforts to roast ethically sourced, fairly priced beans. The best third wave companies have carefully avoided some of Starbucks' growing pains, but the true test of their business model lies in the future.

This vision of hybrid capitalism, balancing the profit motive with social entrepreneurship, is increasingly common in the specialty coffee world. From Stumptown to Intelligentsia to my own *alma mater*, Columbia Street Roastery in Champaign, Illinois, such hybrids are reaping the benefits of their dual commitment to ethical practices and a delicious cup of coffee. As we enjoy their products, we coffee snobs are both literally and figuratively in their debt.

NOTES

1   Here I follow Trish Skeie in her drawing of distinctions between first, second, and third wave coffee. Briefly put, the first wave involved the industrialization of coffee roasting and production. The second wave saw the birth of specialty coffee, including Starbucks. The third wave emerged largely as a

reaction to the excesses of the second wave, emphasizing artisanal roasting and a commitment to ethical practices over and against commercialization and commodification. See Skeie's "Norway and Coffee," in *The Flamekeeper: Newsletter of the Roaster's Guild* (Spring 2003).

2   Bryant Simon, *Everything But the Coffee: Learning about America from Starbucks* (Berkeley: University of California Press, 2009).

3   Critics point to the abject lack of recycling initiatives for such consumables, as well as poor in-store water usage policies. See Angela Balakrishnan, "Starbucks Wastes Millions of Litres of Water a Day," *guardian.co.uk*, October 6, 2008.

4   Consider the fact that Intelligentsia, one of the first movers in direct trade, still must rely on coffee purchased from specialty brokers to meet production needs, especially in its blends. Careful observers will note the lack of any direct trade or in season branding on a number of blends and the occasional single-origin coffee.

5   In 2008, approximately 81.2 million pounds of organic coffee were imported worldwide, while another 145.1 million pounds of Fair Trade Certified coffee were sold. (It is unclear as to whether coffees that are both Fair Trade Certified and organic are double-counted in this statistic.) Starbucks could not have bought enough certified beans to meet its production needs, as it reported purchasing approximately 345 million pounds in 2008 on its website. See Ellen Pay's report for the United Nations Food and Agriculture Organization, "The Market for Organic and Fair-Trade Coffee" (September 2009) for more on this topic (http://www.fao.org/fileadmin/templates/organicexports/docs/Market_Organic_FT_Coffee.pdf).

6   Scientific Certification Systems, "Responsible Sourcing Strategies – Starbucks C.A.F.E. Practices," http://www.scscertified.com/retail/starbucks_documents.php.

7   Slavoj Žižek, *The Sublime Object of Ideology* (London: Verso, 1989), p. 33.

8   www.cupforeducation.org.

9   www.croptocup.com.

10   We should not solely attribute the move toward ethical sourcing to Starbucks, of course. Both Starbucks and the third wave are, in part, responding to broader cultural trends toward conscientious consumption. The Whole Foods phenomenon and the popularity of Michael Pollan's work are both symptomatic of this trend.

11   Josh Ozersky, "Is Stumptown the New Starbucks – or Better?" *Time*, March 9, 2010, http://www.time.com/time/nation/article/0,8599,1970653,00.html.

12   TransFair USA, "Trade Overview," http://www.transfairusa.org/content/about/overview.php.

13   Daniel Jaffee, *Brewing Justice: Fair Trade Coffee, Sustainability, and Survival* (Berkeley: University of California Press, 2007).

14 Ibid., p. 198.

15 Ibid., p. 152.

16 Nicholas Cho, "The BGA and the Third Wave," *CoffeeGeek.com*, http:// coffeegeek.com/opinions/bgafiles/04-02-2005/.

17 Experienced cuppers will also note the aroma of the dry coffee grounds before introducing water into the cups. Beginners, however, will often skip this step.

18 Ted R. Lingle, *The Basics of Cupping Coffee*, 3rd ed. (Long Beach: Specialty Coffee Association of America, 2003).

19 It should be noted that I am here describing an educational cupping for consumers or for internal quality control. There is an evaluative process used by cuppers to grade coffees, with scores ranging from 50 to 100. (Specialty coffees are not supposed to receive scores below 80.) Such numerical evaluations, while critical for the grading of large numbers of samples for potential purchase, are not necessary for beginners, and may not be desirable more generally.

20 See Martin Heidegger, *Being and Time* (New York: Harper and Row, 1962).

21 See, for example, Michaele Weissman's dreamy, if otherwise interesting, paean to the third wave: *God in a Cup: The Obsessive Quest for the Perfect Coffee* (Hoboken, NJ: John Wiley & Sons, Inc., 2008).

22 In this I basically agree with Evan Selinger's amendments to Hubert Dreyfus's phenomenology of expertise. See Selinger's "Chess-Playing Computers and Embodied Grandmasters: In What Ways Does the Difference Matter?" in Benjamin Hale (ed.) *Philosophy Looks at Chess* (Chicago: Open Court, 2008), pp. 65–87; and Selinger and Crease's "Dreyfus on Expertise: The Limits of Phenomenological Analysis," in Evan Selinger and Robert Crease (eds.) *The Philosophy of Expertise* (New York: Columbia University Press, 2006).

CHAPTER 14

HOW GOOD THE COFFEE CAN BE

An Interview with Stumptown's Matt Lounsbury

When Mike and I decided it would be to the book's benefit to have an interview with someone from the coffee trade, it was a natural choice to contact Stumptown Coffee Roasters. I grew up in Portland, Oregon, where Stumptown is headquartered, and I've spent enough of the past decade there to see first-hand how it has come to embody, and in a lot of ways define, Portland's specialty coffee and local food aesthetic. Stumptown has a well-deserved reputation as one of the highest-quality roasters in the world. Additionally, through its direct trade model it has come to be known for treating farmers exceptionally well and paying unusually high prices for its beans.

You'll see in my conversation with Matt Lounsbury, director of operations for Stumptown, that I keep trying, but am never quite able, to identify some kind of essence that underlies Stumptown's business model and shapes its operations. Matt insists quality control is the gravitational mass that pulls Stumptown's ethical behavior into orbit, but he never quite convinces me there isn't a more fundamental,

Coffee – Philosophy for Everyone: Grounds for Debate, First Edition. Edited by Scott F. Parker and Michael W. Austin, series editor Fritz Allhoff.

unifying value underneath. The pride in his voice when he tells me how Stumptown has improved conditions for farmers in Rwanda, or after the interview when he encourages me to check out its Ethiopia direct trade video,[1] seems to belie his insistence on the primacy of quality. But he's a businessman and I'm a writer, so maybe it's understandable that we look at the same situation and want to call it different things. Or maybe Matt's just more practical than I am. If he ever got explicit about an intention to make the world a better place, he'd be forced to confront the real-world constraints on specialty coffee's reach. In the near future at least, there will remain demand for lesser specialty coffees, and even bad coffees, that Stumptown cannot fill; that is, there's a place for Starbucks and a place for Folgers. And somewhere in that recognition that not everyone is willing and able to pay for quality and/or the cost of conducting business in an unequivocally moral way, not to mention the natural and absolute scarcity of "the best beans in the world," lies the upward limit of Stumptown's influence. So maybe Matt's right that it all comes down to how good the coffee can be, and that without the high quality there's nowhere to hang the other values.

But all that abstraction aside, it's nice to get the inside perspective on how one of the world's finest coffee roasters operates.

Scott F. Parker: "Philosophy" is a word that gets used pretty loosely in the business world, but it strikes me that Stumptown is a company that actually takes philosophy seriously – even if you wouldn't talk about it that way. What I ultimately want to get to in this interview is the intersection of ethics and aesthetics in terms of the coffee you sell and the moral responsibilities that go along with that. But first maybe we should start with some company background. Stumptown's only been around a little over ten years.

Matt Lounsbury: Yeah, we got started in November 1999. Duane Sorenson, our owner and founder, got his start in Seattle as a barista and worked his way up through the coffee food chain and became a roaster and then eventually a buyer for a roasting company in Seattle. This was in the '90s when coffee, espresso specifically, was popping off in Seattle. They had coffee going on in a way that Portland did not. Duane used to visit Portland and sort of had his eyes set on it. He moved down and worked different jobs while he bought his first small roaster and got us started by building out a little café in southeast Portland with our roaster inside that café. He roasted by night and served coffee to customers by day. He had one or two employees when he started, and just grew it from there.

SFP: When did you come into the picture? And what do you do?

ML: I started in 2003, like a lot of our employees do, as a barista. I was running a startup company that was doing sustainability consulting and I needed a little extra cash, so I took a job working three shifts a week at our downtown café when it first started. At some point a business opportunity came up on the wholesale side and I sort of went all in. Eventually I was running wholesale, and now I oversee day-to-day operations for Stumptown, company-wide.

SFP: What is the third wave of coffee? And how is Stumptown a part of it?

ML: It's a term that's used to describe the way that coffee is now maturing in terms of being treated less and less like a commodity or something that people just drink and more like wine, where people are appreciating the nuances in flavor and also where it comes from, the idea that there are producers and farmers around the world who are associated with this coffee – that there are a whole host of factors that go into making it good.

The *term third* wave refers to the three distinct comings-of-age for coffee in the U.S. The first being when espresso first got its start, and the second being basically Starbucks and what they did with specialty coffee.[2] The third wave is being used to describe what's going on with coffee now, where, simply put, much like with food and wine, people have continued to put an emphasis on sustainably, locally grown, regional-based foodstuff.

As far as where we fit in, we've been doing this kind of thing since we started. We're all about the coffee producers and the relationships and buying the best quality coffee we can possibly find on the planet. That's kind of what we're known for. In turn, we pay the best prices to our farmers with our model of direct trade, which involves working directly with these farmers year in, year out, hands on, on their farms, asking for the best quality they can possibly offer, and in turn giving them the best prices. A lot of times we'll end up breaking the record for the amount of money ever paid to a farmer in a country, just as a normal course of doing business.

SFP: You mentioned buying the best beans. What else goes into quality?

ML: We've got a guy – and it used to be Duane, until we finally hired somebody – who's a green coffee buyer, and all he does is travel. He's gone about three weeks every month, visiting the producers we currently work with, spending time with them, helping influence their processing and the different steps throughout the year that affect how good a coffee can be. Similar to terroir with wine, it's the idea that a coffee can be an individual expression of a place; it's one small hillside, that region's precipitation, all those things can influence how good coffee can be. But so can the producers. The work they put into the coffee has a tremendous amount of impact on the quality. And we're helping at every step of the way to influence that, with the goal being that you see it in the cup. Ultimately, we make our decisions by cup quality, by tasting coffee. We have someone whose job it is to taste coffee all day long, whether it's samples that are coming in from our current farms because it's the middle of harvest season or from someone who's interested in trying to show us new coffee, we're roasting and cupping[3] coffee all day long. Quality is measured in the cup, but it's influenced in a whole host of different ways. We're a small batch roaster, so we do everything by hand. We do everything on these vintage 1950s German Probat roasters that are like really good cast iron skillets. And the way we roast is very traditional, very hands on, specific to each coffee.

SFP: What about the role of education? Say I go into your café on Division St. and you guys serve me a really nice cup of coffee, and I'm used to drinking something ...

ML: We spend a large share of our time educating people about coffee. We have five people at Stumptown who do espresso and coffee education full time, whether it be for our employees or for our wholesale accounts. Because everyone who serves our espresso has to spend an entire day at our roastery going through training not only on how to prepare the espresso and coffee but also learning about coffee from seed to cup, learning about where it comes from, how it's produced, how it's cultivated, how it's processed, everything. And the goal is that they will be able to answer that question from you better than anyone else can.

So, if you said to me, "What's so good about this coffee?" or "This tastes really good. Why is that?" I would explain what it is you're tasting. And if you were willing I would take it to another level and tell you everything I could in a short amount of time about where it came from and the process that brought it to us. The hope is that if you're walking into the shop maybe being a layman about coffee or being used to drinking shitty coffee, you walk out with some knowledge you didn't already have. Even though most people drink coffee, they don't know that it comes from a bush that has cherries that produce once a year, and that those cherries look like pie cherries. That doesn't occur to people as they're ingesting this into their bodies every single day. It didn't occur to me until I really became entrenched in this coffee world.

SFP: You mentioned earlier that you pay premium prices for your beans, and that's one of the things Stumptown is known for. Can you tell me why you do that?

ML: Because money talks. The only way you can ask a farmer for the best beans in the world is to pay the highest prices. There is definitely a price ceiling most people are not willing to go past, but for us there is no ceiling. The question is: *How good can the coffee be*? Most people don't know this, but fair trade coffee usually goes for something in the neighborhood of $1.50/lb. And that's coffee that sells here for $12 or $13/lb. The prices that are being paid for green coffee in the world are inherently depressed and they have been for a long, long time. That said, we don't buy any coffee based on the commodity market, the global coffee exchange. We buy it based on relationships with our producers and what the coffee is worth, which is predicated on quality: How good it can taste. For us, it's a pretty simple mechanism. We have a scale from 1 to 100. We don't sell any coffees that score below an 86. And coffees that get 89 or above are exceptional. Coffees that get 92 or above are really exceptional, and deserve to be bought at exceptional prices.

SFP: Does some of your willingness to pay high prices come from feeling like you have a moral responsibility to the farmers?

ML: Yes, but it's inherent. It's not ever a question that comes up. For many coffee companies, their work with producers means that the owner takes one trip a year to go visit a coffee farmer and take pictures with them to put on their website. Our work with producers is about becoming integrated into their communities and having a full understanding of everything they do, and also an understanding of their challenges. So when we're paying these premiums we can help influence some of those challenges and hopefully get a better cup of coffee, and in turn make their lives better.

I'll give you an example. When we first started buying coffee from Rwanda, it was some of the best coffee the world had never seen, and the only way that coffee could get out was as high-quality coffee that the world would pay high prices for. But they needed to build these washing stations they didn't have, otherwise, the coffee would just go to crap. And in the first couple years we started working some of these cooperatives in Rwanda – these are people that had never even been paid for their coffee, were never able to sell it anywhere but internally – now they're seeing upwards of $2/lb. for green, which is mind blowing. The impact that that has may not seem like much to us, but for them it's the difference between being able to get health care for their kid for the first time, or an education, or maybe even running water in their house. Just little things that we might take for granted are sort of embedded in these relationships.

But another part of it for us is having them come here. About five years ago we started a Meet the Producers program where we brought coffee farmers to the US, many of whom had never left their farms, let alone left their country or been on an airplane. Just to come to Portland, Oregon, to meet with people who buy their coffee – it's really, really powerful stuff. These guys are tearing up when they're seeing their coffee's name on a chalkboard in a coffee shop or on our labels and it's the first time they've ever seen their names in writing.

SFP: When I ask you about aesthetics you slip into ethics, and when I ask you about ethics you slip into aesthetics. Let's talk about this connection explicitly. What you're describing sounds like a win-win-win situation. The farmers are getting a better price for their coffee. Your customers are getting fantastic coffee. And you guys are growing pretty steadily. If you don't mind sort of speculating: What is that model? Does it have applications outside of coffee? And then, if we can go to a bit bigger picture, what unifies your ethics and aesthetics?

ML: There is an explosion of energy in specialty coffee right now that's happening all over the world. Scandinavia is in a huge coffee boom. South Korea, Australia, it's not just the Northwest or the West Coast of the U.S. You asked earlier about the third wave. Right now everyone wants to see independent options besides Starbucks. Everyone wants to have an independent coffee shop nearby where they can get a decent cup of coffee – and they should.

But to answer your question, the idea of relationships and caring about where your products come from and influencing your suppliers is not unique to coffee. It's similar to a lot of what's happening in farms with sustainable food. People all over are really starting to gravitate toward an idea that's really not new. That you grow what you eat locally and care about where it comes from is old as man. And it applies to coffee. It applies to beer, it applies to bikes, it applies to everything. And I would say it's not just a trend. If I were to speculate I'd say we're going to continue this, especially with the economy down people are caring more about things coming from closer to home, supporting local jobs. I hate to get all on the soapbox about this; it's really nothing novel to think about the relationships that support your own supply chain or business.

SFP: You have a similar attitude toward your employees, treating them as valued artisans rather than interchangeable sources of labor. I've heard you say before[4] that your baristas are buying houses in Portland when a lot of baristas are struggling to pay rent.

ML: Stumptown doesn't have a mission statement. But if we did it would say *quality* and *relationships* period. Relationships with our coffee farmers and relationships with our employees. We've always paid the closest attention we can – more than anyone else in our industry, and arguably more than other companies in the world – to our relationships with our employees. We still have a lot of our baristas who were our very first baristas ten years ago. And they do have families, and they have purchased houses. Duane's very first employee had full health care, and it's always been like that. It's not what you typically find in service jobs. We've had full health care coverage since the day we opened, spouses and everyone else included. We also encourage and foster a culture that some people have called punk rock or hipster, but we hire people that have lives outside work. A lot of our employees are either artists or musicians. Duane has twice paid for all the artists and musicians that are represented in our company to go to the recording studio and cut an album on 180-gram vinyl called Workers Comp. And that's pretty cool. And every year we have art shows and our cafés are coveted gallery spaces in town. We have lots and lots of bands play. So there's that whole fabric of our culture that's under our relationship umbrella, if you will. We take care of our employees for sure.

SFP: Well, to try to push the boundaries again to what underlies Stumptown's approach, it seems like that's motivated by a sense of community that is not necessarily related to coffee –

ML: Here's the thing. People like to write about community and "building community." But for us building community is like – I can't tell you the number of people who have met in line in our coffee shops and gotten married. Our wholesale customers and some of our cafés were the first to go into these really crappy neighborhoods and now there are theatres and local restaurants and new retail businesses, and it's all because of the coffee shop. That's building community to me. And I've seen it happen from the ground up, not just in Portland, but in neighborhoods in Seattle, and it's starting to happen in neighborhoods in Brooklyn.[5] Places where the coffee shop is quite frankly influencing the future of the whole neighborhood or community. One of the neighborhoods we moved into had nothing but this crappy bar. Now there are six restaurants, a grocery store, five condominium buildings that have gone up – depending on how you feel about that. But it definitely happens, and a lot of times it happens around coffee shops.

SFP: Well, so, like, are you guys idealists? I mean, what motivates that?

ML: No, we're business people, too. And all of those things beget business. If you're running your business responsibly, whether you say you are or not, it's going to show. If you have the best quality product, it's going to show and people are going to want to spend their money with you, and that's the way it should be. Everyone deserves the right to have options, particularly independent options rather than support large publicly traded corporations. These days people are especially concerned about money. If they're going to spend three bucks on coffee, it better be the best cup of coffee they've ever had, and it better put a smile on their face. It's crappy times. We're in Oregon, where I think we have one of the highest unemployment rates. People are holding onto their dollars. We're seeing a lot more people brew coffee at home. And we'd much rather have them buying coffee from us, so we can tell them all about how we prepare it and where the coffee came from, than spending the twelve bucks at a very large multi-national grocery chain and supporting something that isn't local. So no, it's not idealism. We're running a business. We sell coffee.

SFP: Well, so you're in a business, but you're not out there trying to increase profits by improving your margins and negotiating lower prices for beans. And you're not willing to sacrifice quality for profit.

ML: You're right. It's not a cheap way to run a business. We could have easily gone out of business. It's a little bit of a gamble, but we've been lucky with how we've been able to grow. I will say that. If you've been here in Portland and you've watched us, you've seen it's definitely been growth. But we turn nine out of ten wholesale customers down. We decide we're not the right roaster for them because of different variables that could lead to a sacrifice in quality once it's out of our hands. We want to work with, and we want to sell coffee to, people on the wholesale level who are into making good coffee. We do have to sell coffee, but we're in the fortunate position of getting to be choosy about who we sell to. I just left an appointment where I turned someone down. Meaning they're starting a coffee shop and they wanted to use our coffee, and based on a host of factors I don't think we're the right roaster for them. And that's been something we've continued to do as a matter of course.

If you were to interview one of our wholesale customers, if you were to interview our retail customers, about our product, it would be the antithesis of what the rest of the business world does. And you could probably not say this about any other business that's grown... If you were to interview them and ask them if Stumptown's quality has gotten better or worse over the years, they would say dramatically better. Our coffee has improved based on our methods over the years, and it's getting better every year because of our emphasis on direct trade and everything we do to continually improve our coffee.

NOTES

1 http://www.stumptowncoffee.com/videos.
2 *Specialty coffee* generally refers to coffees that score 80 or above on a 100-point coffee-tasting scale.
3 *Cupping*: procedure for tasting coffee to identify flavor and quality.
4 Michaele Weissman, *God in a Cup: The Obsessive Quest for the Perfect Coffee* (Hoboken, NJ: John Wiley & Sons, Inc., 2008) p. 171.
5 SFP: Visit, for example, Southside Coffee in South Slope, Brooklyn, where you'll be served coffee from Intelligentsia, another specialty roaster.

PART 4

TO ROAST OR NOT TO ROAST: THE ETHICS OF COFFEE

CHAPTER 15

MORE THAN 27 CENTS A DAY

The Direct Trade (R)evolution

It's easy to feel morally superior while sipping a cappuccino these days. At the corner coffeehouse or local Starbucks, in the supermarket, we choose beans labeled to mark us good global citizens. We sip our fair trade dark roast with an easy conscience, certain that on some verdant hillside in the Global South a farmer has received a living wage for her beans. Ethical choices typically aren't as easy as this one. And then you meet Lucy Wanja.

Lucy, a farmer in the coffee-growing region of Kenya, would tell you a slightly different story about your morning cappuccino. She would tell you that despite a few fair trade cooperatives in the region, coffee remains just a means of scraping by. It has not been enough to keep her fifteen-year-old son in school, and it will not guarantee that her eight-year-old daughter can continue past sixth grade. Lucy's world has changed very little despite the label someone in Philadelphia or San Francisco or Santa Fe now sticks on her beans.

Coffee – Philosophy for Everyone: Grounds for Debate, First Edition. Edited by Scott F. Parker and Michael W. Austin, series editor Fritz Allhoff.
© 2011 John Wiley & Sons, Ltd except for editorial material and organization © 2011 Scott F. Parker and Michael W. Austin. Published 2011 by John Wiley & Sons, Ltd.

Fair trade – trademarked so consumers will know that specific economic, social, and environmental criteria have been met – was a concept developed in the 1940s, shaped in the 1960s, and given prominence in the 1990s. By promising to guarantee farmers a fair price and to contribute to sustainable development in their communities, fair trade became the wave of the future for coffee companies with a socially responsible bent.[1] The trademark first appeared on the shelves of health food stores or boutique markets featuring imports from Africa, Latin America, and Asia. Today, shoppers in Wal-Mart can pick up coffee beans marked "fair trade" and head home with the sense of having promoted global consciousness and equity. (Purists use the label fair trade "lite" to describe companies such as Wal-Mart, which have admitted pursuing the certification for its marketing value alone.)

Official fair trade certification is a designation that farmers have received a fair price for their coffee, that basic labor standards have been met, and that practices used in production are environmentally sustainable. This certification is awarded by the Fairtrade Labeling Organization International, or FLO. This alliance of twenty-four organizations sets the international standards that apply to all fair trade producers, as well as companies that market their products.

In the United States, a non-profit called TransFair USA has helped spearhead this process. Using the official Fair Trade Certified label in the United States means being licensed by TransFair USA. In the 1990s the concept of socially responsible production, marketing, and consumption was thrust into the limelight largely as a result of the work done by TransFair USA.

Open the cupboard and check the coffee, the tea, the honey, the sugar. The Fair Trade Certified sticker pops up even when you haven't specifically sought it out these days. And this is undoubtedly an improvement when stacked up against exploitative practices conjured up by images of farmers or factory workers in the Global South. In the absence of fair trade practices – like in much of Kenya, where deep-seated corruption has made it prohibitive for most coffee to be marked Fair Trade Certified – the average smallholder farmer struggles on a daily basis to provide food for his family, to purchase medicine for her children, to afford basic school fees. The fair trade cooperative represents an important step toward something better; but it only takes us so far down the road toward "fair."

Coffee Talk

Coffee starts simply: A farmer plants seeds, cares for the fledgling plants for five to seven years, fertilizes them with goat or cow manure (adding small amounts of diluted chemical fertilizer if the family can afford it), irrigates the field, and with some luck in the end harvests a robust annual crop. Cultivation is not difficult, although neither is it reliable in a year of drought. (A drip irrigation system to reach one hundred farms in rural Kenya would cost about $30 per farm. This price is out of reach, so drought means a bad crop, or no crop at all.) Farmers are typically born into the industry; they receive their agricultural skills from their parents, and they hand the same skills down to their children. (Think of Lucy's fifteen-year-old son, who already farms coffee instead of studying history and mathematics.) Unlike the agribusiness of developed countries, small coffee farmers in the Global South do not study farming techniques at university or attend trade shows on the latest developments in equipment and technology. Most of them have not advanced beyond the fifth grade. And yet, they fuel a multi-billion dollar industry.

The large majority of coffee beans are grown in the frost-free South, while the bulk of the brewed stuff is consumed in the North. The global retail coffee market was worth $54 billion in 2008, and virtually none of this was cultivated in the United States.[2]

Coffee production has become a means of promoting rapid economic growth throughout South and Southeast Asia, the Caribbean and the West Indies, South and Central America, and especially Africa. This crop is enough of a money-maker that countries in the South still choose to place bets on it, often putting national economies and individual livelihoods at risk.

Because coffee is such a temperamental crop, one that thrives under the southern sun but seldom elsewhere, we might assume that the Global South has an economic advantage. These coffee-growing nations could fix their own prices and put the North at their mercy, similar to how oil-rich nations make money off another US addiction. But no matter how we ache for that cup of java each morning, our need for coffee isn't as controlling as our need for oil. Coffee is luxurious and unnecessary, with zero nutritional value. It is consumed primarily as a part of national culture, because of caffeine's addictive properties, or just because we like the routine and the taste. It is not considered a necessity by most consumers, and so price increases would likely be met by declines in consumption. This, combined with the sheer number of producers, means that coffee exporters have to keep prices low in order to sell.

Smallholder Farmers

Coffee is largely cultivated by rural, smallholder farmers like Lucy who depend on it for their sole incomes. They are the backbone of the coffee industry in Africa, but their reliance on this crop alone leaves them in no position to negotiate prices.

The UN Food and Agriculture Organization reports that more than two-thirds of sub-Saharan Africa lives in rural areas; the majority of this population is defined as smallholder farmers.[3] In Kenya, one of the continent's coffee-producing powerhouses, a smallholder farmer is defined as holding fewer than five acres of land; many, however, own less than one acre.[4]

David Gachigi is a smallholder farmer in Kenya's Central Province.[5] He is in his mid-sixties, married, has four children and nine grandchildren, and never finished the fifth grade. David does not read or write in English, and his Swahili is poor, limited mainly to passages from the Bible. His mother tongue is Kikuyu, but all government circulars and official transactions are carried out in English or Swahili. So there is curiosity in David's voice when, during one of my five annual visits to his region to support farmers, he asks me (Shannon) and my interpreter, "Do you know how much they sell my coffee for in Nairobi?"

In fact, David's coffee doesn't sell just in Nairobi, where expatriates and upper-class Kenyans pay around $10 per pound. It is packed off to Europe and the United States, where the average coffee drinker can buy a three-quarter-pound bag of Kenyan AA beans for about $12. That's an exponentially higher price than David is paid in Kenya, where buyers offer between $0.02 and $0.10 per pound.

David is part of a smallholder farming group chaired by a neighbor and friend, Henry Maina. Henry reports similar purchasing costs for his coffee. In 2009 he received less than $0.10 per pound from sales to his local wet-mill, a coffee industry intermediary. At the average density of one hundred trees on an acre of land, Henry's farm yielded around 1,000 pounds, which earned him less than $100 for his entire annual crop. This put him, along with his fellow farmers, far below the global poverty line

  GINA BRAMUCCI AND SHANNON MULHOLLAND

of $1 per day. And this profit came in a year when prices were higher than average due to the regional drought in East Africa. During a year with good rains – and so ample supply of crops – coffee goes for more like $0.02 per pound, or $20 for an entire annual harvest. It's no wonder, looking forward to a year of $0.05 per day for the family, that Henry considers giving up on coffee.

Bill Gates, who has championed the Global South through his Bill & Melinda Gates Foundation, told an audience in late 2009 that "helping the poorest smallholder farmers grow more crops and get them to market is the world's single most powerful lever to reduce hunger and poverty."[6] The fact that smallholder farmers like Lucy, David, and Henry can't aspire beyond the global poverty line in a good year exposes major fault lines in the traditional system. And fair trade, by ensuring the wage needed for basic sustenance, would itself only take us so far toward changing the paradigm.

Mills, Middlemen, and Markets

Unlike a local farmer growing corn or potatoes or sorghum, coffee farmers can't just sell their product on the side of the road. With a few exceptions, local communities in sub-Saharan Africa don't drink coffee unless offering it to a guest from a Nescafé tin. Tea is the tradition here. There is little interest in coffee unless it can be sweetened with condensed milk and sugar. "I don't have enough money to make it taste good," one farmer told us. "Who would ever drink the stuff black?" So the beans that feed our addiction in the North have almost no market locally. Enter the middleman.

Intermediaries play a pivotal role in the supply chain for coffee. Coffee farmers sell their cherries (coffee in its raw form) to a wet-mill, which washes the pulp off the bean, ferments it, and dries it. The wet-mill sells the dried coffee beans to the dry-mill, which cleans, sorts, and grades each batch. The dry-mill often also "cups" each batch, a crucial step in determining the quality of the coffee. (This will tell whether it can be sold for high artisan prices, or whether it will be sold at bulk rates to be added to lower-quality coffee blends.) From here, beans are usually sent to auction and sold to the highest bidder.

This is an efficient system for international buyers since it streamlines sales and guarantees quality control. National authorities typically issue just a handful of milling licenses, allowing a few select intermediaries to act as the powerhouses of the industry. In Kenya, a country that harvests more than 300 million pounds of coffee annually and employs an estimated six million people through the coffee industry, only four dry-mills are allowed to operate.[7] (Wet-mill licenses are easier to obtain and can be owned by farmers' cooperatives, although the cost of $5,000 to get started is often prohibitive. And even when a cooperative does run the wet-mill, profits are rarely distributed equally. In a system that inherently encourages inequity, even cooperatives tend to allow few to profit.)

In order to even the playing field between coffee farmers and the critical dry-mill middleman, smallholder farmers like Lucy, David, and Henry would need some negotiating power. But when we remember that David never studied beyond fifth grade, for example – that he speaks only rudimentary Swahili and no English, that his family is entirely dependent on coffee, that he doesn't have access to knowledge about the broader market or the potential for multiple buyers – we get an insight into his acceptance of whatever price the middleman offers.

Meanwhile, as American and European coffee shops well know, the money behind coffee is not in the cultivation, the wet-mill, or the dry-mill. The real profit (retail aside) is in the roast. This is where the bean gets differentiated and starts its journey toward a brand. But because the cost of a roaster is so high – try $20,000 for a machine that can handle 15 pounds at a time, or upwards of $300,000 for a commercial roaster – the roast typically takes place in the coffeehouse itself or, for a chain like Starbucks, in some central location that ships out to myriad stores. After this step the pound of coffee that Henry sold for $0.02 is worth $7.00. But the smallholder farmer never sees this money-steeped side of coffee.

Abandoning the Bean

Coffee can be an unreliable crop. Drought years, such as those recently seen in Kenya, are a major blow to smallholder farmers (not to mention national economies in the Global South). Add to this the fact that coffee prices float on the international market, leaving smallholder farmers at the mercy of a much bigger system. When export prices drop below production costs, farmers are unable to invest in their processes – to buy fertilizer, irrigation equipment, or basic tools. This kicks off a dangerous cycle for a farmer, resulting in poor quality and/or quantity of the harvest, and further financial instability.

GINA BRAMUCCI AND SHANNON MULHOLLAND

In 2006 Kenyan agriculture officials reported that the country produced approximately 50,000 tons of coffee. That compares to an all-time high of 130,000 tons in the 1987/1988 season.[8] Drought certainly has its share of blame in this decrease, but so too does a simple decline in the number of farmers willing to tie their livelihoods to coffee. When coffee crops are bad or prices remain low for several consecutive years, a handful of farmers inevitably choose to clear the land and start fresh with corn, bananas, or macadamia nuts.[9] Even more common is the practice of "intercropping," or planting between the coffee plants. Because smallholder farmers can't afford fertilizers (let alone high-quality, organic fertilizers), intercropping depletes the soil of nutrients and hurts farm productivity in the long run.

When these options run out, the younger generation starts heading to the city in search of jobs and salaries. Young men like Lucy's son search out relatives or friends, often in sprawling slums like Kibera – a mass of one-room homes surrounded by open sewerage and violent street crime on the outskirts of Nairobi. It's not better than relying on coffee; but because the city at least represents an ideal of work and profit, it is arguably no worse.

Doing Things Direct

It's hard to view the outlook as anything but dire for smallholder farmers, their families, and their communities. But the past decade's upswing in fair trade practices, matched by a newfound coolness associated with being a global-minded, fair and green citizen, can be credited with an evolution in how coffee roasters in the Global North view their trade.

"Direct trade," a term used by roasters who buy straight from the growers and cut out (or in some cases just demand a fair shake from) the traditional middlemen, is now giving fair trade a run for its money. Direct trade roasters typically negotiate a price with farmers, as well as any middlemen that will remain part of the process. Negotiations are transparent – a characteristic that is rare in coffee-growing nations. And unlike fair trade, which fosters a "fair" but minimum price for the coffee, direct trade roasters offer a premium price and then charge more to connoisseurs back at the trendy café or market up North.

The details of how direct trade plays out can vary from one company to the next since there is no overarching body like FLO International and it is not centrally regulated by something like the Fair Trade Certified mark.

Each coffee company develops its own system for engaging with smallholder farmers and offering premium prices. The real advantage is that by creating that link, there is a built-in advantage for these companies to also make an investment in the coffee farmers' long-term capacity and well-being.

There are a handful of direct trade pioneers in the US market. Chicago-based Intelligentsia advertises its belief that any coffee farmer who grows an "award-winning cup is an artisan," and should be regarded as such. The company does not openly confirm how much this artisan farmer receives per pound of coffee, but it has been widely heralded as a leader in the direct trade movement.

Stumptown, based out of Portland, Oregon, puts an emphasis on giving farmers an opportunity to command prices that will allow them to provide for their families and invest in their farms. In 2009 Stumptown paid 21 percent above the fair trade minimum price for its beans; and the company guarantees that the price goes directly to the farmer rather than to a cooperative board.

One of the authors of this chapter, Shannon Mulholland, helped start Safi Coffee, a direct trade outfit that supports farmers in Kenya to become shareholders of their own company. Safi, which means "honest" in Swahili, aims to pay "farmer-partners" a typical fair trade, organic price, and then supports them by facilitating their certification as organic growers and bringing in experts to teach them sustainable, successful growing techniques. (Farmers selling to Safi also have access to a financial literacy class, so they can start independently negotiating prices.)

Safi, still nascent, is working with farmers who are accustomed to earning $0.02 per pound. The bar is set low. But beyond being equity stakeholders, the farmers will be paid at least $0.40 per pound in the first year, a twenty-fold increase over what they earn through the traditional Kenyan supply chain. If Safi is able to reach its goal of paying at least the equivalent of fair trade organic prices, farmers would both own part of the company and make around $1.70 per pound, an increase of 8,400 percent.

Moving Beyond Fair Trade

To break down the equity argument: Why isn't it enough that smallholder farmers get a guaranteed fair trade wage?

It all depends on what we mean by "fair." It is undeniable that the fair trade paradigm offers the smallholder farmer an improved system – and

  GINA BRAMUCCI AND SHANNON MULHOLLAND

many companies promoting fair trade go above and beyond the label. But most Americans, most of us in the Global North, would never describe our vision of equity as enough to survive one more season. And the fact is that a fair trade wage, or what we would call minimum wage, is just that: minimum.

I (Gina) sat in Lucy's one-room home in 2009, her son listening to music on my iPhone, her daughter playing behind the front door, her neighbor's baby stretched out across my lap. Lucy offered me Kenyan tea – not coffee, of course – and then we went outside to walk through her acre of coffee plants. She showed me the crop, but she also wanted to talk about the problem of her children's school fees, the high cost of fertilizer, her lack of knowledge about what happens in the coffee industry after the dry-mill.

Lucy is a strong woman. She has a voice and is not afraid to use it. But she needs a buyer willing to put a little power in her hands, willing to negotiate a better price for her beans and invest in building her capacity as a business-minded farmer. This is more than the "fair" we symbolize with a sticker. Direct trade makes for stronger farmers and stronger communities in the long run. It means we might pay more than fair trade for our beans each month. And that might just mean we've earned that smug glance over a socially responsible cappuccino in the long run.

NOTES

1   Although fair trade and direct trade do not apply only to coffee, this chapter will focus exclusively on the coffee market and the impact of trade on coffee farmers.
2   According to the US Department of Agriculture, Hawaii produced four million pounds of coffee in the 2008/2009 season. This represents about 0.02 percent of the total global production – nearly 17.8 billion pounds in 2008/2009.
3   James Dixon, Aysen Abur-Tanyeri, and Horst Watenback, "Framework for Analyzing Impacts of Globalization on Small Holder Farmers," Agricultural Management, Marketing and Finance Service, Agricultural Support Systems Division, Food and Agriculture Organization of the United Nations, 2004.
4   Kenya Coffee Board, 2009.
5   David died in 2010 from complications related to high blood pressure.
6   World Food Prize, Des Moines, Iowa, October 2009.
7   Coffee Board of Kenya. Available online at www.coffeeboardkenya.org.

8   J. Mulama, "Coffee Profits Not Percolating Down to Farmers," Inter Press
    Service Africa, 2006.
9   If enough coffee farmers cut down their plants, depleting the international
    supply, prices on the global market might see a sharp increase. Due to the
    coffee plant's long gestation period, it would take years for the market to
    recover.

CHAPTER 16

HIGHER, FASTER, STRONGER, BUZZED

Caffeine as a Performance-Enhancing Drug

This coffee falls into your stomach, and straightway there is a general commotion. Ideas begin to move like the battalions of the Grand Army of the battlefield, and the battle takes place. Things remembered arrive at full gallop, ensuing to the wind. The light cavalry of comparisons deliver a magnificent deploying charge, the artillery of logic hurry up with their train and ammunition, the shafts of wit start up like sharpshooters. Similes arise, the paper is covered with ink; for the struggle commences and is concluded with torrents of black water, just as a battle with powder.
Honoré de Balzac, "Treatise on Modern Stimulants" (1838)

When contemplating whether or not caffeine is a performance-enhancing drug, one is tempted to craft the shortest book chapter in history with an answer of only two words: No kidding! But when we consider that this is the world's most ubiquitous drug, and that it has avoided the scrutinizing eye that falls upon other popular drugs, the question evolves from *Is caffeine a performance-enhancing drug?* (which it most certainly is) to the question *Why is it treated differently than other performance-enhancing drugs?*

Coffee – Philosophy for Everyone: Grounds for Debate, First Edition. Edited by Scott F. Parker and Michael W. Austin, series editor Fritz Allhoff.
© 2011 John Wiley & Sons, Ltd except for editorial material and organization   © 2011 Scott F. Parker and Michael W. Austin. Published 2011 by John Wiley & Sons, Ltd.

When we think about performance-enhancing drugs, we think about sport. Every major sport has talked publicly about doping – the name given to practices which include the taking of outlawed performance-enhancing drugs (PEDs). By examining how drinking coffee fits into the categories of doping and performance-enhancing drug use (which are not synonymous) and the distinctions between the two, we can understand the economic and political factors at play in our public discourse about doping. The discussion will revolve around sport and wind it's way through less extraordinary non-sporting contexts, since there are emerging concerns that PED use will become a debate in non-sporting contexts, and it is certain that the ethical debates from sport will be utilized analogously in the discussion of "everyday doping."

Caffeine: A Brief History of the Buzz

When we talk about taking a drug to enhance one's performance in a mental or physical task, we sometimes are drawn up into the sense, usually forwarded by those who find it morally reprehensible, that it is a new phenomenon. That assumption is completely false. As a natural corollary to that assumption, those people may also believe that PED use in sport is an invention of the twentieth century. This too is incorrect. Archeological evidence shows that since 3000 BCE the hunter-gatherer tribes of the Andes chewed cocoa leaves to increase their energy while immunizing themselves against the stresses of intense physical labor at high altitudes.[1] In the ancient Olympic Games, athletes seized on any ingestible plant that might help them win. In this pursuit, athletes commonly ate bread soaked in opium, strychnine, and fungi containing psilocybin and psilocin (you may know these as "magic mushrooms").[2]

Caffeine was also a staple of the pharmacopoeia of the ancients. Tea is mentioned in ancient Chinese mythology, with its first medicinal use by Shen Nong in 2737 BCE. The apocrypha of Shen Nong's innovations in Chinese medicine came about from ingesting seventy-two types of poison. Laid prone by a fit of illness brought on by this experimental self-poisoning, Shen Nong ate some falling tea leaves, which brought him energy and rid his body of toxins. He recorded his discovery of tea by noting, "Tea tastes bitter. Drinking it, one can think quicker, sleep less, move lighter, and see clearer."[3] The Europeans were introduced to tea by the Dutch, who began importing it in 1610. The Dutch lost

KENNETH W. KIRKWOOD

command over the tea trade to the British East India Company, who expanded trade during the 1700s when duties were relieved on tea, making it an affordable pick-me-up for all. By the late 1700s, yearly tea consumption in England and Wales reached two pounds of tea leaves per man, woman, and child, which translates into four hundred cups of tea a year.[4]

In North America, coffee is the preferred source of caffeine.[5] Coffee came to North America through Europeans who imported it from the nations of the Ottoman Empire (comprising many nations, including modern-day Turkey). Coffee beans first appeared in Venice around 1615, and were chewed in the fashion of the original coffee bean consumers – the Ethiopians. Coffee as a brewed beverage came into more popularity by 1640. Throughout the seventeenth and eighteenth centuries coffee became the reason for which men gathered to debate the major issues of the day. Coffeehouses, as they came to be known, were a staple of elite European male society, and the consumption of coffee as the beverage of choice explicitly acknowledged the enhancing effects of coffee on their mental faculties. One advocate for the enlivening effects of coffee was the French Enlightenment essayist Voltaire, who downed between fifty and seventy-two cups of coffee every day, and credited that consumption for the production of his magnum opus, *Candide*.[6]

Colonialism obviously played a major role in the diffusion of coffee drinking throughout the West. In the present day, caffeine is the most consumed drug in the world, with alcohol and nicotine following behind at second and third, respectively. The anthropologist E. N. Anderson spoke to the global acceptance of caffeine when he observed that virtually every language in the world has words for the four caffeine-bearing plants: *coffee, tea, cocoa,* and *kola*.[7] A cursory glance outside my high office perch on the main street of one of Canada's largest cities alerts me to the fact that on one city block, there are fifteen outlets representing five major beverage businesses whose primary stock and trade is caffeine. A quick trip through any major food or beverage retailer offers a boutique selection of caffeinated products. And for those in North America who find brewed coffee unpalatable, there is that dietary staple of the university student in exam season: coffee beans coated in chocolate.

Clearly, those of us who punctuate our daily life around the timing of our caffeinated buzz share that desire in common with our distant forebears.

Caffeine as a Mental Performance-Enhancing Drug

When we look at North American culture, there is a clear and widespread acceptance of the performance-enhancing properties of coffee. The "pick-me-up" effect of coffee is engrained in Western cultures. But one primary function of philosophy is to examine and challenge accepted beliefs with evidence or other reasons we can say we know. This is especially important for those beliefs we hold that seem the most obviously true to us. So, let's look closer at whether or not coffee is performance enhancing.

When researchers study the effects of caffeine on non-coffee drinkers under experimental conditions, as we would assume, the effects are significant. Among the most reliable effects are temporary increases in blood pressure, increase in free fatty acid content in the bloodstream, and frequent urge to urinate.[8] By contrast, regular coffee consumers only see one of these effects, and those of you who are coffee drinkers know which one it is.[9] If we're talking about mental effects of coffee consumption, and that's the benefit most people seek when they drink coffee, coffee drinkers score higher on cognitive tests of memory, reaction time, and visual-spatial reasoning than non-coffee drinkers (this includes you, tea drinkers!).[10] When we look at the place of coffee in North America, we can see that there is an institutionalized belief in coffee's power to energize our minds. In the classic wage-per-hour workplace, there is often one or two (often legally required) periods in a workday set aside for rest, and known as "coffee breaks." You can take these breaks no matter what your beverage of choice, but it is perfectly acceptable and understood that you might consume some of this brain tonic to fortify your spirit for another bout of work.

Coffee consumption is not just some necessity we undertake to get through our dreary workdays, it is also a profoundly social event, around which we create and maintain friendships and social networks in an open way without any second thought. Even though other drugs that are commonly consumed in social environments are considered illegal or socially deviant, coffee and tea are consumed openly and unabashedly. At a luncheon hosted by the most puritanical religious group, you will likely find coffee and tea offered as part of the hospitality and as a lubricant for fellowship.[11] In many settings, not only is coffee drinking a largely unquestioned social practice, the type of coffee consumed acts as a form of conspicuous consumption. We can distinguish the social class of a person and seek commonalities based on the features of the coffee one drinks.

KENNETH W. KIRKWOOD

For example, one who drinks only fair-trade organic Arabica coffee from Costa Rica might look down upon someone drinking low-grade coffee from the local diner or, *God forbid*, instant coffee made from crystals.

Caffeine as a Physical Performance-Enhancing Drug

If the function of caffeine in the non-sporting world is to increase performance in socially accepted ways, the function within the sporting world is nearly identical. The one major variance is the social acceptance of the performance-enhancing drugs commonly used by athletes. While coffee and tea might be staples of Bible-belt potlucks, people of many different religious and political inclinations harbor deep objections to the drug intake common among high-performance athletes.

The story of how drugs end up being used by athletes is entirely a story of the struggle between enhancement and therapy. Drugs that have therapeutic value to the ill sometimes offer the ability to boost the functioning of healthy athletes beyond their normal capacities. Anabolic steroids, for example, are medically indicated as treatments for various illnesses, but they also came to be used as a way to boost athletes' functioning beyond what is called "species-typical functioning." Caffeine has some medical uses, but has been primarily a social drug since its inception. Clearly, athletes saw something in caffeine that could do more for them than merely fuel creativity and intellectual activity. But does caffeine boost physical performance?

Research on the physical performance-enhancing nature of coffee has been ongoing since the late 1800s, mostly by highly caffeinated research subjects riding bicycles in laboratories.[12] Over more than a hundred years of research, we can safely say that the research indicates that coffee offers its athlete-consumers increased endurance and delay of fatigue, so long as it is consumed with food and not in excessive quantities.[13]

Caffeine as Doping

Since we've seen that coffee is a performance-enhancing drug in both mental and physical functioning (if those things are separate, but we won't go into that here), it might be interesting to know if sports leagues have viewed coffee as a banned substance or not. In the 1930s some sports prohibited the consumption of caffeine prior to and during competitions because it was thought to be cheating by the Victorian codes of gentlemanly competition that dictated the norms of that age. When the International Olympic Committee (IOC) created its first doping control policy in the 1960s, caffeine was included as a banned substance. In the early 1970s the medical commission of the British Commonwealth Games deemed caffeine "as consumed in coffee" to not be a doping agent. Following this lead, the IOC removed caffeine from its banned substance list in 1972. The IOC had a change of heart prior to the 1984 Olympics in Los Angeles when caffeine was reentered into the list of banned substances. Testing positive for caffeine would require an athlete to consume between five and six cups of coffee in a two-hour consumption period, or in more modern quantification: one 20-ounce serving of brewed coffee from a major international coffee retailer.[14]

In the history of Olympic sports, there has never been a drug scandal surrounding the consumption of caffeine. One celebrated caffeine user was American marathoner Frank Shorter. In winning the gold medal in the marathon at the 1972 Munich Olympics, Shorter was given regular doses of caffeine through decarbonated Coca-Cola.[15] Athletic success agreed with Shorter, and his post-athletic career included a term as chairman of the Board of Directors of the United States Anti-Doping Agency from 2000 to 2003.

By 2000, Olympic anti-doping policy was now coordinated by an agency created and primarily funded by the IOC, called the World Anti-Doping Agency (WADA). In January of 2004, WADA removed caffeine from the banned substances list and relisted it into a "monitoring program" to see if the new legality of the substance would lead to a massive uptake in its consumption by athletes. A number of studies show that athletes use caffeine as a performance-enhancing substance. In one study, 60 percent of elite British cyclists used caffeine specifically for performance enhancement, while 33 percent of British track and field athletes did the same.[16] In another study, the rates of detection of caffeine in urine tests of elite-level athletes showed no increase in caffeine consumption since 2004, except for cyclists, who nearly quadrupled their positive tests for caffeine once the drug was permitted.[17]

Given that caffeine can improve your athletic performance if used correctly, and that it has been used by a large number of athletes through the years, it seems reasonable to say that coffee boosts athletic performance. So why isn't coffee considered doping?

One of the key things that people misunderstand when they talk about drugs in sport or listen to public debate about the issue is conflating doping with performance-enhancing drug use. Performance-enhancing drugs are drugs that improve your performance in some way. Doping often involves performance-enhancing drugs – but PEDs are only part of the definition of doping, not the whole thing. Now all we have to do is figure out what doping is so we can determine if coffee should be banned.

WADA uses a three-point criterion for determining what doping is. Doping is any method or substance that meets any two of the following three elements: it is performance-enhancing; it could be dangerous to health; and it violates the "spirit of sport."[18] If we review what we know about coffee:

1   It enhances performance.
2   It can be dangerous to health: There are established connections between caffeine abuse and peptic ulcers, pancreatic cancer, endocrine tumors, coronary artery disease, arrhythmias, and birth defects.[19]

That seems to satisfy the required two out of three score required by WADA to qualify excessive coffee drinking as doping, and yet it still isn't banned (again). We didn't even have to try to use the third criterion of the "spirit of sport" – which is good, because it's not at all useful.

Since the official means of determining what doping is don't seem to lead to the banning of coffee as doping, it behooves us to look at some more philosophical analyses to try and find our own answer to the question *Is coffee drinking doping?* There are a number of arguments people have forwarded over the years to defend a ban on doping in sport. It suits our purposes here to discuss three major groups of arguments about what doping is, and why it's bad.

Cheating and Unfairness

One major problem with typical debates about doping being cheating and unfair is that often the two concepts are argued using each other, and each is not defined by itself first. In philosophical argument, it is often referred to as *circular argumentation*, and is treated as a logical fallacy. In the case of drugs, it is common to hear people say that doping is cheating because it breaks the rules, and that doping is against the rules because it is cheating. Breaking the circularity of this logic requires us to establish clearly *why* doping should be against the rules, and then use this foundation to justify the moral judgment of cheating. If we could establish some kind of understanding about why a rule against doping should exist, then we could speak about cheating. On the other hand, if we could demonstrate why doping is inherently unfair, we could support a rule against doping by appealing to this virtue.

So, is doping inherently unfair? No, it isn't. When we say something is fair or unfair, we usually speak of one person breaking a social agreement for his own advantage. We call it unfair because one person gained an advantage at the expense of his promise and the social bond that a promise creates. To say that doping is unfair ignores the fact that it is equally fair if everyone dopes. When we think about coffee, can we really say that the consumption of one 20-ounce cup prior to competition constitutes a violation of mutual agreement? I guess it is conceivable that if a group of people made a pact that they would not drink coffee, then sneaking a cup when no one was looking would be cheating. But we still have no reason to say why such restrictions on individual behavior should exist in the first place. Given the popularity of all caffeinated beverages, it is entirely likely that fairness is found in the acceptance of coffee rather than the attempting to eliminate it from an athlete's diet.

Unnaturalness

Another line of argument against doping involves the unnaturalness of the substances and methods used. On first glance, there is something inherently unnatural about the vast array of chemicals athletes can use to stimulate superior athletic performances. Even in the case of blood doping, which sees athletes store their own blood for reinfusion before competition, there is a sense of this not being in accord with "nature." While we can allow for argument's sake the idea that such drugs aren't "natural," it's a *non sequitur* to say that such things are therefore unethical. Think about everything that is unnatural in our world today; can we say that those things are all unethical? The first time you open an umbrella on a rainy day, you have, in essence, violated the natural state of things. A strict adherence to all things natural means no umbrellas, no shrink-wrapped meat in the grocery store, and a rejection of most medical advances.

KENNETH W. KIRKWOOD

Oddly enough, coffee products seem natural. When we think of the Ethiopians who chewed the raw coffee beans thousands of years ago, we think of a lifestyle as devoid of "unnatural" technological advances as one could live. This makes coffee natural in this sense, and therefore not subject to sanction.

Harm

One major ethical concern is about the harm that doping has on a variety of people and organizations. We have seen how coffee abuse can be damaging to one's health, and in this way, one could make a claim that coffee is harmful. After all, coffee is one of the first things doctors want patients with blood pressure problems or heart disease to dispense with. But the ethical claim here relies more on intuitive appeal than it does on reason. If the doping control testing threshold for caffeine was high, to the point where it would capture only those consumers who were approaching serious medical consequences caused by caffeine abuse (a syndrome called *caffeinism*), then this argument could continue onward to further analysis. But the quantity of coffee one could consume one or two hours prior to a positive test is one 20-ounce serving of brewed coffee. This leads us to a very large problem – we'll call it the "*Venti* problem" – if you aren't testing at the level of harm, then it is disingenuous to appeal to harm as the justification for your test.

Another form of harm that is often appealed to is the harm that doping athletes perpetrate upon the sport itself. Many sports suffer from image problems related to their histories of widespread drug abuse. Think of 100 m sprinters, and how every world record brings with it some commonly held sense of reservation. One example I can offer is when people said on the occasion of Usain Bolt's world record runs during the 2008 Beijing Olympics, "I'll wait until after the drug test before I believe it." Could coffee or other caffeine products bring this sense of disrepute? I think it is fair to say that it could not. Coffee is the drug of choice for many who are morally opposed to drug use. It doesn't carry with it the same emotive response as other drugs, and therefore couldn't create the kind of harm to the image of an organization. In non-sporting contexts, we are seeing the emergence of discussions around neuro-doping, which is a supposed explosion in the misuse of psychostimulants used in the treatment of attention deficit-hyperactivity disorder by healthy university students to enhance their normal levels of mental functioning. I had a very detailed discussion with a colleague who was deeply opposed to students' use of drugs to enhance their mental functioning, but apparently I was the only one aware of the irony that our discussion occurred in the lineup for our local outlet of the university-contracted coffee retailer. It probably didn't occur to my dear colleague that we were also lined up to receive a drug with psychostimulant properties because coffee is the drug everyone uses, and when everyone uses it, they stop calling it a drug.

When we talk about doping, we talk in very emotive terms. During the most recent scandals at the Tour de France, a diehard cycling aficionado cried out, "They are killing the most beautiful thing ever created!" Not everybody is so maudlin, but much of what passes for argument about the reasons to ban doping is equal parts reasoning and passion. I would speculate that deep down, after much reasoned argument and debate, advocates for anti-doping policies feel that drug use tarnishes what they remember fondly about sport. Some probably see some of the great athletic experiences of their lives precluded to others, because they see current sporting experiences as fundamentally degraded by doping. The foundational basis – acknowledged or not – is that doping conjures up strongly negative feelings in these people, and their distinction between right and wrong is how they describe it – either with negative or positive language and emotion. I've thought this for some time as a description of the current debate over doping, and the examination of caffeine and coffee has offered some insight into why I'll be thinking that way for a little while longer. We've seen that, according to WADA's own regulations, coffee should be a banned substance, but it isn't. Why? Because using the language of "drugs" or "banned substances" or "doping" evokes fundamentally negative reactions and moral judgment from the community at large. When you remind the members of that community that ibuprofen is also a drug, they will often wave their hands and exclaim that it "wasn't what they meant by *drugs*." On one side of this, we can see that terminology such as this is powerfully motivating to a population, members of which may cast aspersions on a perpetrator and question that person's moral aptitude. On the other side, when we hold people to a standard of reason and conceptual clarity, we discover that people want to change their own terminology and make arbitrary exclusions or exceptions. Why? Because if we cloud oversimplified worldviews with fact and precise arguments, it can mitigate the outrage people feel over issues, and makes them less prone to manipulation, which is a good thing – unless you're manipulating people.

KENNETH W. KIRKWOOD

Having said all of this, is caffeine a drug? Yes. Is coffee use by athletes performance-enhancing drug use? Yes again. Is it doping? According to WADA's definition it is. Is it officially recognized as doping by WADA? Not currently. Why not? Because it's not an issue of morality, it's an issue of public acceptance, and since no one would consider a regular coffee habit morally problematic, then popular opinion – including the most important opinions of major Olympic sponsors – says there's nothing unethical about it.

NOTES

1   D. T. Courtwright, *Forces of Habit: Drugs and the Making of the Modern World* (Cambridge, MA: Harvard University Press, 2001), p. 46.

2   B. Grecian Gordon, "Athletic Training in the Third Century (AD)," *Annals of Medical History* (1935): 513.

3   L. Tong, *Chinese Tea: A Cultural History and Guide* (Beijing: China Intercontinental Press, 2005), p. 4.

4   Courtwright, *Forces of Habit*, p. 22.

5   D. Grigg, "The Worlds of Tea and Coffee: Patterns of Consumption," *GeoJournal* 57, no. 4 (2002): 283–294.

6   A. Wild, *Coffee: A Dark History* (New York: W. W. Norton, 2005).

7   E. N. Anderson, *The Food of China* (New Haven, CT: Yale University Press, 1990), p. 163.

8   B. A. Weinberg and B. K. Bealer, *The World of Caffeine: The Science and Culture of the World's Most Popular Drug* (London: Routledge, 2002).

9   Greetings non-coffee drinker! The effect is "more frequent urges to urinate."

10   M. J. Jarvis, "Does Caffeine Intake Enhance Absolute Levels of Cognitive Performance?" *Psychopharmacology* 110 (1993): 45–52.

11   Very few religions prohibit caffeine use. Two well-known exceptions are the Church of Latter-Day Saints and Rastafarians.

12   B. H. Jacobson and F. A. Kulling, "Health and Ergogenic Effects of Caffeine," *British Journal of Sports Medicine* 23 (1989): 34–40.

13   L. M. Burke, "Caffeine and Sports Performance," *Applied Physiology, Nutrition and Metabolism* 33 (2008): 1319–1334.

14   In researching this chapter, I noticed that there has been a remarkable increase in the reported concentrations of caffeine in coffees available from restaurants and coffeeshops over the past forty years. What was considered an excessive amount of caffeine in 1962 is now just what many people enjoy as their first hit of the day.

15   W. M. Brown, "Paternalism, Drugs and the Nature of Sports," *Journal of the Philosophy of Sport* 11 (1984): 14–22.

16 N. Chester and N. Wojek, "Caffeine Consumption Amongst British Athletes Following Changes to the 2004 WADA Prohibited List," *International Journal of Sports Medicine* 29 (2008): 524–528.

17 W. Van Thuyne and F. T. Delbecke, "Distribution of Caffeine Levels in Urine in Different Sports in Relation to Doping Control Before and After the Removal of Caffeine from the WADA Doping List," *International Journal of Sports Medicine* 27 (2006): 745–750.

18 World Anti-Doping Agency, *World Anti-Doping Code* (Montreal: WADA, 2009), pp. 32–33.

19 Jacobson and Kulling, "Health and Ergogenic Effects of Caffeine," pp. 34–40.

STEPHANIE W. ALEMAN

CHAPTER 17

GREEN COFFEE, GREEN CONSUMERS – GREEN PHILOSOPHY?

All theory, dear friend, is gray,
but the golden tree of life springs ever green.
Goethe, Faust (1832)

The central question around which this chapter flows is relatively simple: Is coffee green? However, as soon as one begins to think about this question, the complexity of the answer becomes apparent – as does the difficulty in answering the question satisfactorily. To start, we must unpack the specific meanings of *green*. From there, we might wonder what sort and amount of information does one have to acquire to determine if coffee is green?

As an anthropologist and ethnobotanist, I'm as fascinated by these questions as I am by the general history of coffee as a botanical entity entwined with human lives, actions, and discourses on a larger scale than is any other plant substance on earth. As an anthropologist and ethnobotanist who works in a philosophy department, I find it invigorating and challenging to have the opportunity to explore the meaning of greenness in coffee.

Philosophy, as a branch of knowledge or study, examines the basic components of human experience – such as truth, existence, reality, causality, and freedom. A philosophical consideration of coffee consumption based on its relation to the concept of *greenness*, then, entails thinking about coffee and greenness as they partake in these basic components. But philosophy can also be a set of basic concepts underlying a particular subject. In this capacity, philosophy is interested in examining how the underlying principles of coffee production and consumption are aligned or at odds with greenness.

Taking a look at some of the aspects of coffee production and trade – its growth, processing, transport, preparation, marketing, and consumption – will help us understand the interplay of the various aspects that come with the designation "green." But let's start with the history of coffee, which gives much to think about in terms of ethics – the philosophical category to which the green question mostly belongs – and one may decide that any commodity with a history as "dark" as coffee's could never be considered green. Looking through the literature of coffee, we discover a plant connected to human suffering, slavery, and colonial power. For example, Antony Wild tells us:

> The history of coffee and colonialism evolved together over the last 500 years to forge an unholy alliance that still exists for the benefit of Western coffee consumers at the expense of people of the third world countries – more often than not former colonies – that produce coffee, and at the expense of the plant itself.[1]

These historical injustices surrounding coffee can leave one reluctant to even consider calling it green. A recent book on the subject of fair trade coffee reminds us that the ethical concerns surrounding the coffee industry are as prominent as ever: "In each cup of coffee we drink the major issues of the twenty-first century – globalization, immigration, women's rights, pollution, indigenous rights, and self-determination – are played out in villages and remote areas around the world."[2] Certainly, if we're going to affirm our central question we must find evidence that these inequalities are being rectified.

One final question I want to ask before turning to the concept of *green* is: Who is asking? I've stated my professional interest in the question, but who else cares if coffee is green? I suspect the thoughtful coffee drinker (the reader of this book, for example) will be interested in the question of greenness. There are other concerned stakeholders of course, including

STEPHANIE W. ALEMAN

environmentalists, social justice advocates, and local producers, not to mention corporate markets that are dependent on the idea of greenness for niche sales. But coffee is also the world's second most traded commodity (after oil). This is one of the most commonly referenced bits of data about coffee, and it takes on different nuances in light of current trends in understanding environmental damage and global consequences caused by the procurement and transportation of the most heavily traded commodities. And just to set the larger stakes around this issue, I want to suggest that the coffee industry affects the whole social and geophysical world, not just those directly involved in its production and consumption. So, for everyone's sake, it is necessary to answer the question "Is coffee green?"

The Meaning of *Green*

Before we can determine if coffee is green we must attempt to define what *green* means – and it means a lot of things. In terms of coffee, green doesn't first mean environmentally friendly, socially conscious, economically viable, or sustainably grown and consumed. It first means raw coffee, as the beans are green in color before they're roasted. Green, raw coffee that has not been roasted is sought after more frequently in niche markets where retailers prefer to roast their own and skip the added cost and potential damage to the beans that come from outsourcing roasting.

Colloquially, *green* can mean *new* or *naïve* – as I suggest many consumers may be with regard to the consequences of their own coffee consumption.

Green is also part ethic and part aesthetic, relying at once on several moral principles connected to perceptions of fecundity, lushness, and vigor, as well as health across ecosystems, including the human consumers involved. The environmental and conservation movements both hold a potent aesthetic of greenness as healthy, desirable, and fulfilling. As a color, *green* has come to symbolize health and vigor. In relation to plants, *green* also refers to being leafy, or having edible green parts or leaves – which becomes, symbolically, another potential ethic/aesthetic term for food consumption more generally (such as in vegetarianism and veganism).

Of course, *green* also refers to money. One can imagine asking our initial question, "Is coffee green?" in terms of a reference to money. The answer would vary from producer to producer, trader to trader, consumer to consumer – but, generally speaking, it might be answered, respectively: no, yes, and (given the proliferation of conspicuous coffee consumption) it's the proof of green.

While this partial list of definitions is important to keep in mind, for the immediate purpose, it is the currently vogue meaning of *green* – the one you understood when you saw the title of this chapter – that is of greatest interest. *Green*, in this sense, can be taken to mean advocating for protection of the environment from damage; acting in ways that protect the environment from damage; production methods that do minimal (possibly no) environmental harm; or being generally ecologically friendly.

Growth

If we focus first on the narrative of coffee *growth*, there are trends toward greenness that involve the basic botanical realities of coffee. Its specific growth habit as a large berry-producing woody shrub rather than a herbaceous root crop or leafy crop means that habitats can be created rather than destroyed through planting coffee. This makes coffee perhaps greener than other monocrops. The next level of green in terms of growth concerns the concept of organic. If coffee is produced inorganically – that is, with pesticides and chemicals for fertilizing – it probably does not qualify as green. As an industry term, "organic" is entwined as usual with ethical and aesthetic imperatives. It can mean simply *related to*, *derived from*, or *being* a living thing. It can refer to developing "naturally" without being forced or contrived. Even more fundamentally, it can mean carbon-based. For our purposes here, organic refers to the practice of agriculture without synthetic chemicals, specifically ones that force plants to grow in certain ways. While organic in its label designation may indicate growth without synthetics, ideas of "natural" cultivation can sound oxymoronic, or even obvious.

Climate, in terms of where coffee can actually be grown, is also an immediate issue, since the sites of production differ so greatly from sites of consumption. The consumers and marketers of coffee are overwhelmingly in the Global North, with producers and farmers in the Global South. This situation itself can provide a partial answer to the green question when considered as a transportation and energy consumption issue, which we'll get to shortly.

This leads to the next green issue in coffee growth: the *local production* of coffee. What happens at the local level, where coffee is produced? A recent focus on areas of production stemming from two disparate concerns – environmentalism/conservationism and fair trade/social justice – has been responsible for highlighting more specifically what happens where coffee is grown in terms of the mostly damaging affects to working populations and environments. The introduction of non-native plant species to different parts of the world was a major part of early European colonization. Indeed, botany was critical to colonial European trade ambitions. Effective cultivation in the colonial tropics was a focus, but not green cultivation certainly.

Modern ideas about production of coffee, such as organic and fair trade, are meant to mitigate environmental and human social damage that may have been present in the past. But can these production-site initiatives then lead to the green designation for coffee? Or is there far more to consider?

Sustainability, Shade-Grown, Fair Trade

In terms of behaviors or dispositions in relation to environment and its protection as an ethical responsibility, green has a companion term – sustainability. The idea of sustainability is centered on value ascribed to systems that can replicate desired results for relatively long periods of time. To sustain means to nourish or keep alive, to support (from below), to give moral support, to withstand or continue in spite of pressures, and even to experience a setback, injury, damage, loss, or defeat without collapse. For the purposes of coffee production and consumption, sustainable means a practice that allows for maintaining ecological balance without destruction of environments. When applied to economic or productive systems, it can also indicate the maintenance of social or economic balances without destruction of culture, well-being, and modes of acquiring the basic necessities of human existence.

Coffee growing of course then assumes a green designation in its shade-grown method, as the practice protects environments (migrating bird habitats) from destruction. Shade-grown refers to the agricultural practice of growing coffee under a canopy of trees, in opposition to the Green Revolution methods of the 1960s, 1970s, and 1980s that focused on large full-sun monocropped plantation-style growing methods for coffee. Shade-grown also implies a practice that is closer to natural ecology or natural ecological methods. So again, a "maybe" emerges in response to the question "Is coffee green?" when we consider that shade-grown coffee is at least green at its site of production. The shade itself, the habitat, is good for humans too, and the conditions of labor are vastly improved in smaller, family operated, local farms. This satisfying result might be enough to allow certain consumers to decide to judge coffee as green.

Terms like the "fair" in fair trade also suggest ethical and aesthetic relationships to balance, reason, impartiality, and freedom from bias. The idea of fair trade for a variety of globally traded commodities is centered on ideas of organized social movements and highlights market-based approaches that aim to help producers obtain better trading conditions. Fair Trade certification indicates that a minimum price was paid to producers and that social and environmental standards were met. Fair trade also focuses in particular on exports from developing countries to developed countries, and includes not only coffee, but other tropical to northern commodities such as cocoa, sugar, bananas, and flowers as well. Ethically, fair trade, as a green-laden aspect of social justice through social and economic health for producers, has changed from an "alternative trading network," which sounds potentially green, to a "niche market driven by the interests of giant conventional corporations with minor commitments to fair trade given their overall size."[3] Thus, market-driven social justice is precariously green because of the market itself. But this still does not address the issue of how green is the *journey* from the shade-grown, fair trade, organic, Global South farm site of production.

Globalization

Since the coffee trade is a microcosm for globalization, we might ask if worldwide trade itself can be green. Here we are confronted with the reality that human globalization is not perhaps so very green in some aspects. Globalization can be divided into many different forms – economic, political, cultural, etc. While cultural globalization, such as new media and communicative technologies that allow the world a greater connectivity, don't seem particularly threatening to greenness, the human desire to travel and be in other places requires transportation that is decidedly not green in its use of fossil fuels and creation of exhaust

STEPHANIE W. ALEMAN

pollution. Physical human globalization damages environments. Economic globalization struggles with the effects of uneven access to markets and profits as well as the many challenges to social justice globalization entails.

But other global processes in "nature," such as biannual north/south–south/north bird migrations depend on green behaviors and efforts. Migrating birds land in the trees incorporated into shade-grown coffee farms. In farms without intermixed native trees, these birds have nowhere to land and become effectively crowded out of their natural habitats.

The promise and billing of trade as a lever of development for poorer nations has come to be seen as the elusive promise of development, as the commodity value chain is let out link by link. The paradox is that it at once produces opportunity for their tropical producers and perpetuates their oppression. Tropical producers shifting to export production, are also victims of shifting consumer trends and this is sometimes referred to as the "coffee crisis."

These are not new ideas. In 1983 William Roseberry identified the state of synergies between sites of production and consumption in his study of coffee in the Venezuelan Andes.[4] He uses the narratives of physical and social environment as well as the colonial and capitalist economic systems that have shaped the coffee realities for both producers and consumers.

In 1994 Robert Williams argued that coffee offered potential "social evolution" for Central American governments and states – paths of opportunity or paths of dependence for Guatemala, El Salvador, Nicaragua, Honduras, and Costa Rica.[5] A focus or shift to large-scale coffee production was seen and recommended as a key factor in the global emergence and economic stability of these Latin American nations. But these paths to opportunity could also lead to trade-dependent relationships with more wealthy, buying states, and the whims of a consuming market far from the site of production.

The impacts on peoples and environments are just two strands in the complex decisions of individual consumption. One might well ask for guidance in the ethically and aesthetically laden sphere of coffee. There are increasing numbers of Web references to green coffee consumption, but it appears these considerations do not get at the heart of coffee realities. In an article entitled "Top Green Coffee and Tea Tips," the first piece of advice is to use the Local Brew: "Seek out the coffee and tea that have traveled the least distance to reach you and also aim at supporting local, independent farms, cafés, and roasters."[6]

Other advice centers on the kind of mug one uses to drink coffee, the filters used to brew it, avoidance of the use of milk or sugar, suggestions for avoiding cafés and brewing at home, as well as composting the grounds responsibly. But whatever consumers do at home or locally, there is no avoiding the fact that coffee is produced in the relatively economically disadvantaged tropics and consumed largely in the economically dominant northern hemisphere, and so has to depend on the global links that are necessarily formed through its very consumption.

With regard to how coffee gets from there to here, does one need to be an investigative journalist to have enough information to make the judgment regarding the green aspect of coffee? Does one have to travel, producing trendy Anthony Bourdain-like travelogues centered on ancient coffee routes, witnessing local production and cultural vignettes?

In transportation, new threats emerge to contemplate. For example, how could a giant ash cloud or massive oil gush from a deep ocean bed affect coffee acquisition? In a world full of emergent global transport issues around energy, emissions, carbon credits, and global air/sea transport, the issue of coffee movement around the globe comes into better focus. Ultimately, the mandate to "Eat (consume) locally" results in starved global dependencies and responsibilities. So one may wonder if desire is enough to make coffee green.

Value Chain

Another useful idea in the contemplation of green coffee production comes in the form of the value chain. Value chain refers to the value added to a commodity as it goes from its site of production to its site of sale and consumption. The idea of the value chain places an emphasis on the ethics and symbols of consumption contained in the commodity in question. One of the most under-examined parts of coffee is the quality of the transportation methods used to bring the product to northern markets. There are no readily available sources of information for consumers regarding how their coffee reaches them. Along the journey, coffee follows a value chain that adds ethical and symbolic meaning to the ultimate product. The end point of sale offers views of the site of production in the form of small-scale villages and children, who are dependent on northern consumers for their livelihoods. Consumers are then able to suppose a connection between their desire for coffee and the altruistic advancement of the less fortunate. In addition to the coffee itself, modern-day value chains from port sites to roasting plants, and on to packaging and delivery and display marketing, offer increased opportunity for the consumption of ethical symbols in coffee.

So many of us consider coffee that is shade-grown, fair trade, and sustainable to have significant added value – and we're willing to pay extra for it. Some people do not consider these ethical efforts added value and continue to prefer coffee that is cheap and exploitive. But those of us who do think ethics play a role in coffee will agree with Vandana Shiva, a leading Indian ecofeminist who argues that "drinking coffee is a political act"[7] and Rigoberta Menchu, Nobel Laureate from Guatemala, who says, "Coffee is more than just a drink. It is about politics, survival, the Earth, and the lives of indigenous peoples."[8] It would be hard to find a more value-laden commodity than coffee.

A Personal Conclusion

Is coffee green? In philosophy, logic and critical thinking suggest that one can ultimately decide yes, no, or to withhold judgment until further knowledge or information is gained, or until a change in the circumstance under question can be adequately considered. If pressed to answer yes or no, I would answer, "No, it is not. Or at least only parts of coffee are green." Coffee as a commodity is currently not green in the way we want it to be. It is not wholly green in its environmental or economic sense, if the idea of green is one that relates to the environmental aspects of its production and/or the social justice of coffee's economic markets. Coffee is also not green in the sense that it is sustainably profitable to producers. It seems to be least green in the *actual journey* from farm to cup.

A relevant and slightly different question than the one I set out with is "Could coffee become green?" To this I would answer that it is possible to improve its greenness across the production, transportation, and consumption continuum. Green at the source seems to be making the most headway, along with green containers at the point of consumption. But this leads to another related question: "Will coffee become green?" Here I withhold judgment in part for the reasons given above. I do not have enough information about transportation costs and trends to predict if coffee will ever be delivered green, and I cannot envision a green method of transport. Neither can I see through the somewhat black box of coffee production and delivery for each pound of coffee I buy. I have to take marketers' word for it in some cases.

But in withholding judgment about the future I cannot withhold action. In other words, I have to decide to drink or not drink coffee (or decide which coffees to drink) based on my determination of whether or not coffee is green – and whether greenness matters to me. If I, and if we, decide to not drink coffee that isn't green it could make all the difference in the world to the global markets.

There is a possible disconnect between judgment and action, though – many or even most people will determine coffee is not green and that they therefore shouldn't drink it, but will anyway. This type of disconnect – or cognitive dissonance – can be seen in our current global conundrum over our use of, and dependence on, oil. In the face of decades of ungreen behavior, including environmental and human damage (not to mention loss of life), there seems to be relatively little action to reduce the "addiction" and put more effort into alternative energy sources. This sort of disconnect can be frustrating, but resisting the disconnect is a worthy goal.

To take the matter personally, what will I do now, after absorbing so much knowledge regarding about the way coffee is grown; its effects, both positive and negative, on disparate populations; the cost of shipping and roasting and shipping again; and the extra ethical and aesthetic shot of flavor added to each cup? I will continue to drink from a refillable mug; I'll drink fair trade, organic, shade-grown, direct-shipped coffee from single source, single-bean producers (I prefer the Oromia Cooperative-produced Ethiopian Harrar when I can afford it); and I'll continue to do my part to help bring about a greener future for coffee. For the rest of the coffee-consuming population, the individual nature of consumption and the formation of ideologies of practice make the central question of the greenness of coffee subjective, even in the face of certain economic and global environmental and social realities. So truly the answer to the question "is coffee green?" lies both in how one understands and values all the various factors that go into *green* and in the subjective experience of each drinker and their cup.

NOTES

1   Antony Wild, *Coffee: A Dark History* (New York: W. W. Norton, 2004), p. xi.
2   Dean Cycon, *Javatrekker: Dispatches from the World of Fair Trade Coffee* (White River Jct., VT: Chelsea Green Publishing, 2007).

3 Gavin Fridell, *Fair Trade Coffee: The Prospects and Pitfalls of Market-Driven Social Justice* (Toronto: University of Toronto Press, 2007), p. 3.

4 William Roseberry, *Coffee and Capitalism in the Venezuelan Andes* (Austin: University of Texas Press, 1983).

5 Robert G. Williams, *States and Social Evolution: Coffee and the Rise of National Governments in Central America* (Chapel Hill: University of North Carolina Press, 1994).

6 Online at http://planetgreen.discovery.com/go-green/green-coffee-tea/green-coffee-tea-tips.html.

7 Daniel Jaffee, *Brewing Justice: Fair Trade Coffee, Sustainability and Survival* (Berkeley: University of California Press, 2007), p. 7.

8 Cycon, *Javatrekker*, p. 32.

CHAPTER 18

COFFEE AND THE GOOD LIFE
The Bean and the Golden Mean

I assume the reader is a philosophically minded coffee lover – the author certainly is. As coffee lovers we are likely to agree that coffee and the good life are deeply relevant to one another. As philosophers we might wonder about the way in which this is so. Aristotle's conception of the good life is one way to approach the question. Aristotle never tasted coffee, much less wrote about it.[1] Nevertheless his views on the good life have a lot to offer coffee drinkers. Moreover, I suspect that if Aristotle were lucky enough to know about coffee, he would have almost certainly considered coffee a necessary part of the good life.

Aristotle was the first philosopher in the Western tradition to write treatises investigating the good life. *Nichomachean Ethics* is his most complete and most widely read treatise on the subject. Aristotle recognizes that understanding the good life is not simply an academic endeavor. We ask questions about the good life not simply because we find the knowledge we gain interesting or because we enjoy the pursuit of such knowledge, but because in working to understand the good life we improve our chances of achieving our practical goal of *living* the good life. Aristotle holds that as we identify the good life we become "like archers who have a mark to aim at"; that is, "more likely to hit upon what we should."[2] Aristotle's answer to the question of what role coffee plays in the good life would be very short: *It depends*. No surprise there – instant philosophy is as disappointing and ineffective as instant coffee. The long answer, however, is rich, bold, smooth, and stimulating.

Eudaimonia, Ergon, and Espresso

It is best to get clear on what Aristotle says about the good life in general before taking up questions about how coffee and Aristotle's theory of the good life are relevant to one another.[3] Aristotle recognizes that people's opinions about what sort of life is the good life will vary. Some envy the pleasure-filled lifestyle of a hotel heiress, while others aspire to be honored as the next American Idol, an NBA superstar, or president of the United States; there are also those who seek to live the relatively quiet contemplative life. However, despite any disagreement about what sort of life is the good life, Aristotle believes that all agree that the good life is what the ancient Greeks called the *eudaimon* life.

The Greek word *eudiamonia* is usually translated as *happiness*, but *happiness* does not quite capture the full meaning of the term. Our contemporary understanding of happiness can be understood as corresponding to a pleasant mental state. For example, the mental state one experiences when drawing in a first whiff of freshly ground aromatic coffee beans. Such mental states are private in the sense that no one except the person having the experience can access, or experience, the mental state. To know whether or not someone is feeling happy, we have to ask her. *Eudiamonia*, in contrast, is a public state of being, in the same way that being accomplished or successful are pubic states of being. In other words, *eudaimonia* is an evaluative term that the ancient Greeks used to describe a state of being they recognized in each other. *Eudaimonia* is made up of two parts: *eu*, which literally means *good* or *well-being*; and *diamon*, which means *spirit* or *minor deity*. So, *eudaimonia* literally means something like *blessed* or *well favored by the gods*. But a more appropriate translation for our purpose (and for Aristotle's) would be *well-being* or *human flourishing*. Thus, when Aristotle talks about the eudaimon life, he is concerned not simply with a lifetime of *feeling* happy but with a life of actually *being* well or flourishing. Of course, establishing that the good (or eudaimon) life can be understood as the life of well-being does not settle disagreements about what the life of well-being will be like.

Some behave as if making money is the greatest goal in life. But Aristotle quickly rejects the life of money-making as a serious contender for the eudaimon life because a life dedicated to making money is only "undertaken under compulsion" and wealth is "merely useful for the sake of something else."[4] In other words, no one would spend their life making money unless they had to do so, because money is only as good as the goods and services you can get with it. According to Aristotle, we do not really want money; what we *really* want are delicious four-dollar lattes.

Another view of the good life Aristotle rejects is the *life of enjoyment*. Most people – including both people of the most vulgar type and many prominent people – aspire to the pleasure-filled life.[5] On this view, those with the best lives might pass their time riding shotgun in speeding convertibles, gulping sugary-sweet blended, frozen coffee drinks with extra whip cream, or sipping divinely balanced cappuccinos after seven-course gourmet meals on Italian terraces. Either way, Aristotle argues that such merely pleasure-filled lives are "suitable for beasts," and those living such lives are slaves to their appetite.[6] Thus, the pleasure-centered life of enjoyment cannot be the life of human flourishing.

In contrast to the most vulgar, people of "superior refinement" say the eudaimon life is the life of honor. Contemporary American culture seems to honor political heroes, professional athletes, entertainment stars, business big shots, the occasional artist or intellectual, and to some extent just about anyone famous, including those famous for dishonorable behavior. But Aristotle cautions that the life of honor (and we could add the life of fame) "seems too superficial to be what we are looking for, since it is thought to depend on those who bestow honor, rather than on him who receives it."[7] Eudaimonia is not something that waxes and wanes in accordance with public opinion.

Moreover, Aristotle argues that those who seek honor (and not just the pleasures that might accompany honor) are really in search of some sort of affirmation of their excellence (*arête*).[8] But if this is the case, then it is not honor but excellence that we are seeking. Thus, as anyone who prefers a good local coffeehouse's freshly roasted and brewed coffee over the very latest cherry-chocolate sensation available at Starbucks knows: Excellence is superior to honor.

However, excellence alone will not be enough for the most eudaimon life. After all, it is possible to be both excellent and *asleep* either in the

LORI KELEHER

sense of being a total slacker, or in the sense of being clueless about our excellence. Talented slackers do not exhibit a life of human flourishing. Talented slackers coast through life without daring to see what they could do if they actually focused on developing their talents. Consider Randy Moss, the NFL receiver of whom the Raiders offensive coach Tom Walsh said: "Randy was a great receiver, but he lacked the work ethic and the desire to cultivate any skills."[9] Similarly, as endearing and accomplished as the title character of the 1994 film *Forrest Gump* may be, we do not want to argue that his life is the best life. Gump lacks the ability to truly appreciate the significance of his accomplishments and to *fully* relate to other people. Moreover, one could be both excellent and tormented. It would be difficult to argue successfully that talented and tormented geniuses like Edgar Allan Poe, Vincent van Gogh, and Ludwig Wittgenstein had the good life. Thus, neither excellence nor honor is sufficient for the eudaimon life.

Aristotle is not disputing that wealth, pleasure, excellence, and honor are goods that can contribute to a life of human flourishing. Rather, he holds that the human flourishing is a higher good at which all these goods aim. In other words, we work to secure wealth, seek out pleasure, cultivate our talents, and strive for honor *in order to* achieve a life of human flourishing. So the question remains: What is the life of human flourishing?

The key to answering this question lies in identifying the *ergon,* or distinct function, of human beings. The function of the eye is to see; a good eye is one that sees well. The function of the knife is to cut; a good knife is one that cuts well. The function of the barista is to make espresso drinks; a good barista is one who makes good espresso drinks. The function of the human being is rational activity in accordance with virtue (*arête*). No other known thing can engage in reason the way human beings do. This ability is what makes us special. It is our hallmark quality. We are rational animals. Moreover, the greatest use of this special power is to understand and act in accordance with virtue. Thus, the good (or flourishing) person is one who actively recognizes and acts in accordance with virtue.

"But," as Aristotle famously says, "we must add 'in a complete life.' For one swallow does not make a summer, nor does one day; and so too one day, or a short time, does not make a man blessed and happy."[10] We might add one perfect cappuccino a good barista does not make. After all, the good barista does not just occasionally get espresso drinks right; she consistently – or even habitually – gets them right. Likewise, the good person does not merely occasionally act in accordance with virtue; she lives her life consistently engaging in rational activity in accordance with virtue.

The Golden Mean

We now know the good life is the life spent in "rational activity in accordance with virtue." But what does this mean, and how do we do it? According to Aristotle, being morally virtuous (that is, being just, courageous, generous, sincere, etc.) is like having a good habit or disposition (*hexeis*). We are all born with the potential to become virtuous, but actualizing this potential requires proper education in childhood. Specifically, it requires an education that includes learning good habits. For example, we might become habituated to help our friends with their troubles by being encouraged, or even required, to tutor a struggling friend after school.

Then, once we are mature enough and our faculties of reason are fully developed, we must acquire the intellectual virtue of *phronêsis*. *Phronêsis* is Greek for *prudence*, *(practical) wisdom*, or practical reason, which is a cardinal virtue. Cardinal virtues are virtues upon which other virtues hinge. Within Aristotle's account, all moral virtues hinge upon practical reason. As we acquire practical reason we rely less on the external pressures and generic codes of appropriate conduct for any given situation and more on our own increasingly fine-tuned deliberative skills. When well developed, the skill of practical reason allows us to respond to our emotions (for example, sympathy or pity for a friend's troubles) with insight and to identify the appropriate action to take within a particular moral situation (for example, giving a troubled friend a cup of coffee and a shoulder to cry on).

The appropriate, or virtuous, action in any particular moral situation, Aristotle says, will always be a mean between two vicious extremes of deficiency and excess. For example, *courage* is the mean between the vices of cowardice (deficiency) and rashness (excess); *temperance* is the mean between the vices of insensibility (deficiency) and self-indulgence (excess); *generosity* is the mean between stinginess (deficiency) and extravagance (excess); and so on. As we go through life we practice navigating moral situations and develop the virtue of practical reason, thereby becoming increasingly adroit at recognizing the so-called golden mean and acting virtuously.

We may make mistakes. For example, it would almost certainly be a mistake to send an old high school friend a $5,000 espresso machine as a wedding present. Such a gift would be extravagant for all but a very few people and a very few weddings. It would also be a mistake for most of us to send a single coffee mug with a business logo to most weddings. But if we are to become virtuous we will learn from our mistakes. We will reflect about what a more appropriate – more virtuous – action would be. We would consider things like whose wedding it is, how well we know the person, what we can afford to give, what would make them feel honored but not embarrassed, and so forth. The more we practice acting virtuously the more excellent, or virtuous, we become. It is literally a virtuous cycle. Of course, if we have bad habits and routinely act viciously, then we ruin our ability to make good judgments and become vicious. This is the vicious cycle. The vicious person is one who has come to believe the wrong actions are the right ones. He has given so many tacky coffee mugs that he comes to believe that such things make a really great gift. As Aristotle explains:

> The man who flies from and fears everything and does not stand his ground against anything becomes a coward, and the man who fears nothing at all but goes to meet every danger becomes rash; and similarly the man who indulges in every pleasure and abstains from none becomes self-indulgent, while the man who shuns every pleasure as boors do, becomes in a way insensible; temperance and courage then are destroyed by excess and defect, and preserved by the mean.[11]

The virtuous mean is not an objective and uniform concept like a mathematical mean. It is not the case that boors never drink any coffee while all self-indulgent people drink ten cups a day and all virtuous people drink five cups a day. Rather, the mean is relative both to us as individuals and to the very specific situations in which we find ourselves. Consider, for example, Katherine and Samantha. They are both virtuous coffee drinkers. But Katherine drinks around six or seven cups of coffee every day, while Samantha typically drinks no more than two cups a day. Of course, Samantha might have a third cup of coffee if she knows she will be out late that night. Similarly, Katherine might cut back to one cup a day while she is pregnant. Each temperate coffee drinker engages her practical reason in assessing her individual circumstances, including her tolerance to caffeine, her plans for the day, her current health requirements, etc. As the Mayo Clinic reports: "Some people are more sensitive to caffeine than are others. If you're susceptible to the effects of caffeine, just small amounts – even one cup of coffee or tea – may prompt unwanted effects, such as anxiety, restlessness, irritability, and sleep problems."[12] Likewise, there is no one-size-fits-all formula or moral calculus that we can use to determine what action is the right action for every person in a given situation.

Simply performing the right action is not enough. Instead, being virtuous requires us to *actively* use practical reason to find the golden mean for ourselves in our current situation. Without the *active* use of practical reason informed by our emotions, we are unreflective slackers who just happen to do the right thing. As we have seen, such less than fully rational activity is less than fully human and results in a less than fully flourishing life. Thus, truly virtuous activity is more than simply performing the right actions. It also requires having the right state of mind and acting for the sake of virtue alone. We have to act in the right way for the right reasons with the right feelings. A pound of your sweetie's favorite coffee beans and a box of chocolate truffles may be the perfect Valentine's Day gift, but it is only a virtuous (that is, generous and sincere) gift if you bought it out of love after thinking about how to honor your beloved and for the sake of doing so. If you buy the same gift but do so either because it was the first thing you grabbed after the sudden realization that today was V-day, or because you hope that you will somehow be rewarded for giving such a gift, or because you feel pressured to do so, then your actions are not undertaken in the right way, or for the right reasons, or with the right feelings. Consequently, they are not virtuous.

Finally, for the virtuous person, this rational activity in accordance with virtue is both habitual and pleasant. Only when we habitually exercise the intellectual virtue of practical reason to deliberate about our actions and then act in accordance with moral virtue are we virtuous people. Furthermore, acting in accordance with virtue is pleasant for the virtuous not unlike the way in which playing the piano is pleasant for the pianist, or running is pleasant for the runner. According to Aristotle, if we thoughtfully do the right thing but take no pleasure in doing it we are not virtuous. For example, if we follow our doctor's advice and refrain from drinking the extra large, extra sugary, 750-calorie frozen, blended cream coffee beverage with extra whip cream and extra cherry-chocolate sprinkles, but we still really, really, *really* want one, we have done the right thing, but we are not virtuous. Instead, we are *continent*, or self-controlled (*enkratês*). It is not until we are so disposed to making the right call that

LORI KELEHER

we no longer even want the once-tempting drink, and in fact enjoy refraining from it, that we are virtuous. Of course, if we give in to our appetites and drink the forbidden drink, then we are incontinent, or weak willed (*akratês*). Once again, we can draw an analogy to the pianist or the athlete. After a few lessons or workouts we might play a few notes or run a mile, but it is difficult and we have to force ourselves to engage in the activity. If we are continent, we will practice. We might even mechanically play a few songs in a recital, or enter and finish a 5K fun run. But we are not yet a pianist or a runner. Only when we are so in the habit of playing or running that we miss it on our day off are we truly pianists or runners. Notice that neither the pianist, nor the runner, nor the virtuous person stops challenging himself or herself. If they stop practicing, they will lose their skill. Yet another point can be drawn from this analogy: Just as the runner's body will be fit, according to Aristotle the virtuous person's soul will be in harmony, which like physical fitness, is pleasant.

We now understand that the good, or eudaimon, life is the life spent in rational activity in accordance with virtue. That such a life requires using practical reason informed by our emotional insights to actively evaluate our specific and personal circumstances and identify and act in accordance with virtue – where virtue is a mean between two extremes. And that the virtuous person acts this way habitually throughout her life and gets pleasure from doing so. We are now ready to talk about coffee.

The Bean

Now that we have a full-bodied understanding of the good life we are prepared to ask both (1) how can this theory of the good life inform our understanding of drinking coffee and (2) how can our understanding of drinking coffee inform our theory of the good life. At the very least, Aristotle's account of the good life offers coffee lovers some pretty good advice: For the best coffee-drinking experience, drink coffee in moderation[13] – drink enough so that you are not a zombie but not so much that you are an irritable jitterbug – and while exercising your higher faculties, for example, by reading moral philosophy. However, I think we can take Aristotle's view even further. I submit that drinking coffee can be understood as a virtuous activity.

I am not claiming that excellence in drinking coffee is a cardinal virtue like prudence or courage. Nevertheless, I submit that those who consistently, actively, and habitually engage practical reason as they drink coffee the right way for the right reasons with the right feeling are virtuous with regard to coffee and, consequently, posses the minor virtue of drinking coffee, or what we might call *javavity*. Let us sketch a portrait of the virtuous coffee drinker.

The virtuous coffee drinker thinks about what she is drinking. She does not buy the store's generic brand of coffee in bulk and drink it day after day for a year without thinking. Nor does she drink whatever concoction she happens to find in the coffee pot of the employee break room. And she never buys coffee from a machine that also dispenses chicken noodle soup in a hospital waiting room. She makes discriminating choices about what sort of coffee she drinks and selects fresh, high-quality beans. However, she is not persnickety in her coffee selections, refusing to drink anything less than Panama's *Hacienda la Esmeralda Geisha* (an award-winning coffee that retails for more than $100 per pound).[14]

The virtuous coffee drinker is temperate in her coffee consumption. She neither deprives herself of coffee's rich aroma and flavor nor chugs mug after mug just because it is there. She drinks exactly as much as benefits her. She drinks coffee for the sake of drinking coffee. She does not drink it simply because doing so is trendy or because she wants a caffeine rush. This is not to say that she cannot enjoy the stimulating feeling she gets as a part of the coffee experience, but there is a worthwhile distinction between drinking coffee and doing caffeine. The virtuous coffee drinker has the right feeling when she drinks coffee. She enjoys holding the warm cup in her hands, smelling the vibrant aroma, sipping the warm liquid, tasting the creamy, full-bodied flavor, and thinks this is the good life.

Naysayers may argue that I have merely described one form of temperance, namely temperance with regard to drinking coffee. But I am confident that the coffee lovers reading this chapter will agree that although temperance may be a cardinal virtue on which the relatively minor moral virtue *javavity* hinges, there is something special – indeed, something excellent or virtuous – about the habit of coffee drinking. It is with this excellence of coffee drinking in mind that we now take up the question of how coffee drinking is relevant to the life of human flourishing.

We learned above that, according to Aristotle, to flourish as human beings we must use our practical reason to act in accordance with virtue. We also learned that this is a pretty tall order. Aristotle, like many of us, is only too aware that it is difficult to do all that virtue requires of us. He argues that if we are going to be successful in being fully virtuous and

LORI KELEHER

living the eudaimon life, then we'd better have some things going for us. As Aristotle writes: "it is impossible, or not easy, to do noble acts without the proper equipment."[15] He goes on to list several external goods that make up the proper equipment, including good friends, wealth, political power, a nice family, good luck, and several others.[16] Aristotle's point seems to be that it is difficult, if not impossible, to have the good life – or at least the very best life: one with the luster of flourishing – if we are not fully in control of our lives. It is hard to thoughtfully deliberate about the perfect Valentine's Day gift if you are distracted by practical troubles like paying the bills.[17] I believe that if Aristotle were writing today – or in any environment where regular coffee consumption were a real option – that coffee would make the list of "proper equipment" for doing noble acts. It is in this way that our understanding of drinking coffee can inform Aristotle's theory of the good life and we can recognize coffee as a necessary good for the eudaimon life. After all, who among us is not better suited to thoughtful deliberation and action in accordance with virtue after their morning cup of coffee?[18]

NOTES

1 Although there is some debate about when humans started to consume coffee, there is no evidence that the ancient Greeks, including Aristotle, knew about coffee. Poor Aristotle.

2 All citations refer to Aristotle's *Nicomachean Ethics* translated by W. D. Ross with revisions by J. O. Urmson as it appears in *The Complete Works of Aristotle: The Revised Oxford Translation*, ed. Jonathan Barnes (Oxford: Oxford University Press), here p. 1729 (1094a24).

3 Aristotle was a hopeless sexist who believed that women were deformed men and that only men had a shot at the good life. Sparing the reader my tirade on Aristotle and sexism, I have decided to simply extend his view to *people* – that is, men and women alike.

4 Aristotle, *Nichomachean Ethics*, p. 1733 (1096a15).

5 Ibid., p. 1731 (1095b15).

6 Ibid., p. 1731 (1095b20).

7 Ibid., p. 1731 (1095b25).

8 The Greek word *arête* literally means *excellence of the soul*, and is typically translated as either *excellence* or *virtue*. I use *excellence* here because I want to make clear that the scope of excellence is not limited to moral virtue.

9 *ESPN.com news services.* 2007-05-12. http://sports.espn.go.com/nfl/news/story?id=2871527. Thanks to the talented and hard-working Jeff Horty for suggesting Moss as an exemplary talented slacker.

10 Aristotle, *Nichomachean Ethics*, p. 1735 (1098a18).
11 Ibid., p. 1744 (1104a20).
12 See http://www.mayoclinic.com/health/caffeine/NU00600.
13 Medical experts agree with this advice. The Mayo Clinic says: "Coffee may have benefits, such as protecting against Parkinson's disease, type 2 diabetes, and liver cancer. But this doesn't mean you should disregard the old maxim 'Everything in moderation.' Although coffee may not be harmful, other beverages such as milk and juice contain important nutrients that coffee does not. Also, keep in mind that coffee accompaniments such as cream and sugar add calories and fat to your diet. Finally, heavy caffeine use – such as four to seven cups of coffee a day – can cause problems such as restlessness, anxiety, irritability, sleeplessness, and headaches." http://www.mayoclinic. com/health/coffee-and-health/AN01354.
14 Forbes Magazine: http://www.forbes.com/2006/07/19/priciest-coffee-beans_ cx_hl_0720featA_ls.html.
15 Aristotle, *Nicomachean Ethics*, p. 1737 (1099a30).
16 In addition to the external goods I mention here and being a free male (see note 3, above) Aristotle requires "a good birth, satisfactory children, beauty; for the man who is very ugly in appearance or ill-born or solitary and childless is hardly eudaimon" (1099a31–b8). It is interesting but beyond the scope of this essay to consider whether or not Aristotle is correct in his belief that these external goods are necessary for the good life.
17 Recall that we seek money, pleasure, honor, and excellence so that we can have the good life. It is because of this key instrumental role that these external goods play in allowing us to be virtuous that some people mistake having such goods for having the eudaimon life. The requirement of external goods in general, as well as the inclusion of particular goods on the list of what goods are necessary is debated among philosophers. See Martha Nussbaum, *Fragility of Goodness* (Cambridge: Cambridge University Press, 1986).
18 Thanks to Mike Austin, Scott Parker, and James Sharpe for help editing this chapter. Thanks to Michael Bursum for making good coffee.

HOW TO MAKE IT IN HOLLYWOOD BY WRITING AN AFTERWORD!

In West Hollywood, California, on Sunset Boulevard and Fairfax Avenue, lies a "hot spot." It is not a club or an expensive restaurant – it is The Coffee Bean & Tea Leaf. Walking into The Coffee Bean – on any given day, at any given time – you shouldn't be surprised to see Perez Hilton (popular gossip blogger) typing away in the back, or some of Hollywood's elite ordering soy lattes in the front, or people talking about how they will soon become Hollywood's elite in the front, back, outside, in the bathroom, and even in the parking lot. (The valet guy has what it takes! Translation: He's going to be a FUCKING star!)

More importantly, you can see the Coffee Bean Guys – James "Moving" Kirkland and Dan "Shaking" Levy (a.k.a.: us, the writers). We are two best friends who have lived in LA for fourteen years and have accomplished … nothing (yet). We sit at Coffee Bean from 9 a.m. to 5 p.m., and sometimes 5 p.m. to 9 a.m., developing absurd projects and taking meetings regarding our latest plans of attack on Hollywood. Recently, though, we've gotten something done. We have come together, brainstormed, and developed what we believe is the ideal afterword for this book. You are welcome.

It wasn't easy. When approached to write the afterword for a book on coffee and philosophy our first thoughts were: (1) Can we hybrid this?

*James Kirkland and Dan Levy

Coffee – Philosophy for Everyone: Grounds for Debate, First Edition. Edited by Scott F. Parker and Michael W. Austin, series editor Fritz Allhoff.

(2) We will explain hybrid in an endnote.[1] (2.5) Endnotes are great; they're like numbered previews for the best parts of the book which are written smaller at the end.[2] (3) We do not know how to do endnotes.[3]

Next, we wondered: what is philosophy? We didn't know the first thing about it. But then we Wikipedia'd it (coincidentally, also the title of a reality movie we're developing for a freelance freelancer) and realized we were in our comfort zone. Most of the world's philosophers are highly caffeinated thinkers who think very hard and critically, and do very little. Turns out, we are overqualified to write an afterword about philosophy.

Philosophy is basically the science of getting high and asking: Why?[4] Which is what we do at the Coffee Bean for twelve to sixteen hours a day. For those of you who don't think coffee is a drug: Wake up and smell the coffee you spilled on yourself as you passed out resting a latte on your chest! If coffee is not a drug, why did we spend three years in Coffee Anonymous? Why do we each have a rap sheet longer then a venti frappuccino? Why are we not allowed to operate heavy machinery anymore? Why? The answer is coffee. A conclusion we only came up with while doing coffee.

You see, coffee is the answer, but it's also a question. Coffee? Coffee.

Our third serious thought was: Can we make this into a movie, reality television program, webisode, mobile downloadable content platform, Twitter feed, or telenovela? The answers to all of these questions are, of course, Yes, Yes, Yes, Yes, Yes, and Si!

The amount of projects we discuss at the Coffee Bean is unimaginable. That's right, you can't imagine it. Don't even try to imagine it. STOP TRYING! Because, as we previously explained, it's unimaginable. You could hurt yourself trying to imagine it. Not even John Lennon could imagine it, and he was like the Lady Gaga of his day.

Now, the amount of those projects that we actually work on at the Coffee Bean is a more imaginable number: zero. Easy to imagine because there's nothing there.

Hanging around in a Coffee Bean is not about doing work. It's about making moves. It's about multitude tasking. Thinking HARD about LIFE. Watching people through the corner of your Blackberry camera. It's a chance to read a screenplay, write a TV show, beg for money, play a game of chess, drink espresso till your entire body vibrates, surf the Internet on your iPhone while petting your dog under the table, or, ideally, do all of the above simultaneously.

As a Coffee Bean Guy you must always look busy but do nothing (which is harder than it looks). In fact, it's the cornerstone of our philosophy. Flatly stated: Appearances are more important than reality, so if you look incredibly busy, people will give you money. In conclusion, if you would like to turn this afterword into a major motion picture please contact our agent, Harry Anderson. (Yes: the magician/actor from Night Court.)[5]

NOTES

1 Hybriding is a technical term referring to the act in which two things are combined and therefore made better. Some people call our writing team the perfect hybrid. We agree. Another example of a hybrid might be a cup of philosoffee: a delicious, thought-provoking think-drink.

2 [Eds. note: Endnotes are great, and numbered, and small. And they do go at the end. But preview? Who would look in the small print way down here near the end of the book for a preview? Well, just in case: In *Coffee – Philosophy for Everyone: Grounds for Debate* writers and philosophers from around the world get together to offer up an intoxicating blend of their deepest loves: wisdom and the brain juice that gives it to them. Read, as these philosoffers reflect on the ethics, aesthetics, even metaphysics, of their favorite drink. Special guests include Donald Schoenholt, Matt Lounsbury, and the Coffee Bean Guys!]

3 [Eds. note: This is true. When this afterword was originally submitted, the endnotes were mixed in with the main text; they appear down here where they belong thanks to our advanced understanding of MS Word.]

4 A Unicorn princess told us this.

5 Harry, if you read this, call us! We'll get some coffee.

NOTES ON CONTRIBUTORS

STEPHANIE W. ALEMAN is Assistant Professor of Anthropology and Ethnobotany at the University of Wisconsin-Stevens Point, specializing in shamanism, healing, women's lives, and gender in Amazonia. Her current anthropological work centers on the use of communicative technology among the Waiwai – a Carib-speaking group of Amerindians who inhabit the deep south of Guyana and the forests north of the Amazon in Brazil. She is also engaged in research that relates the large-scale global production of non-subsistence plant products such as coffee, sugar, and tobacco to deeper histories of human cultural significance and use. Stephanie enjoys her coffee strong, with a splash of evaporated milk, and thinks she can tell the difference between new world and old world grown coffees.

MICHAEL W. AUSTIN is Associate Professor of Philosophy at Eastern Kentucky University. He has published such books as *Running and Philosophy: A Marathon for the Mind*, *Football and Philosophy: Going Deep*, and *Wise Stewards: Philosophical Foundations of Christian Parenting*. He owes the first cup of coffee he enjoyed to a philosophy professor at Kansas State University, a paper assignment, and procrastination.

ASAF BAR-TURA is working on his PhD in philosophy at Loyola University Chicago, and is a board member of the Humanities and

Coffee – Philosophy for Everyone: Grounds for Debate, First Edition. Edited by Scott F. Parker and Michael W. Austin, series editor Fritz Allhoff.

Technology Association. His main interests include the philosophy of technology, political philosophy, and the public sphere. Putting his belief in social justice and participatory democracy into practice, Asaf also does organizing work with the Jewish Council on Urban Affairs. A frequenter of many coffeehouses, the best name he's encountered for one is the "Bourgeois Pig Café," which, luckily, is right on his block.

GINA BRAMUCCI has spent nearly a decade working in humanitarian relief programming in Uganda, Sudan, Central African Republic, the Democratic Republic of Congo, and Haiti. She currently works as a consultant, supporting programs that address and prevent violence against women and girls. Gina, who received a master's degree from the Missouri School of Journalism, uses photography and writing to communicate what she learns through her work, and her esteem for the people she encounters. In early 2009, she spent a week visiting smallholder farmers in Kenya to learn about their struggles with local crops, local politics, and the heavyweights of the coffee industry. Whether at home in Oregon or on the road in rural Africa, Gina brews her coffee in a Bialetti Moka, adds a little sugar, and savors each sip.

WILL BUCKINGHAM has a PhD in philosophy from Staffordshire University, and currently lectures in creative writing at De Montfort University, Leicester. He is the author of the novel *Cargo Fever* and a book on ethics, *Finding Our Sea-Legs: Ethics, Experience and the Ocean of Stories*. He is frequently to be found in his local Turkish café, a cup of coffee in one hand and a philosophy book in the other.

KENNETH DAVIDS has published three books on coffee: *Coffee: A Guide to Buying, Brewing & Enjoying*, *Espresso: Ultimate Coffee*, and *Home Coffee Roasting: Romance & Revival*. He co-produced, hosted, and scripted *The Passionate Harvest*, an award-winning documentary film on coffee production. For the past fourteen years his influential coffee reviews have appeared monthly on the prize-winning Worldwide Web publication www.CoffeeReview.com, and he has written for most major industry print magazines, including an ongoing column in *Roast Magazine*. His workshops and seminars on coffee sourcing, evaluation, and communication have been featured at professional coffee meetings on six continents. His consulting company, Kenneth Davids Consulting, has performed coffee sourcing and quality control for both producers and buyers, trained cuppers, designed coffee programs, and performed marketing work for producing country organizations. He is also Professor of Critical Studies at the California College of Arts in San Francisco, where he teaches a seminar on critical theory.

STEVEN GEISZ is Associate Professor of Philosophy at the University of Tampa. He has published straightforwardly academic work in *Philosophy East & West, The Philosophical Forum, Journal of Applied Philosophy*, and a few other places. He has also contributed chapters to *Whiskey and Philosophy* and *Johnny Cash and Philosophy*. He likes his coffee bold and almost undrinkably strong, but at 7.00 a.m. he'll take what he can get.

JOHN HARTMANN is completing his doctoral studies in philosophy at Southern Illinois University at Carbondale. He is writing on issues related to the theological turn in contemporary phenomenology, and has broad interests in American philosophy and speculative realism. John has, while dissertating, worked a number of coffee jobs, including stints in production, marketing, and roasting. While he is partial to African varietals for brewed coffee, John is becoming increasingly interested in espresso, and has been promised that he can buy a fancy espresso machine once he defends his dissertation.

JILL HERNANDEZ is Assistant Professor of Philosophy at the University of Texas at San Antonio. Jill publishes primarily in ethics, early modern philosophy, and existentialism. She is the author of the textbook *Themes in Ancient and Early Modern Philosophy*, and is currently editing a book on ethics and epistemology entitled *The New Intuitionism*, and finishing a manuscript on the ethics of the twentieth-century existentialist Gabriel Marcel. Her favorite coffee is Caribou French Roast – but since Caribou is not available in San Antonio, she has to rely on family, friends, and excursions to the North to keep it in stock.

LORI KELEHER is Assistant Professor of Philosophy at New Mexico State University in beautiful Las Cruces, New Mexico. Her main area of research is international development ethics. Lori has published several articles in this area and is working on two books, *Ethics and the Capability Approach* and *Development Ethics: An Introduction*. She also publishes a bit in ancient philosophy because it is so much fun. Lori takes her coffee like her philosophy: strong with a splash of Aristotle and a heaping spoonful of Amartya Sen.

JAMES KIRKLAND has been a professional comedian in Amsterdam, the Netherlands, starring in the improv comedy show Boom Chicago and appearing on the *Dutch Comedy Central News*. On the other side of the world, James is also one half of the Coffee Bean Guys, movers and shakers in Hollybiz-tainment-ville who spend most of their waking and some of their sleeping hours at the Coffee Bean & Tea Leaf on Sunset Boulevard. You can catch their antics on YouTube, where they're still trying to figure out how to monetize their content. James's favorite coffee is Stumptown, from his native Portland, Oregon. He likes his sugar with coffee and cream.

KENNETH W. KIRKWOOD's mother was horrified to hear him described on national television as "an expert on drugs." Ken studies a number of issues related to the history and ethics of recreational and performance-enhancing drugs. In his day job he's an Assistant Professor at the University of Western Ontario in Canada. His loves include coffee, his wife, Susanne, and his daughter, Solange.

DAN LEVY got his start in comedy performing at open mics where people were more focused on their beers than what the wannabe comics were saying. As a sophomore in college, Dan was named the Funniest College Comedian. Since then Dan has appeared in several television shows on Comedy Central and MTV, including *Comedy Central Presents: Dan Levy*. His big screen appearances include *Mardi Gras* and *My Sexiest Year*. He was in *The House Bunny* until he was edited out during production. He recently sold the television series *My LDR* to MTV (the webisode version, featuring James Kirkland, can be found on YouTube). He is also the executive producer of E!'s reality series *Pretty Wild*, but that is a very long story that he will have to explain to you in person. Dan lives in Los Angeles where he is writing more television shows and collecting sneakers and knives. He understands those are two very weird things to obsess about.

SHANNON MULHOLLAND attended Trinity College in Ireland, where she lived for seven years and completed a master's thesis titled "African Coffee Economies: How Cultivating Coffee Encourages Political Instability, Economic Devastation and Social Upheaval." Shannon's interest in coffee has spanned more than a decade. The Specialty Coffee Association of Europe named her the third best barista in Ireland in 2003. Beyond coffee, Shannon worked for six years in the fields of humanitarian relief and international development. She has worked for the United Nations and international non-profits in Kenya, Pakistan,

Myanmar, Sudan, Paraguay, and Haiti, among others. In 2009, Shannon founded Safi Coffee and began working with Kenyan farmers to gain direct access to markets in Nairobi and overseas. She drinks her coffee true and black, brewed in a Bodum French press and steaming hot.

SCOTT F. PARKER has contributed chapters to *Ultimate Lost and Philosophy*, *Football and Philosophy*, *iPod and Philosophy*, *Alice in Wonderland and Philosophy*, and *Golf and Philosophy*. He is a regular contributor to *Rain Taxi Review of Books*. His writing has also appeared in *Philosophy Now*, *Sport Literate*, *Fiction Writers Review*, *Epiphany*, *The Ink-Filled Page*, and *Oregon Humanities*. He is the author of the forthcoming *The Joy of Running qua Running*. All his work on this book, not to mention everything he's written since 1999, was done under the strong influence of Sumatra coffee and caffè americanos.

MARK PENDERGRAST is the author of *Uncommon Grounds: The History of Coffee and How It Transformed Our World*, as well as four other critically acclaimed nonfiction books (see www.markpendergrast.com). He writes a regular column on coffee for the *Wine Spectator*. Contrary to what you might think, he usually drinks only one cup of coffee a day – but it is brewed from extraordinary beans.

KRISTOPHER G. PHILLIPS is a doctoral candidate at the University of Iowa, where he studies the history of early modern philosophy, with a special focus on the works of Descartes and Spinoza. He is the co-editor of *Arrested Development & Philosophy*, and is the author of an article on the problems of personal identity (and *Arrested Development*). He is also a Master Barista for the Iowa City Coffee Company, and has worked in at least six cafés over the past eleven years. He has a particularly crippling addiction to both philosophy and coffee, which means that he sees his contribution to this volume as one of the coolest things ever.

BASSAM ROMAYA is Visiting Assistant Professor of Philosophy at Gettysburg College. He works in social and political philosophy, aesthetics, ethics, philosophy of sex, and the philosophy of pop culture. His essay "The Straight Sex Experiment" appears in *College Sex – Philosophy for Everyone*, another volume in the Wiley-Blackwell Philosophy for Everyone series. According to coffee legend, upon discovering that no coffee was available during a conference at Furman University, Bassam was rushed to a nearby coffee shop by conference organizers for a quick coffee fix before his early morning presentation.

NOTES ON CONTRIBUTORS

BROOK J. SADLER is Associate Professor of Philosophy at the University of South Florida. She has published in *Philosophy*, *Journal of Social Philosophy*, *The Monist*, *Midwest Studies in Philosophy*, *The Philosophers' Magazine*, and *Teaching Philosophy*, among other places. She once drank seventeen cups of coffee in one sitting, then raced through a semester's worth of logic proofs in one night, and doesn't recommend it – neither the excessive caffeine consumption nor the speed-logic.

Specialty Coffee Association of America (SCAA) Lifetime Achievement laureate DONALD SCHOENHOLT, coffeeman at New York's 170-year-old Gillies Coffee Co. and "Father of America's coffee renaissance," co-founded SCAA, founded the Roasters Guild, and proselytizes for Coffee Kids®, Grounds for Health, and International Women's Coffee Alliance at every opportunity. Donald is an editor at *Tea & Coffee Trade Journal* and serves on the *Roast Magazine* Advisory Board. He has been named among the most influential coffee people of the last quarter century; he was Tea & Coffee Man of the Year in 1998, and is 2010 SCAA Distinguished Author.

ANDREW WEAR is Honorary Associate of the School of Philosophy at the University of Tasmania, Australia. His research interest is aesthetic philosophy, with particular regard for the relationship between concept and form. He is also an experienced coffee insider, having worked as a barista, reviewer, and advisor for nearly twenty years, winning a number of awards along the way. Despite his rallying calls for a return to espresso purism, he must own up to ordering double-ristretto soy lattes. However, in order to protect his identity, he does so in disguise.